The Mystery of You

Kenneth B. Klein

Other Books by Kenneth B. Klein

A Strong Delusion

The Deep State Prophesy and The Last Trump

The Unforgettable Tree

Also by Kenneth B. Klein

Documentary Films:

Twenty-five Messianic Signs
Petra-Israel's Secret Hiding Place
Touring Israel
Cracking the Prophetic Code
In the Shadow of Babylon
Terrorism- America Response
The Great Pyramid-Lost Legend of Enoch
The Great Pyramid-Message From the Stars
The Great Pyramid -Gateway to the Galaxy

Documentary Films (continued):

Trans-Humanism
Invasion of the Dark Stars
Jerusalem and the Lost Temple of the Jews
The Deep State Prophecy and the Last Trump

Table of Contents

PREFACE

What lies ahead is a mirror and a telescope. It is a telescope in that it will help you see things far off. It is a mirror because as you gaze into it you will see your true self. This might seem frightening, and it is because it will shake you to such a degree you will never be the same again. My earnest hope and prayer is after you take this journey you will never come back!

The most important thing in the world is You. At least it is for You! In the consideration of You it is critical to take a hard look at some very important factors about You. The most important is... who are You?

The most dangerous minefield in this present life is our mind! The numerous impulsive thoughts, and the volume thereof, is much like lightning flashing in a bottle. The magnitude of thoughts which course through even in one day is phenomenal. Trying to get a handle on what is at hand is like riding a bucking bronco in a rodeo without a bridle and saddle. If you are honest with yourself it truly is a remarkable phenomenon to say the least. The human mind! But the human mind is merely the television screen upon what is being broadcast. The content is coming from either the outside world or the inner world of your spirit. It is the conscience that is the program director and moderator.

But how does one become objective in order to see and discern one's own thought life? Where does this ability come from to break the wild horse bringing the human mind into the corral?

Like the cowboy that seeks to break the wild horse, without the proper tools the human can only stay on the beast for a few seconds. And without self control the untamed mind is left to create all sorts of obsessions which become habits and addictions.

These uncontrollable strongholds are the spiritual spyware that impregnate the human thought life. They are the internal lightning bolts that flash across the mental gaze. It is time to take authority and bring every thought under control to a master rider! Are you ready to ride?

Before you are the tools in "The Mystery of You."

Chapter 1

Dreaming the Dream

After writing the book "The Unforgettable Tree" I began to have vivid and remarkable dreams. They were dreams that were clearly not from my own imagination. The Unforgettable Tree seemed to open a spiral staircase to a more direct channel into the unseen spiritual world. They came not infrequently. I am certain they were angelic visitations.

On one specific night, during a dream event, I was confronted with a remarkable vision. It was a peculiar distraction, because at the time I was deeply immersed in writing another book. Nevertheless, it was very clear that I was to shift my attention onto what was being brought before me in the dream state.

It was as though a compaction of knowledge and information was being downloaded into my inner man. (The inner man is called throughout the entire following treatise as the spirit, or the heart) The power of the interruption was so pronounced and significant there was no mistaking, it was to take precedence.

The entire compendium of the dream was transferred into my spirit. Yet I only retained in my conscious mind a vague recollection of what had occurred the night before. I had a sense of what had happened, but until I began to put hand to pen did the knowledge flow out from my inner man and onto my word processor.

The following has come to be called .... **"The Mystery of You"**

It is important to take note that the visitation came as an interruption. In other words, the interruption was a critical part of the meaning of the message. God wanted to interrupt my life.

Throughout the whole of this book there will be tangential concepts colliding with preexisting ideas about God. In fact, many tables of the heart/spirit which have been set will be overturned.

The most remarkable is that which the Christian religions teach concerning heaven. The prevailing provincial view is that after one dies heaven is what awaits the faithful believer, but the bible actually teaches something far different.

The following makes clear that the initial destination for those who love God is not actually heaven. I repeat it is not heaven! But don't get nervous, it's not bad news! It is exciting news, and wonderful! It is about our destiny!

As will be seen, the generally accepted belief for the afterlife is not quite correct coming from the traditional church view. It is important to state this from the outset because the consequences are truly enormous. Are you ready for this?

The revelation makes crystal clear what happens when people leave this life departing from their earthly bound bodies. But it is also an instructional guide in preparation for what lies ahead; our actual true destination.

But if it is not heaven then where? Where do we go when we die?

Chapter 2

Vision of Two Gunships

"And I saw, as it were, two gunships. The gunships were two helicopters. The first was flying aimlessly above a grove of trees and had no purpose of direction. Then soon thereafter, when it cleared the trees, it came to be joined by a second helicopter. They flew in close proximity to each other, but not in tandem as one would assume. The second ship seemed to have fire burning in its center, but this ship had the force of direction and was succeeding in a projected vector. Whereas the first ship was aimless, the other with the fire in its center was prevailing in flight. And I sought the meaning of the two gunships."

What lies ahead is the meaning of the vision.

There is a great mystery concerning the number seven. There are also many mysteries concerning other numbers such as three, ten and twelve. There is no doubt spiritual meaning to these numbers, but what is about to be discovered is the mysterious spiritual meaning concerning the number two.

The Power of Two

Today, one of the most, if not the most defining characteristics of our present time and culture is the practice of selfies. A selfie is a picture taken of oneself from his or her cell phone. The selfie is then usually posted on a social network such as Facebook or other internet platforms.

The present phenomena is important to analyze, because it is reflective of the general state of mind of the public. This is especially true of the youth.

People are wrapped up with themselves. At least where the younger generations are concerned, but the older folks are drifting in that direction as well!

As the superficial preoccupation with self seems to be the general state of mind, it is difficult to break in on those habits with even a sliver of spiritual light! How does one sober up those drunken with themselves as the real issues of life remain unseen behind the curtain? Every day it is the same, as precious time is wasted. We seem to be too busy to ask, what is this life all about?

Where did we come from? What am I supposed to be doing here on this earth, and what happens when our short life span concludes? Why do these most deep and significant questions go unanswered?

Could the habitual selfies be a sad commentary on a collective identity crisis? Nevertheless, the questions are what this life's journey is all about. We have been given a lifetime to find the answers!

For those who really want to drill down, the answers are encrypted in the number two. But ground zero for investigating this most mysterious number is to first recognize a fundamental fact. And it does not begin with the polemic of heaven and hell. It begins here on earth.

Unless we pause and take courage to look reality in the face, the truth is on earth, we are blinded by self. We are earth bound! The full understanding of the mystery of the number two is the first step to overcoming the blindness!

The truth begins with accepting human beings cannot see far off. We are nearsighted! We must come to grips with the fact that we have a kind of spiritual myopia. Another way to say it is we are short sighted. And it is because we were born into this blinded and deaf condition. We are virtually unaware that this is our spiritually impoverished state.

Even if a bolt of divine light were to flash across our mental gaze, we tend to ignore the celestial thought defaulting back to our earthly condition. This is the common short circuited habit. This is our condition! And so, we are locked into a preoccupation with the love of self. The entire human race refuses to notice that we stagger on in a habitual maze in the context of a dark and corrupted world, as our bodies grow older. The most significant questions of life are never answered because they are never asked!

Consequently, spiritual cataracts ensue growing over the inner eye. The cycle is never ending as the blind mob madly tries to fill the void with earthly things, but there is no satisfaction. The itch is never scratched. You name it we do it! Yet wisdom screams out!

But God has given us a lifetime to figure out the missing pieces to the puzzle. It's the puzzle of who we are, what is our purpose, and where we go when it's over!

Laser Light from Above

Where do we begin to pick up those missing pieces? The answer begins with the investigation of Two. The first step is we simply must accept the fact we were born blind and deaf to the realm of spirit.

We were born into a material world and with a material body. If we can rivet this fact to our inner man and build on this foundational thinking, we can begin to establish a more objective understanding. Then the pieces of the missing puzzle will begin to fit together.

There are so many unseen mysteries. We need a spiritual road map to take us home. But first, we need spiritual laser surgery!

If this one fact can be embraced there is hope! There is light at the end of the tunnel!

Herein lies the prescription for the new optics. And herein lies the power of Two.

Prepare yourself for you are about to discover who you are!

Chapter 3

The Inner Eye Exam

First let us test the strength of the inner eye. How far off can you see? We all have vanishing points, but what is yours? Paul the Apostle once prayed for the Ephesians, "I pray the "eyes of your heart" to be opened." May his prayer apply right now!

Here is the first exam to test the eyes of your heart; your inner self. This is the beginning of the restoration from near sighted to far sighted.

What is in a Name

What is in a name? What is in your name? I have always disliked my name. But it was just my last name that really bothered me. It was because it was a German name, and it meant small. It seemed as though my last name was defining me. When I was growing up I was the smallest kid in my class. So, when I heard my name called out it reminded me of my physical stature. When people would call me by my last name, I would say, "don't remind me"!

Everyone wants bigger. I was the little guy, and it caused me a great deal of sadness and even depression. Consequently, I had a massive inferiority complex. In fact, my father exacerbated the matter when he would call me "mouse." Man, I hated that!

It was because of my complex I would imagine ways to compensate. It was a futile attempt to overcome my physical size. Nevertheless, I decided early on that I would try to become a football player. I was a fairly good athlete, so why not? All the football players though were big guys, but maybe I could make it. I just wanted to hang out with the big guys. Football seemed like my only pathway.

I set my course early on. Strange as it was, I managed to land a three year football scholarship. After three years at the university level, miraculously, I had three opportunities in the pros. Providentially, however, the football dream came to a screeching halt with career ending injuries.

Yet not long thereafter something incredible happened. I awakened from the improbable football dream! The voice of ancient prophets caught the sound chamber of my inner ear, and a new picture began to form in my inner eye.

"When I consider Your heavens, the work of Your fingers, the moon and the stars, which You have ordained; What is man that you take thought of him, and the son of man that You care for him? Yet You have made him a little lower than angels, And You crown him with glory and majesty!" Psa 8:3

When I contemplated the thought and put my mind on God's creation, the moon and the stars and all that God had made, I was overwhelmed at the enormity of it all. And that is what happened! Something far bigger than I had ever considered came down upon me.

The utter incomprehensible universe is beyond human imagination. It takes thousands maybe millions of light years to cross the expanse of the universe. It would take millions of earths just to fill up the size of the sun. The number of stars in our own Milky Way galaxy is in the billions. And there are thousands of billions of galaxies in the known universe. And then we find that He spans the heavens with the palm of His hand. Not only are we humans barely a breath, but the earth is just a mere dot in a colossal universe. We are barely anything. And yet God loves us!

On earth we seek to find ourselves by pursuing a vocation or a profession. Then we define ourselves by what we do. I am a teacher or a dentist or an accountant. Whatever! Yet what we do is not who we are. Nevertheless, this is how people try to figure out who they are! It is how they seek to define themselves. These roadways to self-realization are giant missteps in trying to discover "who am I."

We must begin to envision that God is all and in all before we can become someone; the right someone! We must really see, in comparison, that in light of the universe we are almost insignificant. And yet God is still mindful of us. We must begin with small. We must see that God made us a little lower than the angels, but with a great promise and destiny, and it is connected to who we really are. We must first become humbled by our smallness.

"Who humbles himself to behold the things that are in heaven(s) and in the earth?" Psa 113:6

So, for every human being on this small earth, we all face an enormous identity crisis and, today especially, it is at critical mass. It is our lifelong dilemma. It is every day. Who am I? Why do I do what I do? What is my purpose? "Midlife crisis" is the common term, and it is a cliche, but from the moment we are born it is all about who am I!

And yet few there be that understand that God must diminish and break down our false sense of self. It is like a cluster of grapes that must be pressed in order for the sweet extract to flow out. Or a walnut that must be cracked to reach the meat. God must apply pressure to break us down. He is in the process, within the context of our life span, breaking us down so that we may discover who we really are!

How are your vanishing points working? How is your inner eye seeing?

What follows will correct many misconceptions. It is for the equipping of one's life and destiny!

A Greater Context

The fact of the matter is when it comes to heaven there exists not only heaven, but a "heaven above the heavens". And that fact is stated over and over throughout the ancient prophets.

The word for "heaven" is used in various ways throughout the entirety of the scriptures.

The book of Genesis says,

"In the beginning God created the heaven(s) and the earth." Gen. 1:1

then....

*"He separated the waters **(waters from above from waters below)** and in between He placed the "expanse." Ibid*

However, the expanse is also called **heaven**. But the expanse is described as the stars and galaxies. So, heaven, as it is used in this context, is really dealing with the second heaven. The focus is not on the waters above the expanse which is called the "heaven above the heavens," it is dealing with the expanse. Take a careful look!

The great King David of Israel put it this way.

"Lord how can I build a house for you (the temple of God) on earth when your greatness cannot fill the 'heavens nor <u>the heaven above the heavens.</u>'" 1 Kn 8:27

Was King David speaking hyperbole? What did he know that we do not? A heaven above the heavens? Yes, there is a heaven above the heavens!

The particular occasion occurred when King David was musing about the significance of God's temple. It was King David who was given the plans by God for the temple. He came to realize how ridiculous and small an idea it was to build such a restrictive residence for God. In light of his meditations on the universal construction, King David awakened to an incredible fact. There is a heaven above the heavens!

If this statement were taken literally what is the outcome? How does this begin to affect a person's spiritual vision and especially a person's true identity? Our inner eye must be opened!

The Firmament

Once again in the book of Genesis concerning the second day of creation, it was stated that God separated the waters above from the waters below and placed an expanse in between.

"And God said, Let there be a <u>firmament</u> in the midst of the waters, and let it divide the waters from the waters.

And God made the "firmament," and divided the waters which were under the firmament from the waters which were above the firmament: and it was so.

And God called the firmament <u>heaven(s)</u>. And the evening and the morning were the second day." Ibid

So, the firmament called the heaven(s) was and is the visible universe.

"God made the two great lights, the greater light to govern the day, and the lesser light to govern the night; He made the stars also. God placed them in the <u>expanse</u> (the firmament, the 2nd heavens) of the heaven(s) to give light on the earth." Ibid

Firmament Mistakenly Called Heaven

So the firmament was populated with physical objects. Here we see the sun and the moon, and the stars. The point being in the translations the firmament should be clearly understood as "**heavens**".
Heaven in this context, actually means heavens, plural.

But an important distinction must be made here at the outset concerning the waters. It was Jesus Himself who made clear <u>the distinction</u> concerning the waters that were separated.

When He met the woman at the well, He clearly differentiated, that the waters below the firmament were different then the waters above the firmament.

"Jesus said to her, everyone who drinks this water (waters below the firmament) will be thirsty again. He said, whoever drinks the water I give him will never thirst. Indeed, the water I give him will become in him a fount of water springing up to eternal life!" Jn 4:13

These waters Jesus was referring to, were waters above the firmament.

"How majestic is Your name in all the earth, who has displayed Your splendor <u>above the heavens!</u>" Psa 8:9

The expanse separated the waters! The waters above were remarkably different than the waters below. But the emphasis being pointed out is that He placed a firmament between the waters above and the waters below and that firmament was what separated the two waters. The separating expanse was the universe, or rather the heavens, with all its galaxies and stars.

This firmament/universe herein is referred to as the heavens. But for the skeptics who need more proof, there is even more Biblical evidence of this separation between heaven above the heavens in the book of Isaiah 51. Please take careful note.

"I have put my words in your mouth and covered you with the shadow of My hand to establish the heavens and to found the earth, and to say to Zion you are My people" Ibid

"You alone are the LORD. You have made, the heavens, the heaven of heavens with all their hosts, The earth and all that is on it, the seas and all that is in them. You give life to all of them and the heavenly host bows down before you." Neh 9:6

"But who is able to build a house for Him, for 'the heavens' and the highest heavens cannot contain Him? So, who am I, that I should build a house for Him, except to burn incense before Him?" 2 Ch 2:6

And just to drive the point home. There is the famous text where the Apostle Paul is caught up into the 3rd heaven where he sees many things that were unlawful to speak about. So, if there is a third heaven there must be assumed a second.

"I know a man in Christ who fourteen years ago was caught up to 'the third heaven' Whether it was in the body or out of it I do not know, but God knows." 2 Cor 12:2

The first heaven is of course where the birds and airplanes fly.

There are many more places in the scriptures where heavens are mistaken as heaven. There can be no doubt that heavens is a reference to the physical universe of galaxies, stars and planets.

Context for a New Destiny

According to the book of Isaiah chapter fifty-one, when we pass from here, we go into **the expanse** or the second heavens. The heaven above the heavens is eventually where we finally go, but first we must go into the **second heavens**.

When Jesus was speaking to His disciples He said. "In my Father's house, there are many mansions." He was clearly making reference to the second heavens/firmament as the "Father's House." And in Isaiah's prophecy we find a clear directive as to where we are initially headed and our destiny.

"And I have put my words in thy mouth, and I have covered thee in the shadow of my hand, that I may plant the heavens." Isa 51:16

Yet while heavens is pointed out in Isaiah as the initial destination for the followers of Christ, the principal focus in preparation is the inner chamber of the human heart. The nature of God must be developed within our being. That is in our spirit!

Since we must go into the universe to plant them, we must prepare, because we cannot plant the heavens unless God's true nature is established and developing within our hearts/spirits first. This requirement internally is so that we have the seal with which to plant the heavens. There is the absolute necessity for preparation.

So, you see we do not go where everyone thinks we go. We go into the universe (the physical universe) first. It can be seen therefore, that our destiny will begin to reshape the way we think about who we are!
We must prepare properly and why the message interrupted my sleep.

Pre-flight Training

"The days of our lives are three score years and ten (70); and if by reason of strength they be foursquare (80) years, yet is there strength labor and sorrow; for it is soon cut off, and we fly away" Psa 90

What follows will correct many misconceptions. It is for equipping one's life with the pre-flight training necessary to fly. What is at hand is spiritual ground school **preparation for flight** into the universe.

It is time that we take heed and prepare for our mission into the stars. Flying into the stars is not a hyperbole, it is spiritual reality and our destiny.

"Lord teach us to number our days that we might present to you a heart of wisdom." Psa 90:12

And when it comes to preparation it is all about who we are!

Chapter 4

The Father's House

When Jesus spoke the parables about the kingdom of heaven was He speaking about the heaven above the heavens, or was He speaking about the heavens? The answer should be very clear by now!

Since, ultimately, He will fill all in all, both the heavens and the heaven above the heavens, some may think it is not a significant distinction at all. But what if it is a vastly important distinction as a primary motivation for preparation?

Does the point of our destination make a difference in motivation for preparation? Consider the earthly comparison, that there is a far different preparation called for when one is planning a visit to Alaska as opposed to visiting Florida. I am speaking in human terms.

Do you know how to prepare for the heavens, because the parable that follows suggests that there will be those, who even though they believe will not have prepared!

Jesus spoke to them again in parables, saying:

"The kingdom of heaven is like a king who prepared a wedding banquet for his son. He sent his servants to those who had been invited to the banquet to tell them to come, but they refused to come.

Then he sent some more servants and said, 'Tell those who have been invited that I have prepared my dinner: My oxen and fattened cattle have been butchered, and everything is ready. Come to the wedding banquet.'

But they paid no attention and went off–one to his field, another to his business. The rest seized his servants, mistreated them and killed them. The king was enraged. He sent his army and destroyed those murderers and burned their city.

Then he said to his servants, 'The wedding banquet is ready, but those I invited did not deserve to come. Go to the street corners and invite anyone

16

you find to the banquet.' So the servants went out into the streets and gathered all the people they could find, both good and bad, and the wedding hall was filled with guests.

But when the king came in to see the guests, he noticed a man there who was not wearing wedding clothes. 'Friend,' he asked, 'how did you get in here without wedding clothes?' The man was speechless...

Then the king told the attendants, 'Tie him hand and foot, and throw him outside, into the darkness, where there will be weeping and gnashing of teeth.'

For many are invited, but few are chosen." Matt 22:1-14

Preparation

Knowing how to prepare means knowing what one is preparing for! While many think they are preparing for heaven their thinking should be more suitably advised.

The man in the parable was ill prepared. Perhaps had he known more about the kingdom of the heaven(s) he would have taken more heed and care for his preparation, because he was not dressed properly!

And when it comes to preparation it is critical to know just where and what one is preparing for. And the preparation weighs heavenly on "who I am." And who I am weighs heavily on how to be dressed!

Take another extreme example. There is a vast difference in preparation for a Halloween party as opposed to the preparation with close friends to a dinner party. The point is to dramatically illustrate the difference for inner motivation based on the two, quite different, gatherings.

We should take the story and the words of the parable very seriously and think deeply about what is being said.

"Many are invited but few are chosen." Ibid

What will ultimately qualify those that end up being chosen are those who have prepared properly and dressed properly. The preparation is about putting on the "wedding garment, ***the robe of righteousness.*"** We are saved and made whole (dressed properly) through the operation of faith.

17

The robe of righteousness is *"the divine nature"* of Jesus. We need all the motivation possible to robe ourselves. The divine nature of Christ is to be put on here and now. But the sands of time are running down. And while it is all about God's grace, we must use our faith to engage with God's grace and we are made whole from faith to faith.

And now for the deeper immersion into the number Two.

Chapter 5

Two Robes

What prevented the poor soul in the parable from partaking of the celebration feast was that he was not dressed properly. He did not have on a proper wedding garment. It is an inner robe!

But there are **two robes!** Just as there are two gunships there are two robes. In addition, we will find there are two roads, two tracks, two cities and two mountains.

It is all about Two.

Many today are not pursuing because they are not motivated properly, and that is because they have an ill defined understanding for the proper destination. God's people do not realize we are called to the heavens.

The Lines are Blurred

We should begin to comprehend we should be preparing for the Father's House. I know there will be many religious people screaming! But the Fathers house is the expanse. Jesus said,

"In my Father's house there are many mansions." Jn 14:2

and such it is with the untold number of galaxies, stars and planets.

There is more concerning the Father's house...

"My kingdom is not of this world and if it were then would my servants fight." Jn 18:36

Are we to assume that there are wars and conflicts in the Father's house?

This statement by Jesus Himself seems to indicate this is the case! Yet, this view is certainly not commonly held! Most believe when we go to heaven after we die it is all bliss and where we play harps. But it must be clear that the Church cannot be the rule over one's personal faith. The Word of God must be the rule. It is a private matter! It is between you and God!

That is not to say there is no benefit from the organized Church, each must decide for himself, but rather the preparation is about one's own private and personal and operational faith. When it comes to who has rule it must be God alone.

The people who ignited the Protestant Reformation at that time were able to make that distinction. It mattered not what the Church had to say it was Sola Scriptura! It was the Bible only, and so it must be. The Church is not the rule, the Word is!

Are we earnestly preparing for the Father's House or just going through the motions of religion? Religion does not clothe a person with the robe of righteousness. Religion is an external "form of godliness." Godliness is not calibrated by appearances. Godliness must be formed within our inner man; our heart/spirit? Preparation is an internal matter.

"The Kingdom of God is with you and <u>shall be in you.</u>" Lk 17:21

There are countless multitudes who think they are preparing believing they are invited and yet they will not be dressed properly. The parable is scary! Merely going to church does not negate nor release anyone from the use and exercise of their own operational faith. Neither does going to church prepare one for the Father's house!

But stop and notice the difference in the intent of one's spirit when the focus for preparation is adjusted from heaven to heavens. Take time and ponder!

In addition, when the responsibility for preparation is in one's own hands not in the hands of the organized Church, or pastor, the responsibility weighs heavy.

The serious question is what and whose mantle are we putting on? How and with what are we being clothed? Is it a form of godliness or the real deal? Notice again this scripture.

"I have put <u>My words</u> in your mouth and have covered you with the

shadow of My hand, to establish the heavens, to found the earth, and to say to Zion, 'You are My people.'" Isa 51:16

This means to civilize the heavens, or as it is stated in Isaiah fifty-one to "establish the heavens." Our first destination after this life is to go into space.

So, then in the way we live out this light momentary (our lives) affliction, the question we should demand of ourselves is, are we putting on a robe of righteousness or is it some other robe? Will we be disqualified because we are not properly dressed? Think about it!

The man at the wedding celebration did not have on the proper attire. He did not have on the correct clothing. He did not have on the required and specific robe. The man in the story was shocked! He thought he had prepared properly only to find he had not. He was thrown out!

Which robe? There are two. Think deeply about it! There is a great deal riding on the matter. It is an eternal matter, a life and death crossroad!

What is Man?

The greatest and most important questions coming into the human mind, pondered in every heart, is what is the purpose of life? What is my own purpose in being here, and what happens afterward?

The answers seem just out of reach, but the conviction once the answers come into view can be grasped in the mysterious power of the number Two. The number Two and the power of Two contain all the answers. There are two paths, but only one worth taking.

Paul knew this and set his course by selecting one path. He knew the answer to the mystery of Two could be unlocked by the pursuit of one. Paul the great apostle said it this way.

"This __one thing__ I do." Phil 3:13

There was only one thing, and that one thing he would do with all his focus. That one primary focus would unlock all the answers to life's deepest mysteries and questions. And that one focus is...the pursuit and acquisition of the *"Divine Nature."* The divine nature is the "robe of righteousness." The poor soul who was disqualified from the wedding feast was clothed improperly, and it was because he chose poorly. He was clothed with self-righteousness.

While Christ is our righteousness His divine nature must be *"trans-accumulated."* He does not just hand out a robe of righteousness at the end of the day as some think. Putting on the robe of righteousness is the process of trans-accumulation.

Trans-Accumulation

The trans-accumulation of His divine nature is the action and process of putting on the garment of righteousness. It is to occur here and now. It is the very process in the preparation for the wedding banquet for the Father's house. It is daily!

"Not that I have attained it but I press on toward the goal to win the prize of God's heavenly calling in Christ Jesus." Phil 3:12

So even though Paul had salvation and recognized his salvation he lived as though he needed to continue to trans-accumulate and weave the garment of Christ's righteousness into himself. He regarded his whole life as the preparation. The preparation for the Fathers House!

The Shadow of Things to Come

While the divine nature was perfectly evidenced by Jesus, it was initially **prefigured** in the images displayed on the walls of the inner sanctuary of Solomon's temple.

The images on the walls of Solomon's temple provide insight into the Divine Nature. By observing these etchings on the walls of the Jewish temple we can learn the necessity for the exercising of faith. It is by using faith we exercise the ability to acquire the Divine Nature.

If as Isaiah says *"we are to fly into the heavens and establish the heavens"* then we must put on the Divine Nature.

Just what is it and what is it like? How do we begin to grasp such a lofty calling for spiritual reality?

Ascending

Solomon had two dreams from God. In the first dream he asked God for wisdom to rule as King over God's people. Not only was his prayer accepted but God was so impressed with Solomon's selfless request He also granted him a long life along with great wealth. Solomon was also appointed to build the temple of God.

It was King David who assembled the resources for the building of the temple, but it was his son Solomon who was given the responsibility and privilege to build it. In 1st Chronicles chapter twenty-eight all the details for the pattern of the temple were given to Solomon.

"By wisdom, a house is built, and through understanding it is established: through knowledge its rooms are filled with rare and beautiful treasures." Prov 24:3

We tend to think of rooms in an earthly orientation since we are most familiar with houses and castles and so forth, but what about the inner chambers of our inner man? Are there not rooms? Do we not at times say, I have *a place* in my heart for this song or that place or for this person or that person?

Solomon, up to that time was the wisest man that had ever lived. He took from his storehouse of knowledge and wisdom and built the temple with the help of Hiram of Tyre.

The Jewish temple(s) later came to be meant as metaphor and physical examples for God's heavenly eternal temple. They were also to be understood facsimile to our physical bodies. When Jesus challenged the Sanhedrin and said,

"tear down this house and I will raise it in three days," Jn 2:19

He was <u>not</u> referring to the actual physical temple of Solomon. He was referring to His own physical body as the temple.

They of course misconstrued what He was saying calling Him a blasphemer.

"Destroy this temple and I will raise in three days," Jn 2:19-21

and He did. The body is the physical temple for the soul and spirit.

Then we find in First Corinthians that the idea of the temple was transferred and applied to His people.

*"Do you not know **that** you yourselves are God's 'temple', and that God's Spirit dwells in you?" 1 Cor 6:19*

Physical Representations in the Shadow World

By examining the physical temple of Solomon as if a shadow of the heavenly temple, we gain important information on what is to be understood for the trans-accumulation of God's divine nature.

The conundrum of course is that we must seek to acquire the divine nature while we are still currently embedded in these physical bodies. Later in the life of the apostle Peter we find that he had a clear distinct understanding of this temporary temple when he said,

"Knowing that shortly I must put off this 'my tabernacle', even as our Lord Jesus Christ hath showed me." 2 Pet 1:14

Peter was well aware of the distinction between his body and his spirit. The scripture calls them earthen vessels but what is meant is "mud house."

"We have this treasure in earthen vessels" 2 Cor 4:7

And yet they are to be the temporary houses or temples within which we must trans-accumulate God's divine nature.

Nevertheless, as we peer into the far past with Solomon, the wise master builder of the temple, we can begin to grasp not only the meaning of the Divine Nature, but also the imagery which is key to finding it.

Solomon paved the way for understanding for how the temple is to be established; it is through knowledge that its rooms are filled with rare and beautiful treasures, that is...the Divine Nature is to fill the whole house."

The Temple of Solomon was just a shadow of better things to come.

Chapter 7

The Inner Sanctuary

There within the secret confines of the Jews' physical temple, inscribed on the walls of the inner sanctuary, where only the high priest could see, was the Divine Nature expressed in images or pictures.

The inner sanctuary was a cube. The dimensions were expressed as cubits. A cubit was about eighteen inches. So, there were twenty cubits by twenty cubits by twenty cubits. Why cubits? In the book of Revelations concerning the measurement of the city of God it is found...

"And he measured the wall thereof, a hundred and forty and four cubits, according to the measure of a man, that is, <u>of the angel</u>." Rev 21:17

(Keep in mind that the measurement of a man is "the measurement of the angel")

So we find that the cubit is the measurement of an angel, but it is also the measurement of a man. They are one and the same. The twenty cubits of the inner sanctuary that Solomon built were in accord with the measurement of a cubit which was also the measurement of a man/angel.

The preciseness of the design not only in dimensions but also in imagery is deeply significant as a clue for the acquisition of our true identity. Nevertheless, it can be easily overlooked.

The whole inner room was plated in gold from top to bottom. All the images therein were set within the context and covering of gold. The book of 1st Kings describes what only the high priest was once a year permitted to see.

The idea for why the high priest was only permitted to enter once a year was an unalterable fact. God's presence is so holy that a human (clay) body cannot handle much of the divine energy for any extended period of time. That is why the high priest could only go inside once a year without being destroyed. Even then were he not prepared properly he would die.

Outside the temple area was a huge laver (a huge copper bowl) that contained 16,000 to 20,000 gallons of water. It was for the priests to wash. It was also to wash the animals for sacrifice. The lavar along with ten smaller lavars were utilized by the other priests, daily, for washing. Whether it was for going inside once a year by the high priest or for the daily ministry they all had to be clean.

The daily washings were essential before going about the daily chores. But for the Day of Atonement when the high priest would go inside into the inner sanctuary; holy of holies (only once a year) there was more elaborate and extensive preparation. God is holy!

The priests' washings and animal sacrifices attested to the holiness of God and how He would be approached. These washings were called for even when just coming near to the most holy place.

While there is a holy place in the heavens which Jesus cleansed with His own blood, the most holy place of our own being is the heart/or spirit of our deeper inner self. It must be cleansed by the more perfect sacrifice the very blood of Jesus Christ. When our heart is cleansed, it is plated with gold. But the new heart must be maintained!

That is why we are admonished, *"to keep our heart with all diligence for out of the heart flow all the issues of life."* When God enters our heart, the heart is covered in gold, and we see this prefigured in Solomon's temple. (Remember the temple of Solomon is a **shadow** of better things)

The Enormous Cherubim Angels

As the details of the inner sanctuary of Solomon's temple were given, Solomon ordered the construction of two enormous Cherubim angels. The angels stretched across the room. Their wings touched each other as they spanned the distance from wall to wall. It was also in this room that the ark of the covenant was placed which also had two smaller cherubim angels covering over the Ark. The whole covering over the ark was called the "mercy seat."

If we assume Solomon's physical sanctuary cube as a shadow and as a representation of our own inner sanctuary, then we must pay close attention to what filled the inner room/cube. In that way we better understand the context for the acquisition of the Divine Nature we should be diligently pursuing. We are the temple of the living God, and with the Holy Spirit our hearts are also attended to by angels. Otherwise, why would they be so prominently displayed within the inner sanctuary of Solomon's temple?

The remarkable size of the Cherubim is a message in and of itself as to how the angels are to have significant access into our inner chamber. They are sent to the heirs of salvation to assist in the development of our inner man and assist in clothing with the divine nature.

The fact that the angels fill the room speaks volumes as to the prominent place the angels are to occupy in our lives, as they did in Solomon's construction, and today, in the inner chamber of our own hearts.

It does not assume that angels are to be worshiped, but only that they are representative emissaries of the divine nature and that they are given to aid the sons of men through their earthly journey, and most importantly with the acquisition of the divine nature. Remember Christ said,

"you will see angels ascending and descending on ben Adam." Jn 1:51

ben Adam is every man/woman. They should be allowed to help in filling all the rooms of our inner man. That they have the divine nature is evidenced throughout all human history and can be attested to from their many recorded journeys to this planet when they interacted with men. There seems little argument to the fact there is divine power that radiates from them.

When men are seen encountering angels they seem overcome often fainting in their presence. Some men are seen falling to the ground in great fear needing to be strengthened to stand and to even hear the messages from the heavenly beings. There is no doubt that there is a divine power emanating from God's proxies who represent and also manifest His Divine Nature.

These enormous angelic replications filling Solomon's room with great stature suggest the important part they are to play for the acquisition of Christ's Divine Nature in the inner chamber of the heart. As an important note also consider the wings and look at this scripture.

As for the days of our life, they contain seventy years or, if due to strength, eighty years, yet their pride is but labor and sorrow, for soon it is gone and

"we fly away." Psa 90:10

After living out this mortal earth life of truly short duration then **we fly.**

The angels' wings suggest flight. Who can forget the fallen angel Clarence in the film "It's a Wonderful Life?" He had to come to earth seeking a way to get his wings. But wings are only suggestive of flight.

The wings of birds for example are designed to create lift from air currents. The curvature of the top of the wings creates the phenomena of lift. This is exactly what allows planes to stay up in the air.

Angels do not need lift because they do not utilize air currents to fly. The wings seen on them are for the benefit from the human point of view. It is to understand that we will fly.

We will not need wings as though like Clarence. The wings on the angels are the images that indicate there will be flight. And that flight will be throughout the star ways in the Father's house and why we need to prepare.

Chapter 8

The Power of Image

"And he carved all the walls of the house roundabout with carved figures of cherubim and palm trees and open flowers, within and without." 1 Kn 6:29

The question that arises cannot but haunt the mind. Why these peculiar carvings exclusively on the walls? Everywhere the eye was met by this threefold ornamentation, everywhere; cherubim, palm trees and open flowers; these and nothing but these. The patterns on the walls were repetitive, over and over cherubim, palm trees, and open flowers. Why the repetition?

The perpetual recurrence of these three, amid all the visible forms that convey ideas of beauty, could not fail to strike and to raise inquiry. And what should that inquiry be?

ben Adam

When Jesus called Nathaniel to follow Him Nathaniel was promised that he would see angels ascending and descending on" the son of Man." But nowhere is there any episode of that promise, recorded in the Bible, where Nathaniel ever saw this actually happening to Jesus. Why?

Nathaniel was jubilant when he met Jesus whom he esteemed with great admiration, but Jesus made an astonishing proclamation which was akin to Jacob's dream given some two thousand years prior. Jesus said to Nathaniel "you will see greater things than these, you will see angels ascending and descending on the son of man." The term He used was ben Adam or son of man, but nowhere in the bible is there any record of this promise ever occurring.

It is because the term "ben Adam" was a reference not just to Jesus. Many times, in the Old Testament, the term "son of man" or ben Adam was referenced. It was a title not uncommon. It was a promise that angels would ascend and descend not just on Jesus, but on Nathaniel as well. In fact, all ben Adams. We are all sons of Adam!

30

*"Are they not all ministering spirits **(angels)** sent to the heirs of salvation?" Heb 1:13-14*

It was the same supernatural manifestation that came upon Jacob. Ah, but that was just an old biblical tale!

When Jacob came to a place called Bethel, he laid his head on a rock as he went to sleep. That night he saw angels ascending and descending upon the earth and when he awoke, he said this is certainly a gate of God and I did not know it!

The term ben Adam was a common term used throughout the Old Testament of other men. Ben Adam means every man. We are all ben Adam. We are all descendants of Adam. We are all sons of Adam. When Jesus promised the interaction of the angels ascending and descending on the ben Adam it was a promise to all. You will see angels ascending and descending on you. Yes you!

Therefore, in the inner sanctuary we see not only the enormous figures of the angels, but the promise manifested, repeatedly, on the walls. The repetition suggests in practical application that the inner sanctuary room would be attended to, over and over again by angels. The angels would affect those that were tuned to their presence. And the effect would be the imparting of the Divine Nature.

Not only is it repetitive, but the relationship is essential for the development of the Divine Nature as represented by the palm trees and the open flowers on the walls of the inner sanctuary.

Chapter 9

Preview of the Divine Nature

The upright palm tree stood for the good man.

"The righteous man will flourish like the palm tree" Psa 92:12

Later in the gospel when Jesus healed the blind man he said,

"I see men as trees." Mk 8:24

There are many types of trees in the world but the "palm tree" is different from all other trees. Principally it has no branches.

Some trees are irregular with no symmetry, they are gnarly, and twisted in growth; some lay along the ground before they rise; but the palm tree is set apart from other trees. It is unique! And there are different types of palm trees. There are coconut palms, banana palms, and date palms to name a few, but they all grow the same way, straight up.

Palm trees grow straight upright and have a crown atop in its palm fronds. And again, they also produce delicious fruits.

The famous scripture that says, "you know a tree by its fruit" is a call to become like a palm tree.

"Blessed is the man that walks not in the counsel of the ungodly, nor stands in the way of sinners, nor sits in the seat of the scornful. But his delight is in the law of the LORD; and in his law he meditates day and night.

And he shall be like a tree (palm tree) planted by the rivers of water, that brings forth his fruit in his season; his leaf also shall not wither; and whatsoever he does shall prosper." Psa 1:1

We can tell the true nature of a person by their fruit. But what is meant by fruit? There are many things. It is character. It is acts of kindness. It is words that are spoken, for words reveal the heart.

"For out of the abundance of the heart the mouth speaks." Lk 6:45

But not only words that come out, but it is the depth of wisdom and knowledge that attend speech. It is also the fruit of a person's life. It is the things that they do. Fruit is also children and their children's character.

"We can know a tree by its fruit!" Matt 7:20

But the palm tree is a special kind of tree, and it was the palm tree that was carved on the walls of the inner sanctuary.

Represented in carved work on the walls and doors of the inner sanctuary, the palm tree represented a man and woman who had been formed by the presence of God in the angelic services of the sanctuary. The carved images on the walls represented divine potential from the Divine Nature.

The good man as the palm tree is well represented here. He is the man who stands upright, who moves heavenward in direction and who is governed constantly by the Holy Spirit and the divine nature personified by the angels. There in the sanctuary he grows to great heights and continues to gain fresh inspirational knowledge and wisdom to fill all the inner places.

"By wisdom a house is built, and through understanding it is established; through knowledge its rooms are filled with rare and beautiful treasures." Prov 24:3-4

The palm tree is an admirable picture of the righteous man. He bears fruit; he is expected to "bear much fruit," and fruit of many kinds. In the spiritual we find the explanation of a life lived in this presence of God producing fruit.

"The fruit of the Spirit *(the divine nature)* is love, joy, peace, patience, kindness, goodness, faithfulness, *gentleness, and self-control."* Gal 5:23

It is **not** through the ordinances of God that the divine nature is acquired and lived out, but rather through the magnitude of the power of the divine nature. For the kingdom of God does not consist in ordinances or laws or word, but by power of the divine nature. If we put on the divine nature, we will live His life. It is the power of an endless life, and that is why we no longer live by rules and regulations which are of the Law. When Jesus died, He did away with the Law and provided in His New Covenant the Power of an endless life. That life is the new energy conveyed by the Holy Spirit and the angels. It is the divine nature.

Those qualities of the divine nature that are found in Him are like the foliage of the palm. They grow not near the ground, where they can easily be soiled and lost, but high up where lower things cannot damage or destroy. The divine nature cannot easily be offended. But it must be reached for with faith.

The good man may have much to depress him and to hamper his growth, but if he "dwells in the house of the Lord," he will rise. Notwithstanding all that would otherwise hinder him from a noble height is overcome by the operational use of his faith.

The Cherubim, Palm Tree and Open Flower

But what of the open flower?

There on the walls there is also the open flower. It is the motif of the feminine. Unmistakably the flower is the righteous woman. She, like a flower in the natural world, is closed to the darkness of night yet opens to the sun.

In a like manner, she opens to the light of God. She is an open flower drinking in the refreshment of God's penetrating presence. She is radiant and lovely because she too is strengthened by the radiating power of God's presence, His divine nature. And she lives large because she is daily, repetitively as the repeated carvings on the wall suggests, taking in and growing as she accumulates more and more of His divine nature.

But it must be clearly emphasized! The imparting of divine energy must be trans-accumulated. The trans-accumulation of the divine nature occurs within the inner sanctuary of our spirit.

Chapter 10

Abuses of the Inner Sanctuary

The Scripture denotes something very unusual concerning the inner chamber. It speaks about a place called the "chamber of imagery." We gain insight into the meaning of this chamber of imagery by reviewing several passages.

"Then said He unto me, Son of man, hast thou seen what the ancients of the house of Israel do in the dark, every man in the <u>chambers of his imagery</u>!' Ez 8:12

But if we backtrack and look at several scriptures before this text we see this.

And he said to me,

"Go in and see the wicked and detestable things they are doing here. So I went in and looked, and I saw portrayed all <u>over the walls</u> of the inner sanctuary <u>round about</u> all kinds of crawling things and unclean animals and all the idols of Israel. In front of them stood seventy elders of Israel, and Jaazaniah son of Shaphan was standing among them. Each had a censer in his hand, and a fragrant cloud of incense was rising." Ez 8:9

He said to me,

"Son of man, have you seen what the elders of Israel are doing in the darkness, each at the shrine of his own idol? They say, 'The LORD does not see us; the LORD has forsaken the land.'" Ez. 8:12

The scriptures teach that all the physical constructs (such as the temple, it's altars and furniture etc.) and even sabbath days and more were mere **shadows** of the real. The real being, the realm of spirit.

So, the inner sanctuary of Solomon's temple was but a mere shadow of the real. But the physical temple even as a shadow tells a story about the real. In this case we are making the parallel between the inner sanctuary of Solomon's temple with the inner chamber of our heart. The scripture calls it the "chamber of imagery."

We all bear within ourselves, in our inner man, a chamber of imagery.

When we look again at the inner walls of Solomon's temple, they were carved with the cherubim angels, palms and open flowers. This imagery, in a figurative sense, should be what is inscribed on the walls of our inner heart. The thoughts of our inner man should be reflective of what these images represent. They should be the basis and bias of our inner thinking and imaginations. They should guide the inner chamber. They should monitor our thought life. It is what we ought to picture within our inner man.

This is what was represented on the walls of Solomon's inner physical temple roundabout.

But in stark contrast we are informed of what was covering over those images on the walls at the time of Ezekiel's revelation. It was something entirely different then Cherubim, palm trees, and open flowers.

Represented in the vision to Ezekiel, the evil priests could not see the original carvings on the walls of the sanctuary because they were predisposed within themselves to vain imaginations of their own idolatry. The fallen priests could not see the holy carvings of cherubim, palms and flowers! They were so caught up with their own agendas they could not see what God had presented on the walls. Those images were covered over!

The idea of this passage is that while the images of angels, palm trees, and open flowers were still there on the walls the religious officials could not see them. They had projected their own idolatrous visions and images over the holy images. Like thick grease on a kitchen wall!

They assumed that God did not see what they were doing. The fact that it seemed He had forsaken the land was proof to them that He did not care. At least they thought he didn't care. The evil fallen priests had blinded themselves by the improper use of their chamber of imagery.

This is what people erroneously assume when they entertain vain imaginations in their inner chamber. They think He does not see what they are thinking or dreaming. They never stop to consider something else should occupy their mental gaze in the inner chamber of imagery. Yet this is what humans do! As a result, they cannot see God or the things of God, nor can they acquire the divine nature. As it was then so it is today!

"And this is the condemnation, that light has come into the world, and men loved darkness rather than light, because their deeds were evil." Jn 3:19

Only the pure of heart will see God. Notice it is the pure of heart, and the pure heart is the one that has cleansed the inner sanctuary, or the chamber of imagery.

This inner chamber formerly portrayed as in the inner sanctuary of Solomon's temple filled with magnificent angels and depictions of majestic palms and open flowers is sadly misused by human beings.

We can think what we please when we please and create all sorts of imaginative inventions. But these are merely "vain imaginations." Nevertheless, the chamber of our imagination is intended for the ingress of the angels, and principally for establishing acquisition of the divine nature. It is for the growth of the palm tree and open flower.

But in the case of vain imaginations of the evil priests of that day, they provide a grand picture that illustrates the same undoing in our present day. Their lack of reverential fear should be instructive lest our inner walls, in like manner, be covered over and darkened by idolatrous imaginations. The inner chamber must be guarded and watched over. This must be a daily regimen and exercise!

"Keep thine heart with all diligence for out of it flow the issues of life." Prov 4:23

Is not this example of darkness reflective of the rampant manifestation of the pornographic industry? Men dream the degradation in their inner man, and then construct those imaginings onto film.

It is the same in the case and use of drugs and marijuana. The inner chamber doors are flung wide open via mind expanding isotropic drugs. Then rushing in are the demonic powers which paint all kinds of sensual images within the chamber of imagery. It is by this flagrant misuse that the inner man is grossly defiled. The chamber of imagery was not created for this purpose. "Pharmakeia" (drug use) accelerates and facilitates the infiltration of vain imaginations. Pharmakeia means witchcraft.

"Because when they knew God, they glorified him not as God, neither were thankful; but became vain in their imaginations, and their foolish heart **(inner chamber of imagery)** *was darkened." Rom 1:21*

These facts are pointed not to condemn our moral ineptitude but rather so people learn to choose the proper use of the chamber of imagery. And use it for gaining the robe of righteousness; the "Divine Nature". We must cleanse our heart via the blood of Jesus and refocus our mind and heart.

Legalism is the vain attempt to legislate morality. It is a legal approach to correcting the misadventures of human folly and misuse of the chamber of imagery. We must be cleansed by Jesus' atonement, but then we must learn to walk. To walk in Christ means not only to learn to keep our inner garment clean, but also to keep the inner chamber filled with its proper inclusions. In that way mortality is swallowed up by life.

It is about proper focus and use. If we are wise and seek to fulfill our destiny, our purpose, and to enter our true identity, we must strive to put on the divine nature. In this way we will be confident to present to God a heart of wisdom prepared to fly into the heavens.

When Jesus Cleansed the Temple

When Jesus came into the Temple during the last week of His life, He overturned the tables of the money changers and those trying to make a buck selling doves for sacrificial purposes to the poor. He was angered because they were corrupting the purpose of the temple. Their hearts were onto something other than God; namely the love of money.

Again, we are the temple! We too can fill our temple with things that are idolatrous, setting our inner chamber on evil imaginations, rather than the things of God. It is utterly amazing how we can calculate everything, and every evil thing. We must learn the discipline of how to set our minds on the things above, not the things below. It is a discipline!

"God has not given us a 'spirit of fear' but of power and love and discipline" 2 Tim 1:7

Chapter 11

Solomon's Improbable Song

It is a terribly sad commentary that Hollywood's masters of imagery habitually perpetuate an unattainable nirvana through romantic, and erotic love.

Truly it is the perplexing dream that comes to all men and women, yet it is in most respects a fanciful dream, albeit an intoxicating dream. It is truly an unsustainable fiction, but one that easily finds its way onto the walls of the chamber of imagery.

No doubt if one pitched a Hollywood producer on the idea of using the "Song of Solomon" as a script to capitalize on the unattainable myth he might jump at the chance. After all, since it is in the Bible with numerous portrayals of sexuality in all manner, why not? Perhaps in a twisted logic many a producer would claim, "since God is underwriting such lurid sensual behaviors why not get on board? We'd have God's approval."

But Solomon's "Song of Songs", is neither about theology or spirituality or morality. It is not God's personal endorsement, as though He is using Solomon for "green lighting" what is sexually permissive. And neither should it be construed as a book about morality, or immorality. But most importantly and certainly, it is not a template for the ideal romance.

Sadly, most biblical teachers and scholars erroneously believe it is about Christ and the Church, while others of the cloth think it is a biblical guide for authentic and true romantic love. Yet truth be told it is <u>none of these things</u>.

The Power of Romance and Sensual Love

Men, women, and Hollywood, as well as all the arts are fixated with the dream of romantic love and sex. It is more than idealism it is the powerful inclination for this most irresistible power. It is the brass ring that cannot be grasped. It is the carrot before the eyes of the jackass. It is the promised mountain top of the perfect relationship between a man and a woman.

The idealism of the dream has always existed. And this idealism is exquisitely expressed, not only in the personal life of Solomon, but also in his "Song of Songs." (Just so that you know, I have been married nearly fifty years)

The Song of Songs was actually a play written some one thousand years before Jesus, but with an all encompassing comprehensive reach. The fanciful notion extends to all men and all women throughout all time. It is the dream that can easily fill and dominate the inner chamber of imagery.

It simply does not exist for the long term, yet the myth is so easily peddled! It cannot and does not die. The people always buy hard the dream no matter what era. Intoxicated with boundless infatuations the temple walls with Cherubim, palm trees, and flowers, are covered over with a miscue of imaginations sponsored by human passion. It is the same idolatry of the defiled priests. Love is blind! And real Love is shrouded over by delusions of romantic love. And it is an endless circle of delusion! There is no escape. It is the quicksand of a soul gone wild. It is not only rampant in films, but also the source feeling sound of most all songs. The exhalation of love. Love makes the world go round. But what love?

One of the most famous songs of all time "Stardust" is a perfect example of the millions upon millions of songs, expressing in refrain, what is commonly held as life's greatest and sweetest reward.

The sound of Solomon's song is everywhere and evidenced in most all past songs but also in contemporary music. Julie Andrews sang "I fell in love with love." Frank Sinatra's famous "I've got you under my skin." Engelbert's rendering "Love is a Many Splendored Thing." On and on it dominates the landscape of human thought and passion for human love. The need for human affection is endless!

While the Song of Songs is polemical to God love it should not be viewed though, as God's total rebuke of human love. But in Solomons epic there is drawn the clear distinctive between God's love and human love! It's critical value is that by contrast human love's pervasive affect over the human soul is clearly illustrated. The Song is like a physician setting a broken bone in place! It is the subordination of human love to God love.

There are three principal words for describing love. One is the word agape, two is the word phileo, and three is the word eros. The word agape is the word most religious people are familiar with. It is best described by a word picture as God extending His love by sending His Son Jesus into the world to rescue the human race. It was the love of God (agape) to make such a magnanimous overture and effort! This is agape love. It is the idea of doing something without anything expected in return. It is sacrificial! It was *agape* love for men to give up their lives at Normandy when they stormed the beaches of Europe in World War Two.

There is another great scripture that drives the point home.

"No greater agape hath a man then he lay down his life for another." Jn 15:13

There were many men who have given up their lives in this type of magnanimous sacrifice. Mothers do this all the time with their children, and these are people who may not be Christian. My father, a Jewish man, went to work every day supporting his family was operating in agape/love.

There are Jews, Muslims, and tens of million of the multitudes of people in general that have an inclination of sacrificial love that routinely function in agape. Not only these facts tell us something about love but the scriptures state that the gentiles agape/love their own.

"If you love those who love you, what reward will you get? Do not even tax collectors do the same?" Matt 5:46

There is resident in humans some semblance of agape or God's love. This fact is affirmed by the bible itself. Agape love is sacrificial love!

Phileo love is a brotherly love. It is a love that emanates and expresses affection. While agape love is motivated by sacrifice, phileo love is derived and driven by feeling.

It is because people cannot clearly differentiate between feeling love as opposed to sacrificial love, we note this mind picture. The greatest visual of sacrificial love was Jesus hanging bloody from the tree. This was the greatest picture of agape.

We know in the story that Solomon does not operate in this kind of love because he does not sell out for the Shulamite girl, and her alone. He refused to give up his seven hundred wives and three hundred concubines, and all his wealth for her. She, on the other hand, cannot deal with her own jealousy and flees back home.

Phileo is best understood and seen in the warmth of a hug. Phileo exists in men and women and children.

Eros love is physical love in that it is sexual. All these levels of love are present in human beings. They exist whether they are religiously devout or not. The confusion; however, is that if each one of these levels of love were seen as water and then each poured into a glass and mixed it would be difficult to see that they are different from one another. Men and women get confused and cannot sort out what is love.

They tend to default to a human comprehension of love. They only understand love from a limited human emotional perspective. Since all these levels of love tend to flow into each other there is the problem to miscalculate what love is, or rather which love it is.

What is entirely astonishing is that while agape to a degree is resident in all humans and while we can have a tremendous mind picture of sacrificial unselfish love, God does not leave us with mere intellectual definitions and categories. Yet this perspective is why mere religion is so damaging.

God does not leave us as though we are orphans. Agape love is more than a religious idea. The perspective of agape love must come from God's point of view and from His nature. That is why God sends into our spirit His Spirit. He overshadows who we are with Himself. Therefore, agape love is not limited to man's interpretations or intellectualizing because God literally floods in with who He is into our inner man. At least He desires to flood into our inner man. This is called the "Baptisms of the Holy Spirit." It is to be distinguished from water baptism. They are not one and the same. The Baptisms of the Holy Spirit is a personal event. It is the real spiritual experience of the powers of the "age to come." It is real and it is experiential.

"And hope does not disappoint us, because He has poured out His love into our hearts through the Holy Spirit, whom He has given us." Rom 5:5

It is the quickening event that begins the lifelong process of the "perfecting of agape love." It is the initial putting on of the Divine Nature. It is the preliminary action of trans-accumulation!

Agape love must be perfected in us. But until the Holy Spirit comes "mightily" into the heart or our spirit, agape love is restrained in its perfecting to a great degree.

"Herein is our <u>love made perfect</u>, that we may have boldness in the day of judgment: because as He is, so are we in this world." 1 Jn 4:7

The love of God must be perfected within us, and that is why these distinctions must be pointed out. The journey of this life should be with the clear understanding that agape love, whom God is, must become perfected within ourselves, in our spirit.

Human beings without the full force of the Holy Spirit become disastrously confused.

Is there no place for romance, affection and sex? Of course, there is! But when human love, supersedes God's agape love, it becomes idolatry.

And people get damaged, and damaged badly!

Falling in love with love, or human affection, even takes a physical toll on our bodies in the most unexpected ways including a racing heart, sweaty palms, and shaky knees. These external signs may even be apparent to the naked eye. But these are minor manifestations.

The mental psychological toll can be catastrophic, and even last for a lifetime. Romantic sensual love is dangerous, and can even lead to suicide and has in countless instances.

Angels or the Love Drug?

What is utterly fascinating about these physical reactions is that they can be easily mistaken and thought to be from heavenly origin.

But what happens to the body internally that makes the "oh so good" feeling, is seldom seen outwardly. Our body's chemistry is rewired when we're in human love. The same chemical processes seen in various addictions are activated when we are with the so-called "right person." The tumblers fall into line and a peculiar type of synapse sparks.

It may be argued that the connection is all about how God has set up the pattern for procreation. Sexuality is not the only attraction that brings two people together and causes a spark. Procreation is certainly a most driving force, but the magnetic attraction to another can be much more. And the falling in love phenomena is overwhelming. It can easily be mistaken for the divine.

What begins as merely a mental consideration morphs and migrates to feelings, and then goes into the heart. The heart is the inner chamber and can be overly focused upon and mistaken as more than just a glimmer of heaven. The small dose is so powerful we want more. But romantic love is not the panacea nor meant to be a replacement for God's entry of Himself into our inner chamber.

Yet the human love intoxication is like wine. We are warned not to be filled with wine which is excess. But when we step over the line and become drunk with love; human love, we are in trouble. It becomes what covers over the walls of the inner sanctuary.

This is the point where critical mass is reached. It is when the glimmer turns to obsession. When that point is reached and then breached it becomes an addiction. When that line is crossed there is no turning back. The longing for the feeling is a craving for life. But it is a lie because it is based upon a chemical reaction we crave in the brain. It is a bodily deception! This is the meaning of the "Song of Songs."

It's All in Your Brain

The moment we meet mister or miss right, the brain's ventromedial prefrontal cortex, the area that judges attractiveness in milliseconds, is immediately activated. This is your body in love!

45

However, falling in love is more than just attraction. Pheromones, chemicals found in human sweat, have an effect when it comes to human sexual attraction.

Falling in love involves one especially important muscle —the heart, the inner sanctuary. It is a muscle only to the extent that it can be exercised.

What comes into the mind if not carefully assayed and screened, can go into the heart. What we allow to fill our heart is what we are taken by and who and what we become.

*"**The good man** brings good things out of the good treasure of his heart, and the evil man brings evil things out of the evil treasure of his heart. For out of the overflow of the heart, the mouth speaks." Lk 6:45*

We are to protect our heart. That there is a close almost inseparable connection between the heart and the mind is without doubt. We can have many thoughts but not allow them into our heart. We have the power to dismiss thought and not allow thought to access into the heart.

"Casting down imaginations, and every high thing that exalts itself against the knowledge of God, and bringing into captivity every thought to the obedience of Christ." 2 Cor 10:5

The Two Computers

There is that number two again.

When there is negligence to arrest certain imaginations and every high thought, those thoughts can drift into the heart. When this takes place strongholds in the heart ensue.

The human mind is like a laptop computer while the heart/ spirit is likened unto a supercomputer.

We are instructed that there are many things from God that cannot presently enter the heart. We cannot bear them yet. But once bitten by the human love bug we have trouble in dealing with our heart. The heart becomes complicated because it has become compromised.

"Eye has not seen and ear has not heard neither has entered into "the heart" of man all that God has for us." 1 Cor 2:9

Whatever the case may be, this is why we are instructed to put on the armor of God. It is of course a spiritual armor that God provides while we live out our lives on earth. The armor includes the helmet of salvation,

46

which is a protection over the mind, but it also calls us to put on the breastplate of righteousness which is a protection over our heart/spirit.

Satan, the opposing force, wants to put all kinds of thoughts into the mind, but his objective is to infect, seduce, and overtake the heart.

It is our duty to keep watch. We have to decide on which thoughts are allowed into the heart. Our heart is the inner sanctuary of our being. It is who we are.

Hence, we are instructed to *"keep thine heart with all diligence."*

"Your adversary the devil prowls about as a roaring lion seeking whom to devour." 1 Pet 5:8

And he seeks to destroy the heart!

Chapter 12

Love and Other Drugs

Norepinephrine, which is similar to adrenaline, produces the racing heart and excitement during the attraction phase which evolves into romantic passion and then to obsession. These two chemicals produce elation, craving, and focused attention which leads to an overwhelming fixation for the object of our desire.

When it comes to matters of the heart, the body can lose control and send a person into overdrive.

"Let the words of my mouth and the meditations of my HEART be acceptable unto thee O Lord." Psa 19:14

When we take a thought and meditate on it we are bringing the thought from the laptop psyche into the supercomputer heart.

When thoughts are brought into the inner chamber and focused on they are radiated. Then issues of the heart come into play, whether they are acceptable to God or not. This is how our supercomputer works.

But momentary romantic bliss can be misinterpreted as an end all. If radiated upon by meditation, they can affect the mental chemical barriers to such a degree that it causes irrational mind sequences turning very dangerous. In fact, it can turn deadly!

How many people have committed suicide because of a broken heart having fallen in love? How many people have thrown away their lives because they cannot live without the fix? What is addiction if it is not brain chemistry altered by chemical? The effect of falling in love is the alteration of brain chemistry and that is why it is a drug.

When we enter states of memories longing for a person with whom we had fallen in love with is it that person we long for, or just the memory of the feeling? Sadly, the memory is a chemical reaction which our brain craves. If we call into mind and meditate on the former feeling of love's refrain, we can actually affect our mental brain waves which is a recalling of the drug.

The Common Myth

The simple fact is that women do not complete men (as though they are the better half) and neither do men complete women. This idea is totally foreign to God. It is confusion and patently false! But the imagination runs wild with the idea when it enters the heart.

The whole phenomena is uniquely and amazingly addressed in the Old Testament's book, "Song of Songs." The Song is the monumental biblical account expressing the earthly sensation.

Our inner chamber of imagery should be wisely focused on keeping the images seen in Solomon's earthly temple in the Holy of Holies. Those images represent glorious representations. For in those images, we grasp the understanding of God's desire for imparting the essence of His divine nature.

Otherwise, romantic love can overpower our inner man and romantic love becomes idolatry. The overpowering feeling obscures the images on the walls of our chamber of imagery. Hence the warning to guard your heart, and the meaning of the breastplate of the high priest.

The proper understanding of what is allowed to occupy the inner chamber is the power that affects the upright palm trees to grow and the flowers to open. It is those images that should impress upon an individual who we are to become, and to whom we belong. It is for certain a profound battle!

Nevertheless, the obsession of romantic love can become so great a fixation that we tend to default calling into the imagination romantic dreams. Sometimes they are even salacious dreams by our own constructions, and thereby misusing our chamber of imagery.

But when the inner man is fully and properly functional and the doorway open to the pathway for the angels, then the Lord can instruct even in the night and throughout the day. Listen to this amazing text out of the book of Psalms by King David.

"I will praise the LORD, who counsels me; <u>even at night my heart instructs me.</u>" Psa 16:7

Chapter 13

A Closer Look

What can become more all consuming then creating a character in a script for the ideal woman? And it can work both ways for both men and women. The romantic film "Sleepless in Seattle" is a classic example where Nora Ephron, the late screenwriter, crafts her ideal man played out by Tom Hanks. He becomes the perfect man of her dreams in the perfect story. Don't get me wrong I thought it was a great movie.

But the great film is the epitome of what people in general allow to play out within their chamber of imagery. It can become the greatest deception that tempts both men and women to excesses and then to obsession.

The fact of the matter, the common temptation is as old as men have been on the earth. And the abiding issue was poignantly and poetically described in King Solomon's terribly misunderstood and woefully misinterpreted "Song of Solomon, or Song of Songs." Let's take a closer look at the classic book in the Old Testament.

One of a Kind

It truly and aptly is titled the "Song of Songs," because every single love song ever written describes the effect of one smitten with the overpowering sensation of human love. And in that respect every love song contains the same essence of the Song of Songs.

Let's take, for example, the classic song in the film "My Fair Lady." "Knowing I'm on the street where you live." Can there be a more powerful aphrodisiac? Listen to the first part of the famous song.

"And oh, the <u>towering</u> feeling, just to know somehow you are near the overpowering feeling that any second you may suddenly appear."

There it is. The "towering" and "overpowering" feeling. This is an obsession, but it is a perfect example of the very premise of King Solomon's

Song of Songs. It was this very feeling that unfortunately captured, occupied and monopolized Solomon's inner chamber of imagery. It was presumably what motivated him to write the "Song of Songs." Solomon was explaining, in his Song of Songs, the towering and overpowering feeling of human love.

I know what you are saying. Wasn't it, though, Solomon who built the inner chamber of the temple? I know! But even the wisest of men (Solomon was the wisest man on earth) can succumb to the intoxicating towering and overpowering feeling of human love. And he did!

The gravitational pull of human love is as hard to overcome as earth's magnetic gravitational pull on every animate object.

The haunting allure of human love, the seductive power of human love is "Just Impossible" sings Vic Damone, as he declares in the song he would "sell his very soul and not regret it." This is the worship of a woman. This is idolatry. Or how about the song "It's love my foolish heart?" The Song of Solomon is the quintessential preeminent character for understanding human affection. The great polemic dichotomy between the love of God as opposed to the love of a woman or man. It's human love versus God love. Solomon is the embodiment and storyteller of the great trap and its deception.

Solomon's story focus in the Song becomes the anti-hero, the antagonist. It's not the woman it is the feeling. Thus, Solomon's fixation with the girl is the inciting incident in this story. Solomon's description of his relationship with this country Shulamite girl is the pivotal point.

But the Song is the siren song for the unsuspecting soul. It is the magic of the magnetism, the plus and the negative that gets you. Gravity is magnetism. It is the magnetic force between man and woman. What would have happened had Adam not caved into *"the woman that thou gavest me"*? Evidently at that point he loved Eve more than God!

The study of human love can be deduced from the innumerable love songs that express the power and allure of what all men and women dream and long for, and most inevitably are taken by.

The power of affection, and the ensuing feeling therein is overwhelming and can easily dominate any person's thought life. No one conquers the siren song. No one returns. It is embedded in the shadow self that we must war against until finally we get to the other side where God wipes away every tear.

The only antidote in this present life is to re-focus on Christ Jesus. If one turns again to the shadow world and the shadow self, it all comes back.

This is the powerful effect of every addiction, and especially human love. And it is one which must be dealt with the rest of our days. It is because it still resides in the psyche of the old man/self.

Closer Focus on Solomon's Temple

It is extremely important to take an even closer look at this most improbable book. The Song provides a clear contrast between God's love as opposed to human love.

The Temple that Solomon built was to be understood later as a type of physical representation of a human being. (The physical Jewish temple was to be an allegory of the human body, as noted in the book of Corinthians)

"Do you not know that you yourselves are God's temple, and that God's Spirit dwells in you?" 1 Cor 3:16

But Solomon filled his own heart (his inner chamber or sanctuary) with the thoughts and feelings of human love. His remarkable Song of Songs reflects the outcome of the terrible miscalculation and misdirected focus. And thus his Song and its meaning created a remarkable contrast. In his classic song we can observe a massive contradiction. Instead of working on his own inner sanctuary of the inner man, Solomon went about his inner sanctuary with vain imaginations.

The Song provides, in remarkable contrast, the many mysteries of the human experience and more importantly the objective spirituality we are invited to reach for.

Dr. Ernest Martin's Commentary

One of my great mentors, the late great Ernest Martin, rolled out one of the most honest commentaries which will serve as a prelude to Solomon's astonishing book.

Here is Martin's commentary. (special thanks to ASK foundation for permission to reprint Dr. Martin's essay)

"Many of you have read it, many, many times no doubt, in the overall reading of the Bible, but have you known what to do with it? Have you really understood it? You see, even the commentators, the theologians and scholars are well aware that the Song of Songs has been the most controversial book in the entirety of the Bible. It is not only because there is sexually explicit language found within it. There are other reasons why the Song of Songs has been disputed over the years. Many people have wondered even if it belongs within the divine library of the books which make up the Bible.

The Jews and others have long ago recognized that it does. It belongs there.

The Song of Solomon has a number of features fundamentally different from other books of the Bible, whether in the Old or the New Testament. For example, do you know there is not one reference to the deity in any place?

This is one of the great difficulties in interpreting the book because, let us face it, it is difficult to discuss at length many of these things.

Song of Songs was a Dramatic Production

Though the Song of Songs uses language that we would normally not use in public, and yet in fact the Song of Songs was a drama performed in public in one presentation and set to music. You and I would say it was something like an opera, a musical, or a stage show. That is why it is called the Great Song, the Song of Songs.

It is because of this fact that people are not very prone to comment on it too much. We should not avoid the Song of Songs if we want to fully understand the overall teachings of the biblical revelation.

In fact, the early Jews (and this is rather humorous but nonetheless true) would not allow a man under thirty years old to read the book, unless he was married, of course. This was because the Song of Songs refers quite openly to parts of a woman's anatomy, and a male's anatomy.

I am not saying at all that I am condoning anything that is stated in the book.

But I am saying that God Himself does not mind talking in very plain and open language. He says it in a beautiful, wonderful setting, a drama set to music so that we can understand and enjoy what He is trying to tell us."

(Note: this was Ernest Martin's attempt at resolving his own conflict with the sexual scenes. Notice how uncomfortable he is!)

"I do not see why we should go around trying to avoid these things like so many people do today. Therefore, it is important to discuss all issues of the Scripture including matters of this nature. However, at the same time we want to use circumspection. We want to be normal and natural about this, and at the same time we certainly do not want to be offensive to ourselves or to you."

I certainly hope that Hollywood does not try to duplicate its theme with all the dramatic scenes being depicted, because if that would be the case you could not take your Sunday school or your Sabbath school class to see it!

I know one thing for certain, everything that is in the Song of Solomon, though it is depicted quite explicitly, is depicted in a way to be uplifting, to give people a beautiful teaching about the relationship between a man and a woman, courtship and romance, and how a physical as well as a spiritual relationship can take place between two people who love each other.
(note: as we will see this was simply not the purpose!)

But I must admit I often wondered how this drama was shown by people in the past in front of the general public.

Many ministers today would not even lecture on this book. Or, if they did lecture on it, they would need to leave out so much that you would not even know what was going on half the time. What we need to do is to look at the general teaching of it and try our best to understand it.

(note: but there are those scenes that are sexual even before marriage)

"This is one interesting thing, some of the scenes are before marriage, then we have the marriage of this Shulamite woman to King Solomon and how she becomes part of his harem, with other wives, and other concubines, and there are other virgins around. I am afraid Solomon did indeed have many wives and many concubines."

"What kind of understanding does this give to us in a spiritual sense?" "I am not absolutely certain."

At this point I must part ways with my mentor. While Dr. Martin goes on to chart the five turns of the plot line, when it came to understanding the premise of the play, he had no idea!

This is what Ernest Martin thinks the book is about.

It is a love song about a virgin girl who goes to Jerusalem to marry King Solomon. She has intimate sex with him and eventually gets married. It turns out she cannot deal with King Solomon having all the other women, so she returns to her home in Galilee, waiting for a time when possibly he might want her solely.

Yes, this is what the story is about but what is the message of the story?

Chapter 14

The Premise of Solomon's Song

Here is what it is not about. It is not about how to go about a proper romantic relationship with another person, though it is tempting to think it might be the case. It is **not** about Christ and the Church, as though in the story we are to see a grand metaphor of Christ wooing His bride to be. It is not a manual for courting a woman. Neither, and far from it, should it be construed as the bible giving license underwriting promiscuous sex, or premarital sex.

For those who attempt to deal with the story it seems everyone is embarrassed, even Dr. Martin. But to his credit Dr. Martin is the most honest of all.

It is so humorous how men blush (even Martin) at the thought of the Song's content. Funny, isn't it? But it is because we do not know how to process and integrate the obvious sex scenes in the Song into our overall sanctified thinking. But this is what men do when trying to figure out the exact meaning of the purpose of this book. Even the great Dr. Martin could not come up with its purpose nor the Song's premise. So, what in the world is God saying here through Solomon?

The Power of Human Love

When you step back and take a hard look at the forest from the trees the weight of evidence supports the view that Solomon was expressing the mystery of the power of human affection, sex, and passion. It had a grip on him. He saw its effect over both men and women in general, and how it dominated consuming almost the entire thought life of an individual. Human love, affection and sex is as the scripture itself says "is a consuming fire."

In a broader sense not only is this evident in the story, but it can be applied to anyone who has fallen in love. It is an incurable addiction. Human affection and love is an aphrodisiac. It is more addictive than drugs. Once the feeling enters the heart, the need for feeling is there for the duration. It will never go away.

In truth it can stay with a person their entire life. It returns time after time to haunt the human soul.

This I believe is the underlying purpose and very backbone of this tremendous book.

The Premise

The premise has a more overarching meaning. The premise can only be deduced by contrasting the human foible of romantic love in the heart with Solomon's inner sanctuary of the physical temple he built.

The inner sanctuary he designed and built for God was real but also to be understood as a representation of the heart or spirit, which is to be set apart for God. But the human heart can become conflicted and compromised, especially when it comes to human affectionate love. If this focus is left unchaperoned by the "divine nature" of God it becomes a usurper and a destructive force. And left unchecked will run wild ruining its participants, as it consumes a life.

Chapter 15

Man Needs to be Worshiped?

The fact of the matter is that Solomon loved being loved and by many women. He knew a great deal about women since he had one thousand partners. He knew what women wanted to hear and how to get them to respond. This is why all the women in the story were so captivated and lovesick.

"We will rejoice in you and be glad; we will extol your love more than wine, rightly do "they" love you." Song of Sol 1: 4

Notice that it is we rejoice and we will extol and that is they who love you.

The whole assembly of women were under his spell. In this singular instance with the Shulamite, we see a snapshot of his affliction, and insatiable need for affirmation. He needed center stage! He needed the attention.

Solomon was able to cast a spell over her too, and she is an example of the seduction which happened to all his women.

The aura of his persona was so powerful neither they nor she could withstand and resist. In his rarefied knowledge and extraordinary experiences with women he was crafty in not allowing his many wives to wake her up.

"Do not wake up my beloved until she wills." Song of Sol 2:7

In her all-consuming delusion and obsession, she could not deal with reality. She was asleep and kept asleep in her delusional dream obsession.

As exemplified in this singular case, it seems as though he wanted to keep her in that sleep state dream fantasy. He did not want her to awaken. He loved the fact she was inebriated and overwhelmed with love. He wanted her to dream on about him in swoons of affection, and admiration. He was consumed with her worship. He was intoxicated by a woman's adoration.

Hence ringing out again and again three times in the dialogue,

"do not wake up my beloved until she wills." Ibid

He did not want her to wake up from what was dominating her mind, because he found great pleasure in her singular admiring focus on himself.

This story's importance and why it is so graphically told is to illustrate the power of human love and affection, and it's inescapable grip on the human soul.

When someone is in love no one wants to wake up!

Not only was the Shulamite unable to escape but neither was Solomon able to overcome the power upon himself as well. It was his insatiable desire for a woman's dotting affections upon him that caused him to fall from God. (He had one thousand partners, consisting of seven hundred wives and three hundred concubines) It is important not to lose sight of his immense appetite.

When he proclaimed to her that she was a lily among the thorns he knew how to make her feel. As though she was his primary love; the one above all others.

Yet, she counters by saying,

"if a man sold all his house for love he would despise it." Song of Sol 8:7

This statement by the young girl indicated that she was beginning to wake up to reality.

What did she mean? She inwardly knew it could not last.

She was beginning to recognize the undesirable factual truth that he could never make her singularly his one and only. She began to realize the inevitable.

It was because she saw the seven hundred wives and three hundred concubines that she could not handle the competition. Jealousy had set in. She fled back to her home but could still not get over him. Nevertheless, she speaks these powerful words.

"Jealousy is as severe as Sheol." Ibid

It flashed like fire in her mind and heart.

"Nothing, (she goes on to say) not even rivers, can overflow and put out the torch," Song of Sol 8:

she laments by saying,

"Love is as strong as death." Ibid7

Even though it was jealousy that caused her to flee home, it was human love upon her so heavily she decried it is as "strong as death."

It was too late! She was ruined, ruined by the emotions of human love.

How unsettling to Solomon was the fact that she was waking up to reality. In her statement she knew deep down in her heart that Solomon couldn't just settle for her alone.

What could she do about it? What would be her resolve? She fled for home.

In the end of course she tries something desperate. It was with her little sister. She moves to protect her little sister from the calamity of her tragic mistake.

Her Attempts at Resolve

She brings up the fact that she has a little sister who was not of the age of puberty. She would seek to protect her from the enormous pain that had been inflicted upon her from her relationship with Solomon.

"What can I do," she asks herself? What she determined was to try to save her little sister from the same fate. She sought to keep her little sister from the incredible agony of anguish upon her heart.

"If she is a wall we will build on her a battlement of silver, if a door we will barricade her with planks of cedar." Ibid

In other words, I will build a defense around her so that no one can bring hurt.

Human Love or Love?

But there is something more which is overlooked and gets lost in the story. If Solomon truly and unselfishly loved and cared for the girl why did he not spare her the anguish. What was it in him that would not allow him to cut short the misadventure, and have the foresight to see what would become a most painful tragic ordeal for her? Why did he not cut it off before she got in so deep? Why did he allow her to get hurt? Where is the love?

There is a horrible reality that lurks in the heart of mankind. It is deeply embedded in the subconscious. It is the need to be preeminent. It is an evil that dwells in our chamber of imagery, but it must be rooted out and overcome. It is in both men and women.

It manifests as a need to lord it over others. It is something that seeks to be higher than another. It is a latent misconstrued idea that presses a person to seek to be worshiped. It is the motivating power of the Nicolatians. It is the spirit of Jezebel. The need to lord it over another. The need to be pre-eminent and supreme.

But what lies at the root of this unconscionable impulse is a massive identity crisis. It is not knowing who we are! Yes, even Solomon!

Chapter 16

The Pearl of Great Price

When it comes to a comparison there is a vast difference between God's love for the world and mans' human understanding of love. There is a massive distinctive difference! Yet the difference is often confused.

The confusion between the two opposites can be easily observed in the parable of the "The Pearl of Great Price."

In the story, a pearl merchant is found traveling the world looking for that one greatest of all pearls. Suddenly, he comes upon a pearl of such beauty that he risks all, investing his entire wealth just to acquire the one magnificent gem.

When Jesus came into this world it was to purchase through His own life, suffering, and the shedding of His blood, the purchase of all humanity. We are the "pearl of great price" in the parable, and it cost the Lord everything.

But in the Song of Songs here is a human description of love that is diametrically opposite. The contrast is startling.

"if a man sold his whole house for love he would despise it" Ibid

In this statement from the Song of Songs the axiom applies only to human love.

The statement written into the dialogue is not the case as it applies to God's love. Jesus sold out for all, but Solomon in his human love could not pay the price for this singular love interest. What a great and remarkable contrast! This fact alone proves that the Song of Songs is not about Christ and the Church as so many suggest!

The two loves are mutually exclusive. They are contradictory. Solomon's love interest with the virgin girl was not worth selling out for because deep down he knew he would need another fix. It would never be enough. This explains his accumulation of one thousand lovers.

The contrast is startling in comparison. Herein is the value of this Song of Solomon. It provides a tremendous comparison and contrast between the love of God and self-centered human love.

In the end the proof of the matter was evidenced by the fact his many wives led Solomon away from God. When it came time to make a decision, he walked. How wise?

Such is this greatest of all temptations that comes upon the "sons of men." But it all begins in the chamber of imagery, and that is why it is so remarkable and ironic that Solomon was assigned the task of building the inner sanctuary of the physical temple of God. It became a gigantic paradox, in contrast with his own heart.

Truth Be Told

What is seen in Solomon's writing of the Song of Songs is the mental landscape of a very active mind. It is the psychological transparency of what all men and women fantasize about. The altruistic elusive notion of finding the perfect person in a human being. Where does it take place? In the chamber of imagery!

If the curtain were pulled back peering into the secret inner chamber of a person's thought life, we would see something similar to what Solomon was writing about in his Song of Songs.

The reason for the knee jerk reactions of all the expositors, theologians and scholars is due to their own embarrassment arising from the Songs lurid sex scenes. The Song exposes the truth concerning a person's inner world of imaginative vividly explicit and secret thoughts. These thoughts lead to powerful emotional bondage, in fact overwhelming emotional chains.

For this reason, it is called the "Song of Songs" as it displays a mindscape that dominates and overtakes the human heart. It is the inner song/vibe of men/women obsessive focus for the unattainable. Consequently, the truth is left to itself alone in solitary confinement because the uncontrollable passions obscure the truth. Truth is left bleeding on the roadside. You cannot take what becomes idolatrous and somehow transmute it into God's love.

For women do not complete men and neither do men complete women. Once again, the scripture saves the day.

"for ye are <u>complete</u> in Him who is the head of all principality and power." Col 2:10

It is the answer for the common malady for love sickness. But try telling that to the afflicted! Good luck with that!

In real life Solomon never learned to master his obsessions giving way to the uncontrollable bias; hence he fell.

The Song of Solomon is the portrait of his obsession.

The Song of Songs is the divine explanation of the powerful aphrodisiac of human affection, sexual pleasure and adoration. It overwhelmed even the wisest of men. Solomon could not overcome his lower self!

Solomon was not condoning anything in this play, and neither was the Lord, but rather the Song is the observation concerning the power of human love. It may not have been his conscious motive or his purpose, but this is what the Song reveals.

The power of the ideal perfect women, he pursued throughout the course of his whole life, he could not accept was futility. In his emotional longings He could not perceive that they were mere insatiable lusts of the flesh. Here was a man lost in his imaginations.

The Song is a sad parody of the idealism of men and women fallen in love. He did say all is vanity, so give the lad some points, and yet he could never get over it himself.

Which robe will it be?

Chapter 17

The Union of Earthly and Heavenly

On the walls of the temple the Cherubim angels appear representing heaven, and the palm trees and flowers represent men and women. They are brought together on the walls of the house of God expressing the potential for connection between heaven and earth.

There were three kinds of "life" portrayed on these walls. Life was represented there from two domains.

These images show forth God's desire and intent to produce elevated human beings.

Jesus said it this way. "Is it not written in your Law, I said,

"Ye are gods" Jn 10:34

But what is fascinating about this text from the Scriptures is that Christians turn away and flee from its consideration much as many flee in fear from an infectious disease!

And yet, it is on the walls which show forth a moving picture of faith for producing a godly man and a godly woman. It is faith which opens to the revelation of God. It is our devotion to God which brings us to know our true identity.

Life-The Grand Source

The temple of Solomon explains this, but remember the physical temple is but a mere shadow of better things.

As Solomon the builder of the physical temple once said,

"there is nothing new under the sun." Ecc 1:9

And yet there is very much that is new, fresh and revelational with God!

Whatever station of life we find ourselves in, God does all His work from the humblest to the highest according to the same focus.

"Eye has not seen, the ear has not heard and neither has entered into the heart of man the things that God has prepared for them that love him." 1 Cor 2:9

And Jesus, Himself said,

"I have much to tell you, but you cannot bear to hear it." Jn 16:2

There is much we have not seen. And when we are set on human definitions, traditional doctrines, and man's opinions we become closed off to God's revelation.

In Pursuit of the Divine Nature

People who become set in their own ways find it terribly difficult to integrate a fresh insight into their own way of thinking. This is a common human foible. Unless they can find a means to qualify new vantage points by categorizing and finding some common ground, or from a so-called authority, they are simply rejected. And when it comes to qualifying authority, they define authority within a context they understand. They must have handles before they can entertain anything outside of accepted views.

People such as these are bound in their mind circuitry. This is not just characteristic of today but has been the general condition of mankind from the beginning.

Jesus when He said,

"Ye are gods and the sons of the most high God." Psa 82:6
He was quoting Psalms 82. But the psalm went on to say,

"but you will die as mere men." Psa 82:7

When we are insecure in what we believe and cannot get out of the boat of tradition we run the risk of being like mere men. Yet the truth is we are more than mere men! But it takes courage of faith to walk on the water!

Instructive Example

One of the most glaring but instructive examples of bound mind circuity was during the time of the great astronomer Galileo. His ideas were so foreign to the Church they even branded him a witch. They could find no common ground. It has taken hundreds of years to see that he was absolutely correct in his discoveries.

In the first century those who followed Christ were branded with the name Christian. The term was not invented by the followers of Jesus. The name came from the people who lived in the city of Antioch who were not able to come up with a way to define those peculiar people. How could they refer to them without some means of classification? Thus, followers of Jesus Christ were branded with the title Christians. It was the unbelievers who called them Christians.

Though these outsiders were not of the faith of Christ their definition stuck and has remained until this day. The need to define others is a common human trait but some people are like the wind. They defy human definition.

Beyond Definitions

In the hot pursuit of the divine nature there is a present danger. A person leaving the traditional fold will begin to defy conventional definitions and become like the wind. He is the one who is beyond categorization. He cannot be defined. This was Jesus and all those who live by the Spirit.

Many are the people who struggle to define such illusive individuals. Everyone seeks handles! They will ask, "are you a Christian"? Are you a Lutheran, a Methodist, Baptist or Pentecostal? What denomination are you? They will even try to define one within a political framework. Are you a Democrat, Republican, socialist, libertarian? Who or what are you?

Jesus was beyond definition. He fit no mold. They sought to define Him and categorize Him. Thus, He was falsely accused and defined by the authorities of His day as a blasphemer, whore monger, a winebibber, and sorcerer. They tried to put Him into their own categories and boxes, but they failed. He was like the wind!

The Goal of Our Instruction

The goal is not to become curmudgeons, recalcitrant, or argumentative, but as we follow God, as we live by the Spirit, this will be the world's perception.

At the end of the day the payoff for those who learn to follow the "law of the Spirit" is the acquisition of the divine nature. That is the true payoff!

It is a payoff not of this world. And it remains as a "weight" of glory. It is eternal.

It is who you are and who you are to become!

Chapter 18

Ascent of the Sherpa

I regard myself as "a spiritual Sherpa." In the natural world or physical realm, a Sherpa is regarded as a mountaineer and expert in the local area. They are immeasurably valuable in serving as guides at the extreme altitudes of the peaks and passes in the region particularly for expeditions to climb to the top of Mount Everest.

As a spiritual Sherpa it is my job to assist climbers to the heights of the spiritual mountain tops. Consider this, the highest mountain in the world is Mount Everest. It is a great metaphor for painting the picture of where God wants to take men and women spiritually.

Over the years the mountain has claimed numerous victims as many have perished in their attempt to conquer the compelling heights. In 2014 the hazardous conditions of the iconic mountain claimed sixteen souls. Needless to say, it is dangerous to climb high peaks! Likewise, there are also great dangers in undertaking spiritual ascents.

The Ascent of Mt. Hermon

"Who shall <u>ascend into the mountain of the Lord</u>? or who shall stand in his holy place? He that hath clean hands, and a pure heart; who hath not lifted up his soul unto vanity, nor sworn deceitfully." Psa 24:3-4

In stark contrast and on a mountain of less grandeur, with far less earthly acclaim at only half the height of Everest, there stands Mt. Hermon of Israel. In the days of Jesus there were few interested in climbing that mountain.

Even though it was unknown to the disciples as they climbed, it would yield far far greater significance, and infinitely greater perspective than the view atop Mt. Everest. The Mt. Hermon assent would provide, perhaps, the greatest vision of all time.

They would see the coming of the "Kingdom of God"!

"For we did not follow cleverly devised fables when we made known to you the power and coming of our Lord Jesus Christ, but we were eyewitnesses of His majesty." 2 Pet. 1:16-17

and this...

"He received honor and glory from God the Father when the voice came to him from the Majestic Glory, saying, 'This is my Son, whom I love; with him I am well pleased.' We ourselves heard this voice that came from heaven when we were with him <u>on the sacred mountain.</u>" 2 Pet 1:17-18

But Mt. Hermon, nonetheless, had its own hazards. There are numerous and countless spiritual hazards that can result from climbing the mount.

Only three men were privy to observe the cameo view of God's Kingdom as it came down upon Jesus at the top of Mt. Hermon. It was there they frightfully witnessed an event that today goes virtually unknown. But once experiencing the vision, and then digesting the experience, they would be set apart from all men. Afterwards, on the day of Pentecost after the death of Jesus what they had witnesses on Mt. Hermon would come upon them.

Nevertheless, what came upon them now would have to be worked into them. Now they would be tested! His life, the life of the Spirit, would have to be perfected in them. Now, they would be thrust into violent conflicts with the outside world. These men became like the wind.

There is a natural conflict that exists between the Kingdom of God, and the physical material worlds (the physical world includes our human body). Once the three men were overshadowed by the spiritual it began to transform their consciousness. Their inner man would never be the same.

Now would come a ceaseless barrage of external circumstantial conflicts, from the world outside. The human body is part of and connected to the outside world. The acquisition of the "divine nature," like a magnet, attracts every imaginable contravening conflict.

The divine nature upon its acquisition leads its patrons into great controversies. The controversies and enmities come even from brethren, family, friends, wives, and casual acquaintances. There are even environmental contradictions and conflicts. We live in a perpetual furnace!

Then there were the shipwrecks, confiscations of property, prisons, beatings, stoning and even death by crucifixion. But it is the dynamic of the conflict that drives the movement in one way. Yet there were and are those who would choose to bail out and go back the other way.

The whole process is set in motion by the transformation of Jesus and the coming of the Kingdom of God. We are being transformed because the Kingdom of God is now.

Once the Kingdom comes into the inner sanctuary of the human heart the fire of conflict is inevitable and unavoidable. But it is necessary!

Without the conflict there is no growth! The divine nature must expand and grow! *"The Kingdom of God is likened unto yeast."* Matt 13:33

It is an ever expanding Kingdom and it is to be expanding within!

Chapter 19

The Two Selves

"Therefore, we do not lose heart. Though our outer self is wasting away, yet our inner self is being renewed day by day. For our light and temporary affliction is producing for us an eternal weight of glory that far outweighs our troubles. So, we fix our eyes not on what is seen, but on what is unseen. For what is seen is temporary, but what is unseen is eternal." 2 Cor 4:17

There are two natures. One is the nature of Christ; the other is the nature of Lucifer. There is the God of the universe who is Christ, and there is the god of this world Lucifer/Satan. Human beings are caught in between these two forces. But complicating the conflict is the fact that our human body is wired to the nature of this world.

Conflict drives a person towards God or towards Satan. The ultimate question for each to answer is "am I being transformed into the divine nature or being conformed to the evil nature." It is either one or the other. There is no middle ground. The huge problem we cannot seem to admit is that our body contains the Satanic nature. Life then is about which nature we are accumulating and living out. We live out whatever nature is taking hold. In order to examine which garment we are putting on it is a good idea to look into a spiritual mirror.

Swearing to Your Own Hurt

Sometimes it is hard to evaluate which nature is gaining ground. And again, it is because of the confusion coming from our outer flesh self identity.

When I was a young boy coming from a non-Christian home my earth father, who was of Jewish descent, passed onto me something of great value. It has always played an important part in my life.

As I was growing up around the age of ten, I had a desire to play a musical instrument. My folks asked what it was I wanted to play. I said the drums. But they were not happy with that selection. I guess they did not want to hear the pounding in their ears. So, they asked again, what would be my second choice? I said, the saxophone. Again, they said, "no but you can play the trumpet."

I didn't like the trumpet, but I was forced into it. My father bought me a very cheesy cheap trumpet which looked like it was picked up from a pawn shop. It was not a shiny new trumpet one would be proud of but covered over with dull dross. This further exasperated my dislike for trumpets. He did the best he could, but it was very discouraging.

Anyway, as I began to take lessons, I learned that the valves had to be continuously lubricated or they would stick. Sticky valves prevented the instrument from properly hitting the notes. But there came a problem one day when I couldn't unscrew the valve covers. So, I took a pair of pliers in an attempt to remove the valve cover to lubricate the valves. In doing so, I bent the entire valve. Panic! I didn't know what to do.

I freaked! I put the trumpet in its case and hid it away for a few days, but my father found it. He confronted me, but I lied denying any direct involvement. I told him I had no idea what had happened. It was then my father said to me his immortal words, "word of honor?"

He had said these words to me before and they had been a classic part of my upbringing, but this time the rubber would meet the road. "Is this your word of honor?" Reluctantly, I said no it is not! He was shocked or maybe surprised would be a better way to explain it. How could I not tell him the truth? He was angry, but he did not whip me.

There were other times, if he thought I was lying, he did not spare. But this time he did not correct me with his belt. The point is, established within me there was a such thing as a "word of honor." It is called telling the truth! There is something about it! There is something about our words. It is a good gauge to measure and test the bias of which of the two natures is gaining ground.

A Very Historic Word of Honor

During the historic reign of King David there was a drought for three years. It was a severe drought and David sought the Lord for the reason why the

74

heavens were shut up. Why no rain? It became known to David that it was due to Saul the former king. Saul had killed people called the Gibeonites.

The Gibeonites who lived in the land of Israel were not Jews. Saul in his hatred for these people just killed them off. But in so doing Saul had violated a covenant that Israel had made with the Gibeonites many many years prior.

In fact, it was almost eight hundred years prior. Yet God had not forgotten the word covenant that was made between Israel and the Gibeonite people. But in this case Israel who represented God had given these people their word of honor. Israel had given its word, but Saul had broken the word/covenant.

The whole episode is recorded in the book of Joshua. It should be seen that God does not forget a matter, when people give their word. Even though we may forget things we have said, He does not. Yet He is very slow in dealing out judgment. Thank God!

He is long suffering. But just because He is slow to deal with a matter doesn't mean He has forgotten; it is because He gives time to allow for repentance and the amending of our ways.

"He tests men with His eyelids, both the righteous and the unrighteous."
Psa 11:4

What this means is that unrighteous men think that God's eyes are closed, and He does not see their evil doings or remember their words. They continue to think He does not notice or care. In other words, to them His eyelids are closed. He does not see! The righteous man is tested also, but in another way. He thinks that because God is slow to anger and to bring remedy that He does not hear prayer nor see their dilemma. Both the righteous and unrighteous are tested by God's eye lids.

When one thinks he is getting away with something, especially in the case of lying, it is foolish ignorance to think God does not see nor remember. When He does not deal with a matter quickly, the people are prone to continue to do evil. In this case continuing in a lying spirit. This is how people become pathological liars and put on the garment of the Lucifer/Satanic nature. It is the robe of unrighteousness.

In the case with king David the people who had formerly represented God had struck the deal and had given their word. It was their word of honor. Now it had been broken, and God had withheld the rain. It forced King David to seek for the reason why. It was told to him it was because Saul had violated the word of honor the Israelites had formerly given to the Gibeonites.

The point is our words mean something. One of the defining tests that determine which nature we are growing in is the "word of honor." Do we have a word of honor? Do we tell the truth, or do we lie? Are we putting on the divine nature or the Satanic nature? Which nature is growing?

When Jesus confronted the religious people of His day, He called them liars. He said your father Satan was a liar and a thief from the beginning and you are his children. Those who are the true citizens of Zion swear to their own hurt when they give their word.

In the case of the Israelites and the covenant with the Gibeonites, it was a very bad deal for Israel. But nonetheless they were required to honor what they had said, even though it was a bad deal. They had to swear to their own hurt.

There are times we make agreements that can be a bad deal, but we must honor our word. We must keep our word of honor and "swear to our own hurt." These are the citizens of Zion and those who are living the divine nature.

Chapter 20

The Marriage Connection Test

The greatest arena for the testing and perfecting of the divine nature is within the context of a marriage relationship. (Marriage is only between a man and a woman)

There is no deeper human relationship than that which exists in a marriage. It is the deepest of all human relationships. It is because in marriage the two become one.

Of all the covenants men can make in this world the most prolific and the most significant human relationship is made when two agree to become one in marriage. It is because the marriage relationship is a picture of Christ and the Church. It is a living metaphor of an everlasting bond that God has made with His people.

The sad reality is few there are who recognize the real difference between romantic love which is a feeling and God's love which is entirely different. God's love is sacrificial. This dis-cognitive failure eventually leads to massive disillusionment. When the feelings from romantic love fade away sadly so does the commitment.

God's love is a sacrificial love. It seeks not its own. It is not selfish, bears all things, believes all things hopes all things. It is patient and kind and does not hold onto unforgiveness. God's love seeks not its own way.

Romantic love is not in and of itself necessarily evil, but it is not the same as God's love.

The tragedy of divorce is that it not only disintegrates the living picture of Christ and the Church but the resultant damage to all the family members is devastating. This is why God hates divorce.

Why? Why do people fall apart and flee out from the marriage relationship?

There are many excuses and defensive claims such as "it was complicated. "I did not feel fulfilled." "I did not love him/her any longer."

But the fact of the matter is simple, and it is the same in every case. "We became incompatible and fell out of love." Those that confess such a thought only understand love as a feeling. They only see human love and understand love in a humanistic way. While there can be many such factors when each person is focused properly on Christ it is His power that holds all things together

There are no two people ever compatible because we are all born with a self-centered selfish nature. It is our fundamental flaw and focus. We default to self. Basically, that is why we are incompatible with anyone. We were born with a selfish nature. The truth concerning basic human incompatibility is stated in the text.

"In many ways we offend all." James 3:2

This is a disheartening scripture. We are so caught up with our self love, it is hard to accept that in fact we can and do offend all. This means each person can offend anyone. For those who have a vivacious personality, I hate to break the news. We in our self-centered nature can actually offend.

In the institution of marriage, as in all relationships, human love wears off. When it does people tend to hit the road. That is why without Christ holding a relationship together the chances of a successful union are not good. And, today, the statistics not only bear this out but are getting worse.

Marriage Vows

The people rarely understand the importance and meaning of the word of honor, which was supposed to be in their vows. Vows in marriage should not be just a flowery speech in a traditional ceremony. Vows are a covenant before God. But the sad fact is most do not regard marriage vows as a covenant. In other words, the vows that come are just part of a ceremony, but they do not come from their spirit.

When God made covenants with His people He never forgot, nor will He ever forget. His word is who He is.

"In beginning was the Word and the Word was with God and <u>the Word was God</u>." Jn 1:1

And so, it is with men. What we say is who we are! That is why we must be slow to speak because our words have great significance and meaning. Our word represents who we are.

The dissolution of a marriage is a classic case of an enormous identity crisis. But if we cling to our vow, God will see us through. What is at stake when the fire comes is who we are. Are we citizens of Zion or citizens of Babylon?

But the common logic is not based upon God but self, and it is our outer self. This is the common excuse.

"I am not happy because I am not fulfilled and therefore, I want out."

But the underlying fact is those who think and say such things never really understood that their significant other was never to be the source for their own fulfillment. Humans do not complete humans. Their significant other should have been God.

"And you have been made complete in Christ, who is the head over every ruler and authority." Col 2:10

When we hang our hat on the errant and foolish notion that another human is the one who completes us, we are bound for disaster. Only God can complete a man or a woman.

When people enter marriage without a full understanding of this spiritual reality they are heading for the rocks. Only when this foundational truth is laid down in a person's life will there be a grounding that enables a person to keep to their vow. When both individuals have this foundation then the marriage vows have substance, real meaning, and staying power. It is the grounding for long suffering in the context of marriage.

The Furnace is Super-Heated

In this hyperactive day and age with the external world filled with such political confusion, sexual temptation, and violence, can there be any real expectation for success in a marriage relationship? The real chances are grim and slim.

When difficulties come the strength of the word of honor should take precedence over selfish concerns. At all costs "I will keep my word (my vows) because my word is who I am." But is it any wonder that the success rate for the marriage relationship today has less than 50% chance of survival in the Christian community?

In looking at the big picture, if we cannot keep our word of honor how will we ever trust that God will keep His word of honor.

"With the kind You show Yourself kind, With the blameless You show Yourself blameless; with the perverted you show yourself twisted." 2 Sam 22:26-27

It is always the same. We fight for our own rights rather than swear to our own hurt, but if we have no other gods before Him, we will keep our word.

Marriage is the ultimate crucible for testing "the word of honor." But when vows are made, they should be directed vertically not horizontally. When vows are shared, they should be made unto God.

The growing up into the divine nature is the key and only purpose in this life. All other pursuits allowed to take precedence usurp the priority and are a waste of a life.

So in keeping with this notion of all "other pursuits," and in alignment with the pursuit of the divine nature to consider, there is one last thought before we press on. This is the most difficult issue to master in our climb to the top.

Chapter 21

The Greatest Hill to Climb

The greatest rebuke in history was recorded in the book of Galatians. And yet the greatest rebuke provides the greatest insight into the greatest test for all who seek "the mastery." Let me set the scene.

There were three men who climbed Mt. Hermon along with Jesus as they ascended to the top. These three were hand picked to view the most extraordinary event perhaps in all history. Little did they know it would involve the transformation of Jesus. It was to be an incredible experience and sight. But most importantly a teaching for the ages!

They were Peter, James, and John. These three were the strongest of the strong believers.

It was Peter who was at the garden of Gethsemane the night Christ was arrested. That night was the culmination of walking with Christ for three years. Peter followed Jesus that night all the way to the house of the high priest Caiaphas. He stayed there all night watching to see what would happen. It was that night Peter betrayed Jesus. Yet he saw things firsthand for three years. No doubt Peter was even there at the site of the crucifixion of Jesus. He was there in the upper room after Christ rose from the dead. Later he observed Jesus when He showed His wounds from the crucifixion. Not long thereafter Peter was back in Galilee where Jesus showed up at the seashore and cooked them lunch. And then years later was the remarkable vision that came to Peter which opened the door for the gentiles to come into the kingdom. He saw things unlike any human being in all history.

Peter was a strident follower of Jesus, and though he had his moments, he truly loved Jesus. Why all this background on Peter?

Peter who became the great Apostle was the recipient of the greatest rebuke in history. The event was recorded in the book of Galatians and the rebuke came from the Apostle Paul. Even though Paul never walked alongside Jesus it was Paul who delivered a knockout blow when he sharply rebuked Peter.

It is important to take a very close look at what took place, because it has tremendous implications and ramifications for our own personal lives. We must not fail to grasp its powerful significance. In fact, it is "the knife's edge" we must all learn to walk on. Jesus Himself said it this way.

"Verily, verily, I say unto you, He that enters not by the door into the sheepfold, but climbs up some other way, the same is a thief and a robber." Jn 10:1

The Camel's Nose Under the Tent

But Peter, the great Apostle, who had witnessed all these things who walked so very closely with Jesus was sharply corrected! Consider the magnitude of this rebuke carefully. Because as we seek to acquire the divine nature which is putting on the robe of righteousness there can be dangerous pitfalls, and Peter, the right-hand man of Jesus, fell into the most classic of all pitfalls.

If it could happen to Peter it could happen to anyone! Paul who issued the rebuke was so cognizant of the problem that he walked with great fear before God, because he knew it could happen to him. In fact, he would say,

"I was with you in much fear and trembling." 1 Cor 2:3

He was acutely aware of the problem of slippage from grace. It could be so very subtle. He knew the problem was related to his body. He knew the physical body was an unruly evil. He knew the human body must be understood as having been subjected into a certain disposition. He knew the body was set in opposition and in contradiction to the inner man. He fully understood there is war between the outer carnal man and the inner spiritual man. He knew the pursuit for obtaining godliness had tremendous hindrances. He knew putting on the divine nature was at daily variance.

He said,

"I buffet my body and make it my slave lest after preaching to others I

What actually happened to Peter that caused his slippage and brought on the classic rebuke? The understanding of Peter's demise is critical in grasping the predicament we all face. It is the ball and chain!

Peter's Pitfall

Prior to the many believing Jews coming to Galatia, where Peter was residing, Peter would dine with the Gentile believers. But after the Jewish believers arrived, he decided to eat with only the Jewish believers.
So what was the big deal?

Paul was able to discern from Peter's behavior in dining with the Jewish believers something was amiss. Why? The Jewish believers were keeping the dietary laws of the Old Covenant! This behavior was creating an air and false sense of a superior class of believers. But they were adding the Law to faith. In keeping with the Law, they were seeking to achieve a greater sanctification as a means for holiness. But Christ Himself taught the impossibility of this when He said, "You cannot sew a new patch (the New Covenant) on an old garment (the old covenant)." This common sin is what people do!

Peter, along with these Jewish believers were in essence, diminishing the efficacy of the sacred blood of Christ for a compromised gospel. This is what Jesus referred to as cleaning the outside of the cup. By a return to keeping the Law they were negating the only means and way to holiness. The finished and totally accomplished work of Christ needs no additives.

They in essence were sewing an old patch on a new garment. The death of Christ and the shedding of His blood is the only means for redemption and the acquisition of the divine nature. The acquisition of the divine nature cannot be attained by going back to rules and regulations. This was why Paul was so adamantly and strongly saying, "if any man preaches any other gospel let him be accursed." What the Hebrew believers were doing was an abomination and disrespect to Christ, the finished work on the tree, and the New covenant in His blood!

They were rebuilding the wall of partition between Jews and gentiles.

There is no wall because in Christ there is only one new man. The Law has been made void! It has been erased! By defaulting to the Jewish Law as an additional necessary means for sanctification they were annulling and disqualifying what Jesus had completely accomplished at His death. He had **_totally_** done away with the Old Covenant as a means to being right and holy with God. Jesus eliminated that way when He died.

The Jewish believers who had just arrived in town were still clinging to their purification traditions and rites of washing. This is exactly what the Sanhedrin tried to lay on Jesus when they first confronted Him.

"Why do you teach your followers to forgo the tradition of washing before eating, Jesus responded, Why do you keep your tradition and disobey the commandments." Matt 15:3

(Just a note. Jesus was not teaching that they should keep the Law here. He was only pointing out that they themselves were not able to keep the Law. The very Law they were demanding others keep they could not do themselves. That was why He called them hypocrites)

Peter feared the Levitical Jewish believers. These Jews coming to Galatia had not shaken free from the tradition of the Levitical rite of washing. Not that one shouldn't wash before eating, but they were making it a regulation and determining factor for righteousness and hence fellowship. Paul was incensed! The washing of hands had nothing to do with achieving a pure heart. And neither is a pure heart acquired by any means coming from any religious regulations, or some religious ceremony, including keeping the Sabbath day.

Peter feared them. When he sided with them as opposed to the other believers it was a clear sign he had fallen under the spell of "another gospel" that required additionally the keeping of regulations for attainment to holiness. The Jewish believers made Peter feel uncomfortable and guilty by their religious behavior for attaining holiness.

From this Paul knew that Peter had placed himself back under the Law.

The subtlety is almost imperceptible to the unlearned and can happen to anyone. It is the camel's nose under the tent. And since it is a present danger for everyone it takes the knife's edge understanding to master the ever present problem.

Chapter 22

The Knife's Edge

It was the "knife's edge" that Peter somehow got away from. Peter had opened the door. He was exchanging the full righteousness in Christ's blood by adding the righteousness of the Law or works. This is exactly what people do when they do not walk the knife's edge.

"Let us draw near to God with a sincere heart and with the full assurance that faith brings having our hearts sprinkled to cleanse us from a guilty conscience and having our bodies washed **(water baptism-signifying we identify with Christ's death**) *with pure water." Heb 10:22*

The sprinkling is a reference to the Jewish high priest's sprinkling blood on the mercy seat in the temple to atone for the people's sin. In this case the metaphor of the high priest is utilized to express in a picture what Jesus accomplished by His death when He shed His blood.

Another way to make clear the practical meaning of the works of the Law is derived from the word penance. Going to a priest who prescribes fifty hail Mary's to eradicate sin is a work of the Law. We cannot fix our inner man and conscience by an external behavior. Any attempt to fix ourselves by an external behavior is a work of the Law. It is called penance resulting in "legalism."

We can only fix an evil conscience by the means provided by Jesus. Seeking holiness any other way by keeping or adding the Law or the works, thereof, nullifies the completed work of God. We cannot adjust an evil conscience by any other means than Christ's shed blood. The Law and keeping it will not cleanse our inner man. This is what Peter was attempting as he aligned himself with the Jewish believers. The Law is for the outer man. It is a regulation on the behavior of the body.

In other words when we stray from the path even though it is a momentary lapse due to the impulses of the flesh, we must return to the sprinkling of the blood. If we are to walk in the Spirit we recognize and understand the mercy of God in His atonement. This is the knife's edge!

We are all tempted to respond to our evil conscience (after we sin) by trying to balance the scale. This is what Peter was doing. Instead of the sprinkling of the blood he fell into the temptation to adjust a troubled conscience by doing something good. In this instance washing of the hands. This is the enormous common error of men and women. Anything can be dead works. This is what brought forth Paul's rebuke!

There is no other way, as Jesus said, except through Him. But when we do not walk daily, and assume otherwise, we cannot help but fall back under rules and regulations i.e., Law. An evil conscience requires adjustment. But if it is not in the atonement then it will be in the classic error of adherence to rules and regulations. This is the meaning of dead works!

As long as we live in this body of sin we must daily walk in the faith and faithfulness of Christ crucified. We are prone to sin because of our bodies. If we do not obtain proper cleansing, we inadvertently revert and try to cleanse ourselves by other means i.e., the works of the Law. We do not have a license to sin, but we are prone to it and must learn to obtain our cleansing from the everlasting gospel (the gospel means the good story) which is written in Christ's blood.

We live in a defiled world and inside a body of death. But the Law which amounts to external regulations on the body, as Paul put it, is a "ministry of death." We cannot fix our conscience by being good!

It is because the Law is weak through the flesh. The flesh, although it tries, cannot live the Law. It is for this very reason Jesus had to come to rescue mankind from our untenable hopeless predicament by doing away with the Law as a means of a cleansing pathway for righteousness. The Law is obsolete!

We cannot help for the moment, (our current life) that we are still here in a corrupt world and in a finite and a vain glorious body. We can only deal with it through the faith in the blood of Christ and the washing of the water of the Word. There is no other way. It demands a knife's edge recognition of our perilous predicament. Hence again Paul,

"I was with you in much fear and trembling." Ibid

The "knife's edge" is the present tense recognition of our perilous situation, but it does not mean we should feel insecure. We have an eternal salvation, but we must manage by a continuous awareness of the ongoing battle within ourselves and the repentance we are called to daily. There is no way one can walk in the Spirit without the humility and necessity to repent. Repentance is not merely when accepting Christ, but an ongoing and continuous attitude of faith for the duration of this mortal life.

Dividing Soul and Spirit

There is a call to recognize the dividing of soul (the word for soul in scriptures is psyche) and spirit (spirit is pneuma). There is a great difference!

Our human mind is our psyche, and our heart is our spirit. We must develop the ability to differentiate between the two if we want to grow in Christ. This is the daily call to walk with the Lord and it is "the process." It is literally and spiritually the knife's edge. There is no escaping. We simply must learn daily how to cut it!

"The word of God is quick and sharp piercing even to the dividing asunder of soul and spirit and to the joints and marrow and is a discerner of the thoughts and intent of the heart." Heb 4:12

Just remember. Your body is not the real you. All legalism and walking in the flesh is the result of losing recognition of who you really are. It is an identity crisis. We are not our body. The Law was given for the unrighteous man (the unrighteous man is our body) It is unrighteous because it is cursed as it was conceived in iniquity. The fact of the power of the body or flesh and its influence was accentuated in the book of Jude where it was noted...

"save others by snatching them from the fire; and to still others, show mercy tempered with fear, hating even the clothing stained by the flesh." Jude 1:23

When people such as Peter added the Law (rules and regulations) to grace it is because of unrepentance. People simply do not understand the duality of themselves and that is why legalism is a classic example of an identity issue.

Two Edges of the Knife

Repentance keeps one in alignment with God, but in order to live fully according to the "law of the Spirit" there must come first the "Baptism of the Spirit." The empowering of the Holy Spirit is the infilling of the Spirit. If one is not baptized in the Spirit, how can one walk in the Spirit? There are countless Christians who are <u>not</u> baptized in the Spirit. They have a form of godliness but not the power. That is, they tend to revert to a moralistic idea of Christ. They live by rules and regulations rather than by faith!

These folks are still living according to will worship and not by the power of the Spirit. But even those who have been baptized in the Spirit like Peter can still fall back under the Law as did Peter.

We must walk daily and be ever cognizant that while in these mortal bodies we can and do stumble. Unless we remedy our transgression through the sprinkling of the blood then we will fall back under the tendency to follow rules and regulations. Once we are cleansed through the eternal blood, we can once again return and live according to the Spirit.

Is it any wonder then why Paul would say,

"I was with you in much fear and trembling and endeavored to know nothing among you but Christ and Him crucified?" 1 Cor 2:2

But how can you know the walk in the Spirit if you do not understand the inner man? The inner man is the sanctuary of God as opposed to the fleshly soulish natural mind inclinations of the outer man. These inclinations come from influences of the body. Paul called it the "body of death" for that reason.

Paul's incident with Peter at Galatia is perhaps the single most important spiritual reality to master for daily progress regarding who we really are. It is the one most critical factor in the attaining to the divine nature. We are not flesh; we are spirit sold into flesh.

Chapter 23

Another One Bites The Dust

The title of this chapter is not to be understood as a glib remark. I am in sadness for what I am about to tell. Unless one is vigilant it can happen to anyone.

One of my dearest and oldest friends who accepted Jesus Christ, and was even water baptized, sent me an interesting email. It was after we had a long conversation on the phone. He had discussed his spirituality previously, but I was not certain as to what he was talking about. He sounded all right, but I had an uneasy feeling about the interaction. He said that he was doing well and that he meditated daily.

I was never sure about what he was meditating on. In a subsequent phone call, it began to surface. It turned out that he had adopted a transcendental idea that served him as a structure, but it had nothing to do with the Good Shepherd Jesus.

"Satan can transform his messengers into angels of light." 2 Cor 11:14

Beware and be forewarned!

The stepping stones he had embraced (via Alcoholic Anonymous ten steps) was nothing more than another proffered pathway that was based on another set of rules and regulations. It was another form of legalism. It served essentially as an external control over the body.

It offered another way other than faith and for him it became a regulation. He did not understand that he was trying to regulate his outer man. He didn't know who he was.

Yes, it provided him with a way to escape the ravages of alcoholism, but there was no way it could cleanse his inner man, his spirit. Thank God he is free from his addiction to alcohol, but external steps to follow with a call to meditation does not cleanse the inner sanctuary of the temple. Again, Law or laws or regulations of any kind cannot cleanse the inner sanctuary or rather the inner man, the true self. They may help for regulation of the outer man but have no benefit for the inner man!

Even though the ten steps were not of the Jewish Law, this was exactly what Peter had fallen back into. But Paul said it this way, and it has a comprehensive application.

"If even an angel preaches any other gospel than that of Jesus Christ and Him crucified let him be accursed." Gal 1:8

"For If I rebuild that which I have destroyed I openly show myself to be a transgressor." Gal 2:18

The Law with all its regulations and which Paul called the "ministry of death," cannot in any way produce righteousness. It may produce an outer righteousness or form of godliness but not an inner righteousness. This kind of technique of which there are many today can never qualify for our acceptance before God. Christ Himself had to secure righteousness for mankind because we cannot attain to it in any way.

We do not achieve righteousness by the works of the Law (or any other means) on our own. If we do not walk with this understanding it is certain we will fall back under the Law or other external regulations and abandon the daily necessity for the use and exercise of faith. And this is why organized churches are most often legalistic.

Faith is, first and foremost, a connection with our will. We choose to align ourselves with His throne. This is how our will works with grace. But it is not an external work. Jesus said, "this is the work of God to believe in Him whom He has sent." It is not a dead works type of works where one is trying to earn salvation by penance or by exercising an external form of godliness. No one can work His way to heaven(s) by doing good deeds or by obeying legal obligations, or even trying ever so hard to be a good person. No one either can gain the weight of glory by keeping external regulations.

Since God is not willing that any should perish, He includes all into His kingdom who merely believe in His name. Because even the mere belief on His name is a work of faith. So the exercise of faith in Jesus, whatever the depth, the dimensional scope, or wherever one fits on the spectrum is what qualifies for God's kingdom.

But growth in the Kingdom is another matter!

Growing Up!

Here is a good analogy!

When one picks up the phone call from God and answers the call he is saved! But in keeping with the mind picture of the phone call, the dimension of faith one possesses can be assayed by how long one stays on the call.

Some people say hi and goodbye while others stay for a while and have a good conversation, and yet others stay on for a long-extended period. This is faith, and it is a gift. Each man has his gift! However one chooses to use his or her faith gift is that person's choice. But the longer one stays on the phone call the more he knows the caller. This is how one acquires the "divine nature." Paul was no longer concerned whether he was saved or not, he was concerned with the acquisition of more dimensions of the divine nature.

"If any man's work shall be burned, he shall suffer loss: but he himself shall be saved; yet so as by fire" 1 Cor 3:15

So then the question we want to be asking is how much do we want to use our faith. How much time in our lives do we want to devote to staying on the phone call? How much do we want Christ? The answer relies on the use of faith.

When Jesus put forth the question,

"will the son of man find faith on the earth?" Lk 18:8

It was a rhetorical question and left unanswered. Will He? This is the question each must ask of himself and that must be answered daily. If it leaves a person feeling insecure it is not that they are unsaved again, it is because the answer is based on hearing His voice daily. It takes faith.

"Today if you hear His voice harden not your heart." Heb 3:7

Faith comes by hearing. So hearing means you are on the phone. So, then we use our faith to get into His presence and while in His presence He adds more and more grace to our existing faith. This is the meaning of from "glory to glory."

The reason He asks, "will He find faith" is because His people do not know how to connect daily with His grace. They have not learned how to use their faith.

"Grace works through faith." Eph 2:8-9

Faith Failure

It is a recurrent theme in both the Old and New Testament that God's people continually fall backward.

In the book of Revelation for example all seven churches had their candles extinguished. They were no more! The great apostle Paul when writing to his spiritual son Timothy expressed to him a great sadness concerning this perplexing problem.

Paul spent three grueling years establishing a work in Asia. His headquarters were in the city of Ephesus. Night and day he worked to build a congregation. He wrote from Ephesus to the Corinthians on the other side of the Aegean Sea of the great difficulty he had in Asia stating that he even despaired of living. Eight years later while in Rome, in a letter to Timothy, he wrote,

"all have departed from me in Asia." 2 Tim 1:15

Imagine how discouraged he felt after all the work he had done in Asia only to discover all had departed. What a terrible sense of loss!

What an incredible dilemma we find ourselves in as we peruse history only to find this is the nature and tendency of all people. Each must, therefore, be personally responsible and vigilant in the exercise of his/her own faith. We cannot live off the faith of another.

But the problem is everyone has a ball and chain! People fall away from God because they fail to recognize their body is not who they are. They fail to connect and build up their real inner self. They walk in the flesh. Their ball and chain body pulls them backward.

In order to live according to the inner man identity, we must be renewed day by day.

"Therefore we do not lose heart. Though our 'outer self' is wasting away, yet our 'inner self' is being renewed day by day." 2 Cor 4:16

Chapter 24

The House

It is essential to lock into the big picture. Our permanent body is our eternal body!

"It does not yet appear what we shall be." 1 Jn 3:2-3

The development of the divine nature is a matter of one's own faith, and it is a lifelong process. How we use faith will determine the magnitude and weight of our inner man. It also brings weight to bear on the eternal body into which we will eventually enter.

The house prepared for us in the heavens, our eternal body, is tailor made in accordance with the acquisition of the divine nature. The progress we have attained in the journey through this temporary earthly life has eternal significance.

Even though life here is considered momentary (perhaps seventy years or so) it is critical to the formation of our eternal inner being. Hence let us lock into the pursuit and acquisition of the divine nature. We may get angry with the chaos coming from the outside world, but the principal matter of this mortal life is attaining to the divine nature.

Again, the development of the divine nature, which is by the daily exercise of faith, will determine how the eternal body is tailored. It will be tailored as to who we are, or rather who we become. Hence our destiny is in our own hands, in a sense, using faith! Life eternal is not about what one accomplishes in this life and in the outer world but who we become. It is not about what we do it is about who you are!

Look at this misunderstood scripture in the classic chapter in the book of Romans.

"Not only so, but we ourselves, who have the first fruits of the Spirit, groan inwardly as we wait eagerly for our adoption as sons, the redemption of our bodies." Rom 8:23

Your earthly body is not you! Yet the pervasive effect on the mind and the mind's development and what leaks into our spirit comes from the outside and from our physical body. That is why the psalmist wrote in his psalm...

"create in me a clean heart oh God and renew a right spirit in me."
Psa 23

The outer world and the appetites of the human body tend to dominate occupying most of our conscious daily thought life. The outer man is so very powerful in its influence upon our inner man it can even affect our dreams at night. Since these effects are 24/7 and the outer world is so obviously corrupt and our bodies so lustful, how difficult it is to obtain a pure heart and a clean spirit. Hence, we must strive to enter His rest. Coming to Jesus initially is just the first step.

When Jesus took His disciples to pray, they could not endure in prayer for even one hour. He called their attention to their weak inability to pray and then finished the incident by saying...

"the spirit is willing, but the flesh is weak!" *Matt 26:41*

The Apostle Paul pointed to the same problem when he said in the book of Romans.

"What the Law could not do in that it was weak through the flesh."
Rom 8:3

Both Paul and Jesus were saying that the body is a ball and chain. The body pulls us backward as it wars against our inner man. This is our foremost problem we must come to recognize if we expect to grow and advance spiritually. The ball and chain do not go away when a person comes to Christ. In fact, it remains a great problem for the Lord in helping us.

It is so easy to lose sight of this objectivity and what we must be brought back to daily.

The Sacred Stripes

When Jesus was whipped and beaten, He bore the effect of the scourging in His body. Those marks from the whipping are referred to as stripes. It is written...

"But He was pierced through for our transgressions, He was crushed for our iniquities; The chastening for our well-being fell upon Him, and by His scourging we are healed." Isa 53:5

Notice that the scourging was done to His body. How is it that the stripes in His body produce healing in us? When we hear of Jesus healing blind eyes or deaf ears we immediately think of the physical eye and physical ear. Jesus did do those things of course but look at the bias of our thinking. We apply the meaning of healing to the outer man first. But the outer man is perishing. Should we not think of healing and the stripes He bore was for the inner man first? Is not the eternal inner man of far more significant importance than the temporary physical body which is perishing?

So then how do the stripes that He bore for us work to heal the inner man?

Again, we call to mind the crucial fact that God is the one who is in the process of separating the wheat from the chaff. This is His discipline. As has been mentioned He separates the sheep from the goats, the good from the evil, the soul from the spirit. But how His stripes work for our inner healing, is best explained in the parable of the wheat and chaff.

Wheat is separated from chaff by crushing. In those far off days a very heavy stone called a millstone was rolled over wheat. When the stone rolled over the wheat it crushed and separated the outer chaff that housed the wheat from the meat or the wheat kernel.

When Jesus was crushed by wicked men it was as if a milestone was being rolled over Him. When we see those stripes He bore we begin to understand that we too must bear His stripes as we recognize that life will crush, whip and beat us to separate the bodily influences of the outer man on the inner man.

In that way we bear His stripes and in that way, we are healed because we are being separated from the chaff of our body/flesh and its terrible influence and corruption on our inner man. The classic word used to characterize the millstone is trials. But we must bear up under the crushing by seeking Him. In the seeking under the intense pressures of this life we acquire His nature. This is how we are healed! This is how the divine nature is acquired, but only as we look to the unseen.

That is why when Paul encountered Jesus on the road to Damascus Jesus said to Paul, whose name was Saul, "Saul, Saul why do you kick against the goads"? If we can learn from the stripes that come to everyone as the necessary element for separating the influences of the outer self from the inner self, then we understand we are in that process of the crushing or whippings/stripes that heal. It is the goads that are the stripes and the discipline of the Lord.

Job said it this way.

"Though you slay me yet will I praise You." Job 13:15

At that point we can embrace the words from the book of James,

"Count it all joy my brethren when you fall into various varieties and many colored trials." James 1:2

...because these are the stripes of Jesus wherein, we are healed!

So God is watching to see how we respond and deal with trials and why it is said of Him,

"Precious in the sight of God is the death of His godly ones." Psa 116:15

We are essentially being killed by a thousand cuts. But it's all good!

What is Redemption of the Body

So, then we should have a clear understanding. The body in which we were born into was conceived in iniquity or vanity. Our earth body was ruined even before we emerged from the womb. It is a feeble wreck that must return to the dust. No matter how beautiful the woman nor handsome the man, it is but dust. Yet as second Corinthians tells us...

"to be absent from the body is to be present with the Lord." 2 Cor 5:8

When the scripture speaks of the redemption of our body it is not talking about the redemption of our human body, for there is nothing redemptive about this "body of death." It is so ruined it must be buried in the earth. There is nothing redeemable about these temporary human bodies.

The redemption of our body cited in Romans pertains to the "heavenly body."

We groan within ourselves because we long to be set free from this damnable prison and put on <u>the eternal body</u> that is waiting for our return.

Paul was able to see clearly, that he was preparing to live in the city of God along with myriads of angelic beings in a re-acquired eternal heavenly body.

Physical Exercise Profits Little

But before we press on, look at this. One of the more interesting statements that goes to this reportage is the statement in the scripture "physical exercise profits little."

"For physical exercise is of limited value, but godli**ness** is valuable in every way, holding promise for the present life and for the one to come." *1 Tim 4:8*

What?

Today, what do we see? We see the glorification of the human body. There is a premium placed on good looks, physical fitness, proper diet and the exhalation of the human body. But physical exercise profits little!

Nevertheless, look how much time people spend in the clubs and gymnasiums and the beauty salons. The plastic surgeons make fortunes fixing women's faces and bodies. Look at the colossal effort taken to make the human body look spectacular. Now there are designer diets and hormonal injections just to beautify the human body. Isn't the herculean effort obviously a focus on the flesh or the carnal man. Isn't it all vanity?

It is vanity because the human body at best is like grass that in just a few years withers away like the weeds of the ground and then is no more. All the effort for what? Yet the building of the inner man is neglected while the inner man is eternal and forever.

Are we saying being in good shape is a sin? Is working out a waste of time and all vanity? Of course not! Yet, for some it may be. The idea of physical exercise profits little for the most part, is not profitable, at least not for the acquisition of righteousness and the divine nature. The word righteousness, and the pursuit thereof, can be lost in the grand scheme of things.

What we should understand is that righteousness can be misconstrued unless we keep it within the context of the <u>duality of our being</u>. Righteousness should be seen as the ongoing exercise and strengthening of the inner man as opposed to the outer man, which is the flesh. As an aside, when the scripture encourages the speaking in tongues it is because the man who speaks in tongues strengthens himself. The self he is strengthening is his inner man, and that is why Paul said,

"I speak in tongues more than you all." 1 Cor. 14:18

The Human Body is Wired

What is monumentally important to understand is the body, or outer man, left to itself will default in the direction that leads to the city of Babylon. It is inevitable. It is wired up that way.

When one stops to consider the heavenly body, which lasts for eternity as opposed to the earthly body that is so temporary and lasts for maybe seventy years, the comparison is not worthy of much consideration.

We simply must count the real cost while here and now and build our inner man and prepare for reentry into our real bodies which are waiting in suspension reserved in the heavens.

But it says the redemption of our bodies. Since the human body cannot be redeemed, and flesh and blood cannot enter the heavens, the redemption of our bodies is a great promise awaiting.

Chapter 25

Hidden Portal

In more than fifty years of Christian experience, and literally hearing thousands of sermons, I have never heard even one message about the unprecedented Transfiguration event that took place at the top of Mt. Hermon in northern Israel.

To characterize the event as a mere pinnacle event would diminish the enormity of its importance and spiritual significance, but that is what has happened! It is generally considered just a mere historical moment in the life of Jesus. Few are those who consider it a "spiritual portal."

From the Heavens to Earth

Apart from the death, resurrection and ascension of Jesus, the giving of the Ten Commandments, the fulfillment of Joel's prophecy concerning the day of Pentecost, the Transfiguration on Mt. Hermon was the most important manifestation of spiritual reality to happen on planet earth. Yet the Church is virtually silent to the colossal event.

Why is this incident so tragically ignored and absent from the voluminous endless messages from the pulpit? It seems to have little or no place in the religious conversation? Could it be that it is the doorway into the spiritual reality that all hunger for? And why the powers of darkness fight so vigorously to camouflage hiding its monumental significance?

It is well beyond time to revisit the momentous event and reclaim the key which opens the door for what was promised. It was the promise for the acquisition of the divine nature, the principal objective, and the Kingdom of God.

"I will give you the keys to the Kingdom" Matt 16:19

"You have not come to a mountain that can be touched and that is burning with fire; to darkness, gloom and storm; to a trumpet blast or to such a voice speaking words that those who heard it begged that no further

word be spoken to them, because they could not bear what was commanded: if even an animal touches the mountain, it must be stoned to death. The sight so terrifying that Moses said, I am trembling with fear."
Heb 12:18

"But you have come to <u>Mount Zion</u>, to the city of the living God, the heavenly Jerusalem. You have come to thousands upon thousands of angels in joyful assembly." Hebrew 12:18-22

What does it mean to come to Mount Zion? Is this just a clever metaphor? Is it hyperbole that has been reduced to a mere cliche in Church circles, or was it meant to be a daily experiential reality? Could this not be a powerful image that spiritually beckons like Mt. Everest in the physical, but paints a magnetic image of what it means to be seated together with Him in heavenly places?

Not many have sought to read and personally apply this scripture in Hebrews and sadly it remains just a historical moment in the life of Jesus Christ. Nevertheless, there is something to it that should draw us out!

Let us seek how it applies.

Spiritual Substance

The spiritual substance is supernatural yet remains out of reach for most because the real event has faded from view. In organized church circles the matter has become nonessential.

Superlatives that pump up emotional yelps through bombastic sermons while pick pocketing dollars from ignorant parishioners most certainly is not God's plan. Emotional responses evoked by clever preachers flunk God's call.

The understanding of this key text is the meaning of the <u>process</u> of trans-accumulation of God's glory and the building of the inner man.

Emotion is not Spirituality

God's people characteristically and historically confuse emotion as spirituality. They are not one and the same. In fact, they are at the opposite ends of the spectrum.

But the call of Christ is to come to the mountain and climb Mt Zion. To really climb Mt. Zion is the activity of the exercise of faith and the process for gaining the divine nature.

The Mt. of Transfiguration episode was intended by the Father as an invitation and doorway into spiritual reality. Hello, I am the Sherpa!

Heavens Have Been Shut

Today it is the professional clergy who claim exclusivity to the keys of the Kingdom, but the promise of the keys is to all of God's people, not to just a professional clergy class.

The Holy Mount of Transfiguration provides the guidance and encouragement for ascending and uncovering the many secrets to personal transformation through trans-accumulation and ultimately transfiguration. This is the pathway in preparation for the redemption of our eternal body and flight into the Father's house.

It is far beyond time to ask the hard questions. Questions that have long been dodged by the titled professors and priests who cannot answer tough spiritual inquiry. It is the pretensions of self-exalted men who shut up the heavens who themselves do not enter preventing others from entering as well. The Kingdom is at hand. It is now!

It is on Mount Zion where our spirits are perfected.

Superlatives, dogma or do we have spiritual reality? It is either one or the other. Has man's supposed engagement with God been reduced to unsatisfying dogma, religious tradition, bankrupted doctrine, false history, foolish myths, amplified talk, and mental exercise? It is the difference between empty religion or the revelation of the living God.

Is Jesus and His kingdom really real, right now, today or has it become just a theoretical notion, a mental exercise, a boring cliché, or a meaningless debate? Is this why so many are walking away?

As a result, could today He be saying, as of old, "I hate your gatherings"? And why He has departed from thousands of sects, denominations, and churches?

Let us put on the divine nature and let us not pretend by merely going through the motions of Sunday services. The question we should all be asking is are we growing in the acquisition of the divine nature or just kidding ourselves. Unless you touch the "powers of the age to come" you will never know if your spirit is being perfected!

"Behold I stand at the door and knock. If any man hears my voice and opens the door I will come into him and sup with him and he with Me."
Rev 3:20

In the end Jesus is knocking at the door of the Church to get in. Perhaps to really know Jesus, it is better to be outside knocking at the door with Him.

Let us go on and climb to the highest levels of Mt. Hermon's secrets. As we climb the holy mount there will come the separating of spiritual reality from the conformity to the religious counterfeit forms.

Chapter 26

The Key that Unlocks the Door

"Faith is the victory that overcomes the world." 1 Jn 5:4

This is a remarkable statement in 1st John because it indicates that there is a problem, but it also provides the solution.

The world and the flesh is the problem which must be overcome, and the way of overcoming is through faith. The flesh is also of the world. So while there must be a good explanation for what faith is, there must also be a good explanation for what the world is. But first, why is it so important to overcome the world?

The Satanic Anointing

Please take note: Jesus Christ means Jesus the anointed. Or as it is sometimes put in scripture Christ Jesus, Anointed Jesus.

The book of Ezekiel tells us that there was an archangel who was called the Anointed Cherubim and identifies him as Lucifer. The word anointed, again means Christ. Lucifer was the Christed Cherubim. So not to be mistaken, the degree of the Cherubim's anointing was vastly different from the anointing of Jesus. It had to do with the office.

Lucifer had anointing for the office of the Morning Star. Jesus had the anointing as Savior. Savior was the office for the redeemer. His office as the Son of God required the anointing, but it far exceeded and surpassed the anointing for the Morning Star office.

Lucifer had a brilliance over that office which mere men cannot fathom. But his brilliance became reversed. What was once a brilliance of light became a brilliance of darkness. The best earthly picture of dark brilliance in the last hundred years was in Adolph Hitler. Hitler had a dark brilliance! He had a Satanic anointing!

When the war in the heavens took place those under the angel Lucifer's command were banished along with him to this present prison world. The effect of his anointing has poisoned this world. The darkness of his anointing like a filthy garment has soiled nearly every human agency and earthly

105

institution since the beginning of human time. That is why the scripture calls him the "god of this world." He has been given by God authority to rule over this world. But why would God Almighty allow this?

The answer is lengthy and is answered as we go forward, but for the moment it becomes clearly evident that we must overcome Lucifer/Satan's horrific influences over the planet! We must overcome the world!

Jesus begins to describe this overcoming just before He and His three disciples took their ascent up Mt. Hermon. (Remember Mt. Hermon is the Mountain of Transfiguration)

It was at the foot of that mountain at a place called Caesarea Philippi where He began His discussion. The location was in northern Israel and was dedicated to the pagan god Pan. To the Jews it was known as "the gates of hell!"

When Jesus asked His followers who they thought He was, they gave various answers. But Peter said,

"thou are the Anointed (Christ), the Son of the living God." Matt 16:16-18

Jesus responded by saying,

"thou art a stone and upon this Rock, I will build my Church and the gates of hell will not prevail against it"! Matt 16:18

So we have an Anointed (Christed) Lucifer and an Anointed (Christed) Son of God. These Anointings are in a contradiction!

But just as our Sun is an enormous celestial object in the sky it nonetheless looks equal in size to the moon. Yet, they are far far different in magnitude and volume. So too are the anointings! They are far far different!

Gates of Hell

But Jesus is saying something very monumental here concerning gates.

The term gates had a specific meaning to the Hebrews. It was at the gates of the cities where the leaders and dignitaries would meet to discuss the issues for governance for their particular city. It would be the reasoning of these leaders which would be the determination for the city's policies.

In the United States, for example, the gate for governance, for now, is Washington DC. Also, in each sovereign state of the United States the gates would be the governor, and legislature. But Jesus was talking about the gates of hell. The gates of hell are the reasoning of hell. The reasoning, He was saying, would not prevail over and against His Church.

It did not mean that the prevailing of His Church should be misunderstood as the conquest of the outer world. It meant that the outer world would not conquer the inner Kingdom within His faithful. The outer world governed by the god of this world and his reasoning would not prevail against the believer.

But the only way this could be prevented would be that the faithful would know how to overcome. And that prophylactic would be faith!

"Faith is the victory that overcomes the world." 1Jn 5:4

But if faith is the victory, what does it look like?

Faith is how we must live it by personally pursuing the Throne of God! We cannot use the keys of someone else. We cannot live off another person's faith. We cannot even live off the coat tails of the pastor. It must be our own faith!

Our individual pathway through this life has specifically tailored circumstances. They are unique. Each life is individualized. And each one must learn how to use his/her faith!

So then using another person's keys (faith) to open a door or shutting one is like cheating on an exam or plagiarizing another person's work. We fail the faith test because we are not understanding that what we are dealing with is a personal matter. Neither do we understand that we are called to overcome Lucifer/Satan's world.

Life is dynamic not static, and therefore, as the plot line of the outer world flows, faith must be at hand and exercised continually. Each ensuing trial is a hurdle we must learn to overcome by faith. These tests are specially tailored difficulties designed as obstacles, but are intended as stepping stones to build faith.

"For I will give you the keys to the Kingdom of Heaven. Whatsoever you bind on earth will be bound in Heaven, and whatsoever you loose on earth will be loosed in Heaven." Matt 18:18

The binding and the loosening have to do with what we allow in or not. But the promise of Jesus is that the reasoning of hell will not prevail. The contradiction of the two anointings exists to keep us moving forward and pertains to who we are! It is about who wins! And who wins is a matter of faith!

"Faith is the victory that overcomes the world." 1 Jn 5:4

Without the use of faith, the reasoning and power of the "gates of hell" can overpower our inner man.

So, we must see that the obstacles we daily encounter are the hurdles of God's design essential to develop our faith. And faith is evident or not with how we confess. How we talk! It is not what the pastor says, it is what you say!

"A man believes in his heart unto righteousness and <u>confession</u> is made unto salvation." Rm 10:10

What we confess is the evidence of faith.

The Mind Picture

Everything Jesus said or did was not only literal it was metaphoric. Here at Caesarea Philippi was a vivid picture of the gates of hell. It was to be contrasted with the mountain top's transfiguration event that portrayed the acquisition of the anointing. (Notice the location of the literal event that was also to be a metaphor. It was at the foot of Mount Hermon! Quite a contrast!)

The Holy Mount event in contrast with the gates of hell is a picture of the process for obtaining and growing in the Anointing. We are to obtain the Anointing!

"Speaking the truth in love we are <u>to grow up</u> in Him in all things" Eph 4:15

This is the anointing!

The acquisition of the anointing is to grow up in Him!

"But before faith came, we were kept under the Law, shut up unto faith, which should afterward be revealed." Gal 3:23

Unless we understand that Jesus did away with the Law (i.e., rules and regulations) and made them obsolete so that we could live by faith, we will not use faith and may still be shut up to faith! And that is why so many cannot grasp faith.

Chapter 27

Faith Frustrated

Have we become so sophisticated, overwhelmed, and jaded by the "information age" we can no longer be taught? The information age has stolen our minds and robbed us from knowing God. It has stolen faith!

Even when there is a scarce moment when a divine seed might be planted it is immediately plucked up by the numerous birds of the air of the information age. The world's technological environment has created a blinding effect robbing us of our spiritual thinking. We have become so overwhelmed with temporal knowledge and information that it crowds out any room for the use of faith, the spiritual, and the supernatural.

We fail to come to grips with the fact that our hearts have been hardened and our conscience seared as with a hot iron. We have been robbed, unaware and oblivious to the reality we have been mentally pick-pocketed by a master thief.

God rides silently in the back seat gently tapping on our shoulder, but we are too dull to apprehend, and do not turn to listen. No wonder Jesus had to ask history's greatest rhetorical question!

"Nevertheless, when the son of man returns, will He find <u>faith</u> on the earth?" Lk 18:8

The fact that He will even be searching for faith suggests a grave problem. If we had even a modicum of care, shouldn't we stop and deeply consider the question?

What really do we have going on in our chamber of imagery? What is so important in deference to the use of faith?

Nevertheless, on and on day after day, attention is riveted to I-phones, laptops, I-pads and TV. The focus is tantamount to the same idolatry that brought an end to Israel's previous temples. Yet, likewise we allow the outside world entry and access into our own temple! No wonder the whole world follows, bows down and worships the image of the beast! The image of the beast is the media.

These electronic devices, if not used with wisdom, drown out the voice of God rendering the inner person's mind and spirit unreachable and un-teachable! If that is all we have going on we are wasting a life never developing faith.

"If any man thinks he is wise let him become a fool so that he can be wise." 1 Cor 3:18

The admonition and caution for entrance into the Kingdom is clear. You must become as a child! But honestly who has time to take that seriously? Everyone is just too busy.

"For the Kingdom of heaven is of such as these." Matt 19:14

But it takes a death!

The use of faith requires a death. The motions of the body scream against the flexing of faith. It is almost like a rocket ship lifting off the earth straining to break free from the opposite pull of gravity. People refuse to make the effort because the body wars against the use of faith. We must put aside our fleshly lives daily and this requires that we die to our human nature and passions.

"You must become as a child!" Matt 18:3

A child is teachable. This is what was meant by the Lord for His invitation and entry into His Kingdom.

To become a child must be preceded by a death. A death to self. The death to self means our human outer self. In a day when the common parlance is to love yourself God says the opposite.

"Whoever finds his life will lose it, and whoever loses his life for My sake will find it." Matt 10:39

And so again, comes the great rhetorical question. And this is the question each must ask of himself.

"When the son of man returns will He find faith?" Ibid

There are many scriptures that talk about faith. If Jesus will be in search of faith when He returns to earth and questions will He find faith, then we must look only to ourselves if we desire to have it when He returns. What does faith look like?

There are so many who think that the faith is all about a creed or a mental exercise, a virtual mind game. But faith in God is not mental gymnastics. It is not memorizing a bunch of scripture or debating. It is not about the Apostles' creed. None of those things are wrong but this is not faith.

You can have faith in yourself or another person or in anything. You can have faith that if you climb a set of stairs you will get to the top. Or when you drive your car you know that if you step on the gas the car will go faster and likewise when you step on the brake the car will stop. You have a settled certainty in the car's operation. It is second nature. But unfortunately when people discuss the word faith they think about faith in terms of doctrines. "What do you believe they might ask"? For example, "do you believe in the Trinity or hell or heaven"? But this is not faith. You may believe in these things because you have a mental ascent, but this is not faith.

These are examples of intellectual concepts or theological ideas, but is this what Jesus meant when He said, will the Son of man find "faith" when He returns? Was Jesus talking about theology? Was He talking about religious theory? When the Son of Man returns will He find theology?

Yet when people talk about faith this is what they think, but this was not what Jesus was referring to. Jesus was not talking about theology. He was not talking about becoming masters of theology. He was not talking about brainy religious intellectualism.

Picture of Faith

One of the best examples of faith was demonstrated by a gentile and this was before gentiles were thought to be included in the commonwealth of

God. He was a soldier and had a sickness in his house. Jesus pointed him out as a great picture of faith. In fact, the greatest picture of faith.

"When Jesus had finished saying all this to the people who were listening, He entered Capernaum. There was a centurion's servant, whom his master valued highly, was sick and about to die. The centurion heard of Jesus and sent some elders of the Jews to him, asking him to come and heal his servant. When they came to Jesus, they pleaded earnestly with him,"

"This man deserves to have you do this, because he loves our nation and has built our synagogue."

So, Jesus went with them.

"He was not far from the house when the centurion sent friends to say to him."

"Lord don't trouble yourself, for I do not deserve to have you come under my roof. That is why I did not even consider myself worthy to come to you. But say the word, and my servant will be healed. For I myself am a man under authority, with soldiers under me. I tell this one, 'Go,' and he goes; and that one, 'Come,' and he comes. I say to my servant, 'Do this,' and he does it." Lk 7:1-25

When Jesus heard this, he was amazed, and turning to the crowd following him, he said,

"I tell you; I have not found such great faith even in Israel."

"Then the men who had been sent returned to the house and found the servant well." Lk 7:5

Here was a man who demonstrated extraordinary faith not creed not theology! This man's faith produced something remarkable. Faith is not a mind game for theological debate and discourse. It is not about who has the right doctrine, or eschatological view. It is about a belief in Jesus to such a degree that it produces something.

Does this sound like intellectualism? Does it sound like biblical academia? Does theology by itself produce anything?

What Is Faith?

Did the centurion have hope? Yes. He hoped Jesus would bring a healing. Did He express faith? Yes. He said, "I am a man under authority, just like you." His faith was in the recognition that Jesus was under the authority of God, and He would do it, and he said so. He confessed what he believed!

The resultant effect was the evidence of the healing. It was the evidence that came that was initially unseen. Faith, real faith produces something that manifests in the physical world. It is not about discussion. It is about the manifestation of the unseen to the seen. It comes as a conviction and then manifests as a confession. It was his deep conviction in who Jesus was and what He could do.

Faith works the unseen and even miracles ensue. It has substance. It produces. Again, faith is the substance or conviction of things hoped for, **the evidence** of things not seen. It is the movement from the unseen spiritual world to the physical seen world.

Here it is again.

"Faith is the substance of things hoped for the EVIDENCE of things not seen." Ibid

It manifests beyond mere chatter. But the common man or the natural man does not understand how real God is! The natural man believes and thinks He is just a theological construct or concept. And yet God answers prayer!

Down Payment of the Age to Come

But just as a man gives to his betrothed an engagement ring as a down payment of his commitment, so does God give a down payment on His promise of His Kingdom and eternal life. He does not leave us in mere hope of eternal life, but He proves by demonstrating His love and reality. He gives the Holy Spirit. The very power of "the age" to come. The Holy Spirit is not merely a topic of theological discourse. The Holy Spirit is a real force of His power. It is the experiential reality of the age to come. It is the engagement ring for the future marriage. We get to taste the eternal age now!

The Mount of Transfiguration experience was a monumental preview of what would be experienced very soon thereafter. While the three selected followers who accompanied Jesus to the top of Mt. Hermon did not fully apprehend the Mt. of Transfiguration episode, it represented a phenomenal hope.

Jesus said, "the Kingdom is at hand and <u>will be in you</u>." The visual at the Mt. of Transfiguration episode was a preview and promise. That promise would arrive on the day of Pentecost. It was then that the Kingdom had come from the unseen to the seen. The Kingdom had come down to earth. It manifested. Those who followed Jesus with the hope of His coming Kingdom would become recipients of the power. Their hope turned to faith, and it produced from the unseen to the seen.

It was not a mere hope of promise in the way off future. The evidence of hope came in the overshadowing of His Kingdom upon and within the disciples. This was "the evidence of things not seen." It was the down payment, so that no one was left to believe in a far off theoretical or theological, or eschatological hope of a future Kingdom.

This is the conviction or substance of hope. It is in that conviction wherein faith is energized and activated. It is and was at Pentecost where the evidence of the unseen manifested. Pentecost was real and it is real for everyone. Right now!

When Jesus returns this is what He will be looking for!

Chapter 28

The Two Tracks

The question Jesus asked concerning faith in the preceding chapter must be looked at rhetorically. It was asked as a question which each person must answer for himself. While we have the "earnest of the spirit" (if you have received it) we must come to clearly understand the daily testing.

This life is actually lived, metaphorically speaking, as a train running down two railroad tracks. We are all on board the train. Each rail of the track represents two roads. Each road leads to a respective city. And each city has its citizens. We are all heading to one city or the other.

This is a picture of the trial of our faith, and it must be fully understood. It is because of the conundrum, that our faith is proved each and every day. I hope you heard that! It must be proved each day. To be proved means to be tested. Every single day, throughout the day, our faith is tested.

The citizenship of either city depends on which nature one is acquiring. Inevitably there will be citizens of the city of Zion, or on the other hand, citizens of Babylon. It is inevitable. It will be one or the other.

It is an astonishing fact that each parallel rail of the railroad track leads specifically to one or the other respective cities. Every human being, aware or not, is living out their lives riding on the train going down those two tracks. We are all heading for a city. But the uncertainty and question are which one? Which city? The dilemma is one that must be understood and solved. How is this question settled?

It can be known by truthfully evaluating which track we recognize ourselves to be riding on. In that honest evaluation we can determine the bias of which track, and that bias dominates our life choices. Are we headed to the city of Babylon or to the city of Zion? No one can tell you. It is for your own determination. The riddle is yours to solve! But each day our faith is tested as to which track we ride.

The track we consciously or inadvertently select determines which city, and the city of citizenship. One track leads to the city of Babylon "Mother of Harlots" the other track leads to the city of God, which figuratively is Mt Zion, and the city of angels. It's either harlots or angels. You can call yourself a Christian and still find yourself on the wrong track because each day requires a reset. This is insight into why the Apostle Paul said, "I must die daily."

Both cities cannot be seen with the human eye they must be perceived because while both cities are real, they exist in the spiritual realm, but be assured it will be one or the other.

The City of Babylon Mystically

Many today try to fix a physical location to the city Mystery Babylon. Some say that the city of Babylon in the book of Revelation is New York City. They say this because of all the cities in the world New York is the commercial center of the world. Others say no it is London which is the chief banking center of the world.

Others say, "it is Rome," because of the religious control of the Catholic Church.

And then there are those that say, "no it is Jerusalem where Jesus walked, and that Jerusalem is called Sodom and Egypt where their Lord was crucified."

But Babylon the great was the historical city (around 2000 BC) which existed during the ancient historic time of Nimrod. It was the Satanically designed system which released raw spiritual sewage and corruption into this world with a religious stench persisting even to this day. It is the mystery Babylon Mother of Harlots and the great city! It does not exist today in a physical sense, but its spiritual influence is ubiquitous. It is Rome, it is Moscow, it is Paris, it is Tokyo, it is London, it is the United States. It is everywhere. It is ubiquitous!

In the book of Revelation, it is the by-word that has become a symbol of religious and hence spiritual deception. It is the counterfeit city of God. It is an unprecedented contradiction!

It covers the entire planet and cannot be located by assigning it to any one single physical location. It is everywhere present and remains a pervasive force over the peoples of the earth. It has deceived the inhabitants of the planet from ancient times and continues to this day. All the world has been taken by her seductive power.

It has been carefully designed and crafted by the adversary of all mankind and is made to look so real that it is almost impossible to recognize and nearly impossible for anyone to come out from. But it is a Satanic creation that has been designed to destroy all humans keeping them from the only true God and the correct city of destination. And on a greater scale it diminishes God's people from a greater attainment to the divine nature, and far more exceeding weight of glory. It is counter intuitive to faith! Mystery Babylon is the polluting stench that has corrupted the outside world!

It is real in the sense that it is here and now and sits upon institutions like a cloud shrouding over the land. It is why people are so easily seduced. It is a serious counterfeit of the real city of God. It is a miracle that anyone can wake up and come out of her.

"And the woman which thou saw is that great city, which reigns over the kings of the earth." Rev 17-18

The city of Babylon is described as both a commercial and religious deception that seduces the whole world and has sucked the blood out of the saints.

"And I saw the woman drunk with the blood of the saints, and with the blood of the witnesses of Jesus. When I saw her, I wondered greatly." Rev 17:6

Religious deception is a horrific bondage. It is very difficult for people to accept that they may be heading toward that dark city. This is the reason why the apostle John who penned the whole book said...

"When I saw her, I wondered greatly!" Ibid

Look at how she is described.

"The woman was clothed in purple and scarlet, and adorned with gold

117

and precious stones and pearls, having in her hand a gold cup full of abominations and of the unclean things of her immorality." Ibid

The deception by the magnetic pulsating power of "the city" is great. While most of the Protestant churches point their finger singularly at the Catholic Church they fail to recognize they too are being described in the text.

But Mystery Babylon is <u>not just a religious deception</u> it is also the world of commerce and trade, and of course politics. Politics controls commercial Babylon. In its commercial description, who can deny it is best modeled in the United States.

"For all nations have drunk of the wine of the wrath of her fornication, and the kings of the earth have committed fornication with her, and the merchants of the earth are waxed rich through the abundance of her delicacies." Rev 17-18

Now this concerning her...

"And I heard another voice from heaven, saying, <u>Come out of her</u>, my people, that ye be not partakers of her sins, and that ye receive not of her plagues." Ibid

One of the key indicators of which track one is on is contained in the amazing scripture.

"Win to yourselves those of mammon with mammon so that when mammon fails they will receive you into everlasting habitations." Lk 16:9

What is Mammon?

This was a message Jesus taught concerning the "god of this world," which is the love of money or wealth. Of course, we know that Lucifer/Satan is the god of this world, but people who place the love of money and wealth above God have made money and wealth their god. In that way money and wealth are what people worship. They spend their lives serving mammon. Worship in the Greek language means to bow you knee.

The book of Romans points to the correct priority and it should be our reasonable service of worship which is to serve God.

"Therefore, I urge you, brothers, on account of God's mercy, to offer your bodies as living sacrifices, holy and pleasing to God, which is your spiritual <u>service</u> of worship" Rom 12:1

He was explaining to His followers that you cannot serve two masters. If you try to do this then it amounts to trying to straddle the two railroad tracks. Jesus said this was impossible to do. He said,

"no one can serve <u>two</u> masters: Either he will hate the one and love the other, or he will be devoted to the one and despise the other. You cannot serve both God and money." Matt 6:24

But the idea of the teaching was to use money, if you find yourself in that position, to use wealth to win people over to the true God. Find a way to invest your earthly wealth to build God's kingdom.

This is an issue of everyday testing. Our heart, if we are not paying attention, can flip from one day to the next and motives must be under scrutiny. One can start out on one track and then always flip to the other.

The Only Way Out is Up

But there is the other side. It is the track leading to the city of God. But even for those who initially focus on the correct track, be warned, there is the ever-present allure and pull coming from the opposite track. We must contend daily. Faith must not be allowed to become dormant by going to sleep on the tracks.

"But you have come to Mount Zion, to the city of the living God, the heavenly Jerusalem. You have come to thousands upon thousands of angels in joyful assembly, to the church of the firstborn, whose names are written in heaven. You have come to God, the Judge of all, to the spirits of the righteous <u>made perfect</u>, to Jesus the mediator of a new covenant, and to the sprinkled blood that speaks a better word than the blood of Abel." Heb 12:22-24

While there are two tracks, the two tracks are set in a dynamic tension

and contradiction. They are not asleep! There is a constant conflict between them. But it is the constant conflict that brings weight to the decisions of daily life. The heart can flip flop! The daily tension calls for a constant watchman.

We are instructed to "keep our heart with all diligence for out of the heart
come the issues of life." And then this wisdom from proverbs.

*"A little sleep, a little slumber, a little folding of the hands to rest, and
poverty will come upon you like a robber, and want like an armed man."*
Prov 6:10-11

There must be continuous care as we ride the rails. It is ever so easy to go
to sleep and ignore the exercise of spiritual discipline. The end of that failure is just as the proverb states, to become spiritually destitute ending up
in the city of Babylon.

Like the watchman at night on the wall of the city, or today, the ever-vigi-
lant watchers that keep track of the flights of enemy aircraft, there must
be the watching over our hearts. The enemy powers of this fallen world
are ever seeking whom they may devour. We are, whether we want to or
not, in a titanic spiritual war. That was why Paul, when writing to his son in
the faith Timothy said,

*"thou therefore endure hardness as a good soldier of Jesus Christ, No
man that wars entangles himself in the affair of this life that he might
please Him who called him to be a soldier." 2 Tim 2: 3-4*

We ride the two rails! But when Paul said,

"I was with you in much fear and trembling" 1 Cor 2:3

It was an expression of his constant awareness of the conflict and the concern that he would remain on the right track. He did not want to come
short and become a failure to faith. His primary concern was in the continuous acquisition of the divine nature, the robe of righteousness.

"Will the son of man find faith?" Ibid

It depends on which track. And each track identifies who we are!

Chapter 29

You Must Be Dressed

The proper track one rides requires a specific clothing. We must dress properly as we ride the rails. And when it comes to the track leading to the City of God it is the putting on of the "robe of righteousness." Specifically, the clothing for the city of God is the acquisition of the divine nature. The divine nature is the robe of righteousness, and the daily pursuit.

What an incredible conflict! What an incredible tension! The problem is polemic and every day. The book of Psalms carefully instructs that we are to number our days. Each day is critical.

"Lord teach me to <u>number my days</u> so that I may present to you a heart of wisdom." Psa 90:12

Have you ever put a number on your days? How many days do you think you have? If you live to three score and ten which is seventy years you would have 25,550 days. That's all! Not much time to acquire the divine nature.

Unless we truly understand the extreme pressure, we are under in the daily conflict we will never press into the instruction for the "numbering of our days." We can easily waste a lifetime in futile, empty and vain pursuits.

It is as though two magnets are pulling from opposite directions. Each road set against the other.

One city, the City of God and the other the city Mystery Babylon. The ride along the tracks represents an everyday conflict of choice. It is the choice to exercise faith or not. To which track will be the commitment and decision for this day? It is not just something one can decide on and walk away from when he/she first gets saved! It is an everyday polemical conflict which requires a daily decision. It is a choice for today. It calls into play the immediacy and daily use of faith. This is why it is a "narrow way."

What will your choice be...today? It is so easy for the heart to harden. It is so easy to forget. It is so easy to be like the natural man who looks in a mirror and goes away forgetting who he is.

"Today if you hear His voice harden not your hearts." Heb 3:15

One of the greatest spiritual songs of all time is the hymn "Great is thy Faithfulness." In the song is one phrase that stands out and should be underscored.

"His mercies are new every morning." Lam 3:22-23

If we could just hang our faith on the shelf, then why would we need his mercies to be new every morning? The answer is we cannot! We cannot hang our hat (our faith) on a shelf and walk away. Each day requires the exercise of faith. We must learn to exercise faith today. In fact, the very Sabbath day is today!

Yesterday's mercy does not work for today. Oh yes, we can coast on yesterday's victory, but only for so long. We must be accelerating in faith not coasting. Coasting leads to deceleration.

Just as we eat every day to maintain our body so must we use faith to gather spiritual sustenance for our inner man. And we can because His mercy is new every morning. He is there! But what becomes of those who neglect to gather their spiritual food? They will lose momentum and begin slowing down and eventually go in reverse, or as it is commonly called in church parlance backsliding.

Spark of Life and the Destruction of A Soul

Recently, in an incredible YouTube video, there was a pictorial of conception; the very instant a sperm touched an egg. When the sperm touched the egg there was an explosion of light. It was the precise moment of conception when a spontaneous light flashed. It was the instant the spirit had entered flesh. Incredible!

The Choice is Life or Death

Yet, this gave pause to consider a terrible situation which arose within my own family. It was with my daughter in law. She had become a perfect example of one who had no spiritual discipline. She decided she was not fulfilled in her marriage, so she turned back to the world and became an adulteress. I never in a million years thought this could happen within my own family. But everyone must choose. No one can live their life for another. God gave to each person choice and a measure of faith.

She stepped off the right track and put her foot down on the other; the one leading to Babylon. She chose, preferring this present life, to the eternal life provided by our Father. I still cannot believe it!

It is not as though others have not made the same catastrophic decision, but because this happened within my immediate family it was particularly incredulous and terribly painful.

There are several examples mentioned in the New Testament where people departed from Christ. What she chose to do was not uncommon nor unprecedented. But her fall came after ten years of marriage, and three children. What a disaster! Sin is messy.

Fools Gold

There are many Christians who would say, "yes there but for the grace of God go I." I cannot believe how misinformed that statement is! Yet it is so prevalent. Those who would say such things do not understand faith. They have a view as though it is in God's purview to dole out grace as He pleases, and when He wills. They seem to think, "And if He had not doled it out to me then there would I go as well." They incorrectly and erroneously see grace as a random act of God.

How shallow and utterly ignorant! It comes from not understanding faith! I get angry at the ignorance.

God does not dole out grace as though there are some lucky ones and some unlucky ones. Grace is not flung out like a candy man indiscriminately tossing out sweets to children at a party.

Grace is more than a definition of "unmerited favor." That is what people commonly say in such cases, but it is terribly wrong. Yet, what a powerless and clueless cliche. God is not a candy man!

The grace of God, which keeps us from falling, comes by the daily use of our faith. It is His power (grace) that must be connected to every day. We have to stay on track and keep ourselves in the grace of God. We must "strive to enter His rest." It makes no sense to strive to enter His rest if we falsely assume we can put our faith on a shelf. Striving to enter His rest suggests there is effort involved. It is like seeing the sperm connecting with the egg.

"Grace works through faith!" Eph 2:8

We must press through with our faith and lay hold of the grace that is always there to connect with.

My daughter in law never learned to use her faith and she finally succumbed to the desires and impulses of her flesh. For her it was not about grace it was about her never using her faith.

Yes, there but for the grace of God go I because it is God's grace that keeps me, but grace must be enjoined and contacted with by faith. The two work together not separately. Those people that utter the sad cliche do not have, nor know the proper understanding of how faith works with grace. The ignition of grace connected to by faith is like the sperm touching the egg.

My daughter never understood the word that,...

"Unto us are given exceeding great and precious promises so by these we might be partakers of the divine nature having escaped the corruption that is in the world through lust." 2 Pet 1:4

The "promises" of God were never given to fundamentally acquire anything of this world. Faith is not about getting stuff. They were given to acquire "the divine nature." And His nature conflicts with our earthly nature, our flesh, which is our bodies. The divine nature is also in conflict with the world outside.

It is not hard to understand that when the Apostle John saw in the vision

Mystery Babylon Mother of Harlots why he was, struck dumb, mystified, and incredulous!

Today, there are so many men and women who have assumed that faith should be used in the acquisition of money or homes or cars or anything of this world. But faith is to be directed, not regarding the earthly stuff of this present world, but to the acquisition of the divine nature which does not perish. The divine nature is the true wealth. It is eternal! The acquisition of the divine nature is to be who we are and who we are becoming.

When John gazed at the vision of how Mystery Babylon had insinuated it-self into the very Church of God, he was incredulous. The "so called" faith prosperity teachers of today are guilty of this vision. They are Mystery Babylon. They are on the wrong track! But it is not uncommon. It is what happens when people choose the wrong track because they do not use their faith!

Chapter 30

Knocked Off Track

The woman of Mystery Babylon was described as a whore. She is a seducer. This very woman is referred to again as a Jezebel in the 2nd chapter of Revelation to the church of Thyatira.

"Thou suffer that woman Jezebel." Rev. 2:20

Today, God's people continue to suffer from the "spirit of Jezebel." It is not hard to make the application, because it is so obvious that so many people suffer that woman.

"But I have this against you: You tolerate that woman Jezebel, who calls herself a prophetess." Rev. 2:20

One Fine Day

My initial human response to my daughter-in-law's infidelity was, I wanted justice. The truth is I wanted vengeance. But when God delays acting it is really a trial of faith. When He delays we question if God is really real, and does He care?

Is He there? Why doesn't He act? Surely, He sees the disgusting behavior? At that point, the great temptation is to let anger take its hold by taking things into our own hands. At that point we do not want justice we want vengeance. But be careful.

"When God delays His judgment, the people consider evil." Ecc 8:11

We want justice and we want it now! But in stark contrast to horrible sins God is watching in great grief at the destruction of a human soul. What a colossal tragedy and remarkable contrast!

We should all fear!

Get Back and Stay on Track

God is not willing that any perish. He is slow to anger and long suffering. But for me, in her case, I wanted it now! But God does not lift His hand. Why Lord? What are you waiting for? My prayer cries out. But there is no answer. Silence in heaven. Faith is being tested! It is real! Faith is tested by the fire.

Fortunately, I got back on the right track. And so must all be diligent when we are proved by the difficulties that come our way, whatever and whenever, and however they be. They come to test the track we ride. If we pass the test we acquire more of the divine nature. For just as the universe is in an expansion mode so must our hearts be. The acquisition of the divine nature is a dynamic process. It is not static. It is the trans-accumulation of the Holy Spirit into the white shadowing of the Holy Ghost!

"But we all, with open face beholding as in a glass the glory of the Lord, are changed into the same image from glory to glory, even as by the Spirit of the Lord." 2 Cor 3:18

The angels stand astonished watching the theater below. God is in anguish for one of His own who is slipping away. But for those who wring their hands wanting action there is seemingly no relief. Our prayers go unanswered because we do not know the greatness of our God. Yet it is the cauldron in which we live. It is the crucible for the refinement of faith. Yet the trial persists. It is real!

"Why Lord do you hold back, why won't you fix the problem and give us relief?"

We cry out for justice but there is none. How quick we forget His mercy regarding our own transgressions. He could have meted out judgment on all of us many times, but He did not. Yet we are quick on the trigger for others to get theirs. God help our poor memories!

Our patience is tested and the temptation to become angry with the Lord festers like pustules surrounding a foreign object that has penetrated our skin; only it is our heart that has become infected. Be careful! This is where you can jump onto the wrong track. This is where we overcome or are overcome.

I had failed to comprehend that her sickness had attached itself and spread to all my family. It took faith to overcome the great illness. Over time we did. Thank God!

This is not to pat ourselves on the back but only to offer comfort to any in like manner afflicted. We still wrestle with the trial, but we are on the down slope of the mountain. But it is through God's grace.

Yet, God does desire to stay the plague. He does not desire an illness to become epidemic. We had blindly stumbled not apprehending it was a trial of our faith. In an instant of human time the heavens reached down and grabbed our hands. Thanks be to God for His heavenly host.

"Do not root for her destruction."

Enter into the heart of your Father and weep. God is love. And faith does not work without Love, for faith works through love.

How brazen is a hard heart and how easy it is to fall for the temptation to hate? The trial was the most difficult of my lifetime because the enemy had put his hand on my most treasured possession, my family. Yet for me it was the moment of truth because it is the ongoing trial of faith in the Heavenly Father. I must trust that He knows. And that He knows best. Sometimes, though, I think I know better the He!

"Though You slay me yet will I praise you." Job 13:15

I began to comprehend that the terrible trial He allowed had been de-signed to equip me (if I so choose) with patience. If I could grasp the op-portunity provided by the trial, I could invert the curse.

"Consider it all joy, my brethren, when you encounter various trials, knowing that the testing of "your faith" produces endurance. And let en-durance have its perfect result, so that you may be perfect and complete, lacking in nothing." James 1:3

If we then consider it not joy then the incident, so real, so monumental so personal in life, would not profit nor add weight for eternal purposes. These incredibly deep troubles are the very afflictions of Job. They are the stripes of Jesus. They test the track we ride.

At this point in almost fifty years of believing in Jesus, I can glimpse the heart of God in His great despair for her and all people. But in the horror of her demise, I should not have allowed her sickness to become my own. I must invert the issue so that it works for me and my household a far more eternal weight of glory. And as the scripture points out, that I may be made perfect and complete lacking nothing. The perfect and complete has to do with the adornment of the divine nature. Hatred is so easy, and the flesh dies hard. But it is the price for obtaining the love of God. It is the Holy Ghosting within our hearts. God our Father is Love. We must use our faith. And that is why it is called the trial and fight of faith.

We Are Headed to a City

"Lord, create in me a clean heart and renew a right spirit within me, then will I teach transgressors thy ways and sinners will be converted unto thee." Psa 51:10

This prayer should be every day present in every heart, because in this life and on this side of the heavens we never completely arrive. The process of God creating a clean heart is ongoing daily for the rest of our lives here on earth.

The other extreme is to think that God is weak in hearing. He is not, but people think that since He is referred to as "the lamb of God" that He is meek and mild as a lamb. He is tender hearted, but He is also a Lion.

But the idea behind Him being called the lamb of God is because lambs were used for sacrifices on the altar of God in the temple. Being called the lamb of God meant that he was the perfect and spotless sacrifice. Jesus is not meek and mild in the way people think of a lamb. He never backed down when He confronted by the authorities of the Jewish Sanhedrin.

As a matter of fact, He called them out accusing them of being sons of hell and offspring of the devil. He was never fearful of them. I wonder today if

129

there are any so bold as to confront the snakes in political and religious offices who have sold out for money and power.

When we view Christ in the book of Revelation, He has eyes that are on fire and His feet are burnished brass. This is not the portrait of weakness but of power and strength. We are reminded that He is storing His wrath. But God is not and in no way cruel, and the Lord is working this out in our lives. In the process He is dealing with issues long ago not dealt with, but today He is focusing on these latent but stubborn imperfections. He desires a clean heart.

It is in His hands, but it is up to each individual to keep it in His hands.

As long as we walk and live our lives in the use of our faith, we have confidence with God.

Chapter 31

Stepping Over the Purpose

There are phantoms in the inner chamber! Phantoms that must be expunged.

I can remember very clearly my 2nd grade teacher Mrs. Manny. She would keep me after school almost every day. She did this because I could not keep my mouth shut during class. I craved attention. Why? I had a relentless insatiable inferiority complex. I had a tremendous drive and needed to be recognized.

We need to ask ourselves is it our outer identity or inner identity? Time to wake up! Do I have a need to be loved by mankind? Do we crave attention and recognition? Is this not the fear of man? Why do we do what we do?

So much of our motivation is due to the need to be loved, revered, and honored, and that by mankind. Why? If God is for me who then can be against me? Whom, shall I fear! But we have been born into a sea of uncertainty and instability. But what we do for love!

And neither should we go out and just do something or just anything. The idea of a purpose driven life is a good idea but what purpose? The idea of purpose has become a common theme in many circles today.

A very famous Pentecostal pastor once said, what are you waiting for? If God has called you to greatness go out and do something great for Jesus. Another famous man wrote a best-selling book "A Purpose Driven Life." These messages are both misdirected and misleading.

Yes, we have been called to greatness and yes our lives should be purpose driven. But to what purpose? What is greatness? To just do something or anything is not a good idea. In fact, it is counter-productive and presumptuous. And having a purpose, any purpose is equally erroneous. What is my purpose then? Is it outward into the world or is it upward to God?

It is not about being a great doctor or politician or CEO of a great corporation, or even a great minister. Those things may or may not come but principally it is about being a great person. A great person is one who has escaped the corruption of the world and is putting on the divine nature. A great person becomes a servant to all. The acquisition of the divine nature produces servants. It may manifest through being a doctor or garbage collector, but it is about being great in the Lord.

"Unless the Lord builds the house the people labor in vain." Psa 127:1

It is a mistake to focus on the outer world as though our purpose should be doing something fundamentally focused on the outside world. It is not about changing the world. It is about how God has purposed to change us, His people!

Our purpose should be what God has designed to do in us and cooperating with His purpose. God desires to restore our souls and create in us a clean spirit. We should seek that purpose! This is the correct purpose driven life. This is greatness!

When we abide in Him this way, the life force and power of His glory infuses within our being His divine energy. His energy or glory cannot help but emanate and cause fruitfulness to affect the outside world. But our primary focus should be concerned with the weaving of the robe of righteousness. It is an upward call!

The fruitfulness of our outward lives flows naturally. Just as fruit on a tree grows automatically so it is with those who are abiding in Christ. But men focus on the outside world first. It is because we are carnal and lost in our human identities. We mistake faith for will power. Our whole bias tends to be in the flesh and the outside world. Mere men see greatness in terms of worldly definitions. Jesus, in quoting Psalms 82, defined true identity when He said to the religious leaders you are more than mere men, you are Elohim. And this He says to all!

Enormous Misstep

One of the most instructive stories that underscores this fact occurred when King David was trying to bring the Ark of the Covenant into the City of David. The ark had been lost to the Philistines and David was consumed and overwhelmed with the notion as he sought to recover the ark and bring it into his city.

This was a noble act of honoring God and David was happy to be doing something of great importance. Was this not a great purpose? Yes, but the ark had been placed on an ox cart and was not being handled correctly.

As the ark was coming toward the camp the wheels hit a chuck hole on the road and it began to tip over. One of those who was accompanying the ark, Uzzah, reached out his hand to steady the Ark lest it fall to the ground and be damaged. But suddenly he was struck dead. The scripture recorded he was struck dead because of his irreverence. David became angry with the Lord for striking the man dead.

After three months David figured out why God had done this to Uzzah. The problem was that it was forbidden that one should touch the ark unless he wore a linen ephod. The linen ephod was the clothing of a priest. It was only the priest who was allowed to touch the ark. This was the irreverence of Uzzah. Consequently, after learning why the outbreak occurred, David put on a linen ephod himself and then accompanied the Ark into his city.

What is to be learned from this?

When it comes to doing things for God we can actually create death if we do not first put on a linen ephod. The meaning of the linen ephod is that we are first a priest. The way to approach God is as a priest! David was a king but to approach God he had to see himself first as a priest. He could not approach God as a king. A priest faces God. A king faces the people. To face God means we must be humble and pray. Most would rather be king!

It is assumed by so many Christians the greatest thing is to become a pastor or put on God's armor and go to war responding to the great commission. After all isn't that the greatest purpose one could imagine. But the greatest call is to be a priest. It is one who prays. Yet wait!

"Go into all the world and preach the gospel." Mk 16:15

That is the mandate, and it is ordained by God. Yet even though Jesus provided what can be construed as the greatest purpose that one could achieve with his mortal life, He said wait!

Even before He had given authority to go into all the world. It was because they were called to pray first. Then afterwards God gave them empowerment to go into all the world. Had they gone ahead of the Lord before waiting it would have been a disaster!

If we just go out and do something without prayer, without putting on the clothing of a priest, we do greatly err and commit the sin of Uzzah.

David had to take off his kingly crown and dress as a priest to be able to do something of a great magnitude, and so must all. We approach God as priests not as kings. And before we launch out we must go before God in prayer. Seriously! The Father's house is a house of prayer.

Jesus said it this way.

"I am the vine and ye are the branches, he that abides in me and I in him brings forth much fruit for without me you can do nothing." Jn 15:5

Then there are those who try to motivate God's people by teaching, "why doesn't God do something? The world is falling apart, why does He just stand by? They answer by saying, "He is waiting for you to do something. Get going already! What are you waiting for?" But this call by the ministers is a misstep for God's people even though it sounds right. But if we just do something, anything, it is because we get motivated out of guilt rather than faith. Guilt to do something is not faith!

We must pray to get clarity with regard to our individualized marching orders for what we do in the world outside, orders from our Commander and Chief. We cannot just run headlong just to do something. The problem is powerlessness. My Father's house is a house of prayer. This is faith and in that He speaks. His nature in us is more important than anything that we can do.

In their challenges to just do something, the religious zealots, push people to commit the sin and the irreverence of Uzzah. We must put on a linen ephod. We must use our faith. There are works that come from faith, but we must hear from the heavens. He really is there!

The call of God is ***first upward*** not outward. We cannot pay God back for what He has accomplished out of a sense of guilt. A feeling of unworthiness is not a call to assuming just any purpose, even a presumptuous response to the Great Commission.

Yet, this is the motivation for so many because they do not wait on Him in prayer. He will speak to us as we abide in Him!

We must see the calling of God as first upward!

Political Power of the Outside World

"Let us save America" is the clarion call, but it is nothing more than putting our hands on something out of balance. Politics can be the irreverence of Uzzah!

Politics is merely a collective human effort in the attempt to make sure things do not tip over. It is the putting of hands on the ark. It is the process and way men try to determine how they will be ruled in the flesh. Our precious faith is not under the dominion of worldly rulers good or evil. We are of another King and another Kingdom. We are truly not of this world.

The obsessions of those who push politically one way, or the other are yet fearful of death. Think it through! Are not those who are so politically absorbed trying to maintain peace in the outer world? It is not that external peace is wrong, but Jesus told us that in the world we will have tribulation. Who in their right mind desires tribulation? But the peace that God gives is a different kind of peace then the absence of trouble in the outside world.

But regardless of the political outcomes anywhere on the earth we are not of this world. We do not belong here and are aliens first. We are principally not citizens of America nor any other nation. We are heading toward Mt. Zion the city of God. We are citizens of Zion.

If the politics of this world is the preoccupation, then the direction is toward a citizenship of the city of Babylon. It is the wrong track! So do we abandon the world all together? No, but it must not become our primary

135

focus. It cannot be our obsession!

It is an upward call first! The outer world, if it is to be touched properly will not come by religion, nor politics. It will come by the life of Christ! The life we share is the fruit of the tree that is planted properly in Christ not planted in religion or politics. Just like any city of the world or any nation of the world, they are all infused and stink with the noxious odor of the whore city of Babylon.

We are simply not of this world! Stay on track. It is so easy to get knocked off. Even if there is a promise of a noble outcome we are not of this world.

Chapter 32

Inside the Train Looking Out

"Brethren, I do not regard myself as having laid hold of it yet; but one thing I do: forgetting what lies behind and reaching forward to what lies ahead, I press on toward the goal for the prize of the "upward call" of God in Christ Jesus." Phil 3:14

Earthbound Thinking

As I said, when I was growing up I found myself to be of very small stature. All my friends grew faster. I always looked up to bigger people. When I entered high school, I was 5ft 3 inches and weighed 113 pounds. I was a shrimp!

Somehow, years later, miraculously, I signed a contract with the San Francisco 49ers. I became a pro-football player. But what was it that had driven me towards this improbable outcome?

I always longed to be big and powerful, and here I was playing alongside giants. Man, that was painful! I still carry the scars in my body. Not a good idea!

Now as I look back, I can see this is pretty much what most people go through. Maybe not a career in professional football, but in some way to be more powerful. The whole of this life is the quest to discover "who am I." It is the same for everyone!

When I think of the many heroes I idolized growing up it was always soldiers, football stars, actors, and the super hero. It was always the same routine, but the fantasizing was a kind of a common tendency especially among young people.

Is there something yearning from within the deepest recess of our being? Are we supposed to be something more than we are? As I reflect growing up, the epitome was superman. I could not get enough of the cartoons and programs of the man of steel. Superman seemed to evoke some kind of primeval memory.

When it came to the Bible characters that caught my eye it was Sampson who had supernatural strength, then David who killed the giant Goliath and then His mighty men who slew thousands. What was it in my imagination that gravitated and fixated to these images and characters? But really who wouldn't want to be like them? It seems to be a common fantasy for so many. Perhaps it is why the marvel comics movies became so popular.

There is something stirring within us. And I know what it is! It is the longing for our **heavenly bodies** that are reserved in heaven.

"For in this body we groan, earnestly desiring to be clothed upon with our house which is from heaven(s)." 2 Cor 5:2

And we groan because we who are fallen are weakened and affected by the earth. Earth life is kryptonite to our present and temporary existence. We groan because we are afflicted.

"For in this tabernacle (body) we groan, earnestly desiring to be clothed upon with our house which is from the heavens." 2 Cor 5:4

The preparation for the retaking of our heavenly *immortal bodies* is by climbing the mountain of God, which in a figure of speech, is denoting the effort to put on the divine nature.

This is the purpose of the spiritual Sherpa to guide up that mountain.

Yet we still can do many things without God!

What?

Before I came to the Lord, as I said, I had actually made it to the National Football League. So, to say I could do nothing does not synchronize with Jesus' words. There are many people who can do many many things in this life. This is patently obvious. So what can we make of this?

When I went to my fiftieth year high school reunion one of my old acquaintances said (he had become a highly successful attorney), "Wow, becoming a pro athlete, that was a great accomplishment." And it was in the natural physical world. Not so much in God's economy!

So there are many things people can do even if they do not abide in Jesus, but the sad result is that those things are not eternal and will not endure the fire that will test all men's work. And those things will not inure to the perfecting of one's heart.

What is the Work?

These things mentioned above, are called "dead works." Dead works can arise from taking the wrong direction or wrong track, even from wrong motives, or even guilt.

Dead works can even be highly esteemed careers in the eyes of men and the world, such as an attorney or doctor, actor, or even a minister, fill in the blank. There is nothing wrong with these outer world vocations, but remember those things are passing away. The only thing that really matters is what is eternal and what remains. And that one thing is the "robe of righteousness." This is the principal "work" of God. It is putting on the robe of righteousness. It's an upward call and an inner clothing.

"Where is the wise man? Where is the scribe? Where is the debater of this age? Has not God made foolish the wisdom of the world?" Ibid

"for all that is in the world the lust of the flesh the lust of the eyes and the pride of life is not from the Father, but is from the world and the world is passing away but the one who does the will of God lives forever" Jn 2:17

None of these things in the outer world are necessarily wrong unless they supersede and usurp the upward call and inward identity. Yet if the apostle Paul were the standard, he had one focus. And that was the upward call.

But it is important to keep in mind he had a trade. He was a tent maker. A vocation in the world should be seen at best as a tent making job, no matter how it is acclaimed by men. We are to keep our eye on the prize. This is how we stay on the right track.

Easter's Lament

Every year during the time of Easter there are reports of people allowing themselves to be crucified on crosses. Why do they do this? They do this because they are trying to earn worthiness. This is of course an extreme example. In great error they assume that if they abase themselves enough, the activity will earn them more acceptability with God. This is another gross example of trying to add to that which comes only by faith and that through grace.

This is a horrible example of people who do not apprehend their sins have been forgiven because God also took away the Law. The Law that condemns them. Paul called the Ten Commandments the "covenant of death."

These poor souls in their ignorance are trying to fix a guilty conscience by adding their own work of abasement. In this case having their own bodies crucified. This is a horrific and extreme example of those who are still under the covenant of death.

This activity is an affront to God because it is saying that what Jesus did was not enough. Now, they think, "I must do something more." It is a gross example of what religious people do in more subtle ways. People cannot fathom the magnitude of God's forgiveness in Jesus. In the same way as those who crucify themselves, they ignorantly and foolishly think they can pay God back or add to what He has already done.

Stolen Grace

Even in the religious church world a person can be involved in various things and for the wrong motives and reasons. Here is an indication which Paul points out in the book of Philippians.

"Some, to be sure, are preaching Christ even from envy and strife, but some also from goodwill; the latter do it out of love, knowing that I am appointed for the defense of the gospel" Phil 1:15

Here is an interesting scripture in the book of Philippians where people were preaching the word out of wrong motives. Paul does not call them out by name because he is glad that the word is going out. Why stop them? But it is possible to preach Christ for the wrong reason.

In this case, cited by Paul, there was envy and jealousy. It was because of Paul's successes. Many people were attracted to Paul because of many wonderful things taking place through him. Those who were preaching out of wrong motives wanted Paul's acclaim and his success. After all he was getting so much attention.

Paul was saying that there were people so taken by the power of the Word and how it was affecting others that they themselves would become motivated by jealousy and envy seeking the same attention and acclaim by doing the same. These people were desirous of the same attention and accolades Paul was receiving. A gross example of identity crisis! As Paul was becoming revered others wanted to be part of the show. Just as some people want to be like Michael Jordan these people wanted to be like Paul.

We do not serve Christ to gain the approval and admiration of men. If this is the case, we are seeking to find the affirmation of identity from the outer world. External circumstance whether good or evil does not define who we are. We do not find identity though the adulation and praise of men. Human responses do not define and validate who we are. Outward successes in standing room only crowds is not a vindication of who we are, nor is the lack thereof a proof of who we are not. Men do not define us, and neither do circumstances.

Jesus Defined Who We Are

Jesus said, "Have not I said you are "elohim." How are we to understand this?

If it is men who affirm and define us then how does one explain the life of Jeremiah. He was probably the most hated of all God's prophets. And again, if one were to examine the life of Elijah it would not have been enviable either. But Jesus defines us as elohim!

In the case of the great apostle Paul, he notes the contrast to his apparent popularity. There were some unenviable and terrible problems which followed him wherever he went. He even despaired of life itself. In fact, the greater the revelation by God the greater came the sorrows. One of which came after three years of hard work in Ephesus in which he discovered that all had departed from him. Is this a measure of success? Is this what men aspire to?

Most all of God's prophets did not achieve external successes as we count success. When we see some of today's ministers having large followings we tend to think, Wow! that man/woman is really blessed and called by God! We point out the apparent successes by the outward optics. But Paul did not point to these.

"For it seems to me that God has displayed us apostles at the end of the procession, like prisoners appointed for death. We have become a spectacle to the whole world, to angels as well as to men" 1 Cor 4:9

At the end of the day if the prominent most important people in line preparing to receive their reward are those that are pastors and those who have great followings then God would be unjust. The fact of the matter is it is those who prevail in prayer and the ones who go unnoticed who will be at the front of the line. It is those who put on the robe of righteousness. God judges and rewards so differently than men think.

Here is what the Apostle said about those in leadership in the Corinth church.

"Already you have all you want. Already you have become rich. Without us, you have become kings. How I wish you really were kings, so that we might be kings with you." 1 Cor 4:8

Paul was First a Priest

It is far better to be a priest then a king. A priest is the one who prays standing before God. A king stands before men. Now I ask you what is the most preferable?

"My Father's house is a house of prayer" Matt 21:13

The fact of the matter is that in God's way of thinking, the last shall be first. There will be many who were never known that will receive the greatest rewards. God's ways are not our ways. It is an upward call.

Unusable

"It is true that some preach Christ out of envy and rivalry, but others out of goodwill. The latter do so out of love, knowing that I am put here for the defense of the gospel. The former preach Christ out of selfish ambition, not sincerely, supposing that they can stir up trouble for me while I am in chains." Phil 1:15-18

We must allow God to create in us a clean heart and renew a right spirit within. This dealing by God through the Holy Spirit concerning the motives of the heart is the process whereby we partake of the heavenly upward calling.

Rightly does the proverb say a man is tested by the praise of men.

"The crucible is for silver and the furnace for gold, And each is tested by the praise accorded him." Prov 27:21

Such is the disposition of the heart. But it is always the other guy. We must face the awful truth about ourselves!

There are many deaths one must die as we ride the rails. We must face our carnal self and kill it by putting it on Jesus. We must examine our hearts. This is what it means to put on the robe of righteousness.

We are not made whole through how men perceive us. Our identity does not rest in how we are seen, defined or even appreciated by men from the outside in. We are complete only in Him.

As we climb the holy mountain of God, we must allow ourselves to be rid of all the baggage. God desires to create in us a clean heart, a clean spirit, a clean chamber of imagery.

"Wherefore seeing we also are compassed about with so great a cloud of witnesses, let us lay aside every weight, and the sin which doth so easily beset us, and let us run with patience the race that is set before us"...

and...

"fixing our eyes on Jesus, the author and perfecter of faith, who for the

joy set before Him endured the cross, despising the shame, and has sat down at the right hand of the throne of God." Heb. 12:1

We are called to examine ourselves, our hearts, our inner self, to see if we are really in the faith. Remember the heart is the inner sanctuary and there are pockets of darkness within which must be exposed to the light. We are to be redeemed to the uttermost.

The reasons we do things is based on either a reverence and fear of the Lord or the fear of man. We all need to be loved and accepted for sure, but when we seek our fulfillment first through the admiration of men or congregations or wives or husbands or fans or followers, we have fallen into the need to have our identity established with the wrong focus and in the wrong places with the wrong motives.

One of the greatest achievements in this life is to overcome the fear of man. Perhaps it is the greatest fear of all. But if we walk closely with the Lord we will overcome!

There will be many, when all is said and done, who will be shocked when they discover who they really are.

I want to meet you in the city of God!

Chapter 33

The Forgery of Jesus' Name

One of the most disturbing scriptures in all the Bible, which should cause all to take pause, was quoted by Jesus Himself.

"Not everyone who says to Me, 'Lord, Lord,' will enter the kingdom of heaven, but he who does the will of My Father who is in heaven will enter. Many will say to Me on that day, 'Lord, Lord, did we not prophesy in Your name, and in Your name cast out demons, and in Your name perform many miracles?" Matt 7:21-22

These are frightening words. Hopefully, they will not be regarded with superficiality. We should all be like Paul, take heed, fear and tremble.

The name of Jesus can be used and affect people because of the power in His name. However, His name can be used surreptitiously. It is likened unto spiritual forgery! And in this light, as it is explained in the parable, a warning from the Lord concerning false preachers and false doctrine.

Men can assume doctrines which are false and even some activities stamping them with the name of Jesus. We must be careful in how we use Jesus' name lest we use His name in vain.

I have seen this many times when preachers stand before congregations with a predetermined speech. What if that which they have studied is in error? Then they pray and ask God in Jesus name to help them deliver the speech. The bible teaches there are false prophets and false apostles. We must not be tossed about by every wind of doctrine!

Those who practice lawlessness include false prophets.

"Give unto the LORD the glory due unto his name: bring an offering and come into his courts. The name of God is power. He is God." Psa 96:8

There are many who have come to know the power in the name of Jesus. And sadly, use His name inaccurately and thus inappropriately to validate for authenticity. In a sense this is a spiritual forgery.

What is amazing about the charlatans, whose motives are hidden from plain view and are in it for the money or for fame, is that many remarkable supernatural manifestations do occur at their hands. They are deceiving and being deceived! It is confusing, and those who operate in these ways, and get away with it, makes one scratch their head. "How can this be?" The answer is that there is power in the name of Jesus. When the name of Jesus is raised power is present.

While a charlatan can use the name of Jesus for selfish motives, the Lord is ever present and faithful to <u>honor His own Name</u>. So, while there are those who use His name fraudulently, He is nonetheless present. There are many forgers who do not realize that when they eventually stand before the Lord and protest, as in the parable, "Lord Lord, didn't we do this your name, they will be in utter shock at what He says to them!

"Then I will tell them plainly, '<u>I never knew you; depart from Me</u>, you workers of lawlessness.'" Matt 7:22

The Classic Misuse of His Name

Perhaps one of the greatest misuse of His name is by those who try to couple the New Covenant with the Old Covenant.

Jesus warned against those who would attempt to sew "a new patch" on an old garment. Here is the classic scripture.

"No one sews a patch of unshrunk cloth on an old garment, for the patch will pull away from the garment, making the tear worse." Mk 2:21

He was using a word picture to explain the danger of adding the New Covenant to the Old Covenant. In other words, patching up the old garment. They do this by mixing the Law with the New Covenant of grace which is in His blood. You cannot patch the new to the old.

Many of those who practice lawlessness are they who put themselves back under the Law, while invoking Jesus' name. Sometimes the name Yeshua is used to be more Hebrew correct.

God does not demand the keeping of Jewish feasts or even the very idea of the accurate day for the sabbath to facilitate spiritual growth. There are those who insist that unless one keeps their idea of the specific sabbath day they are not part of God's kingdom. It is a rampant attempt to control the behavior of believers. But it is just another form of legalism. Ostensibly it is just the forgery of Jesus' name.

The tendency is not confined to just one denomination either. The abusive phenomena is widespread. One of the most obvious is the legalistic use of the scripture...

"let us not forsake the gathering of ourselves together as the manner of some is." Heb 10:25

Many ministers use this as a club or law upon parishioners that they be well advised to attend church. Paul did not intend his council to be a law to be used against God's people so that they would be faithful to attend weekly services. He was counseling the elect to be in fellowship with those of like mindedness and those of like precious faith. It was intended as a principle for encouragement not a legal demand. Yet look how it has been turned into a law. It was meant to help God's people to be strengthened by each other's mutual faith. It was not a legal constraint to control God's people.

They are the lawless ones who do so. It is they who use Jesus/Yeshua's name fraudulently doing all sorts of things in His Name. It is sewing the new patch on the old garment. The problem of adding Law to grace is the major source of all heresy. To those who do such things He calls them lawless and "I never knew you." No wonder Paul was in fear!

What we have here is **forgery**. It is the forgery in using Jesus' name. Let's be very clear. Jesus put away by His own death "the Law."

And if the robe of righteousness is weaved by our faith in the gathering of God's nature into our inner man, then false doctrine is a horrible detriment to the development of the inner man. It is why Paul had such an awfully hard rebuke to those who did so.

"let them be accursed" Gal 1:9

147

Hence, we are instructed to study to show ourselves approved a workman that rightly divides the word, so in the Day of the Lord we shrink not back in embarrassment. It is a very narrow road!

"Study to shew thyself approved unto God, a workman that needs not to be ashamed, rightly dividing the word of truth." 2 Tim 2:15

We are the workmen in that it is we ourselves who do the weaving of the garment, i.e., the robe of righteousness. Be careful and study. The robe you weave with the threads of His glory is what you will wear. You cannot afford to allow just anyone to do the work. It is you who are the workman. Jesus said it this way.

"But you are not to be called 'Rabbi,' for you have 'one Teacher', and you are all brothers." Matt 23:8

Both you and I are responsible for what we hear. So, we are warned to be careful. The pastor does not weave the robe for you. At best he is there to assist your faith.

It is we who build on the foundation. It is the carnal man who accepts the idea of building on the foundation of Christ as the responsibility of the pastor or famous preachers and teachers. We tend to think that it is their responsibility and their chore as they go about building the church congregation. Yes, to some degree, but look at this scripture.

"But 'each one' must be careful how he builds. For no one can lay a foundation other than the one already laid, which is Jesus Christ."1Cor 3:11

and ...

"If what 'he has built' survives, he will receive a reward. If it is burned up, he will suffer loss. He himself will be saved, but only as one being snatched from the fire. Do you not know that you yourselves are God's temple, and that God's Spirit dwells in you?" 1 Cor 3:15

It is not singularly and certainly not solely in the hands of the pastors. Each person is called to build.

Chapter 34

The Divine Witch

One of the greatest people of the 16th century was considered a witch!

In the 16th century most of the world, especially the Church, not only believed the world was flat, but that the sun revolved around the earth. To think otherwise was considered blasphemy and heresy!

It was the astronomer Galileo who began challenging those stubborn views, so deeply embedded and entrenched in the Church. Through his scientific studies he proved those traditional views were dramatically incorrect. For his courageous work he was branded a witch by the Church. He barely escaped from being burned to death. It took many many years before the Church would come to accept his breakthrough discoveries. The Church had a stranglehold over the masses.

Imagine the ire of the Church leaders because of the powerful control they wielded over the people. Imagine when their authority was threatened by Galileo's discoveries. It was the same phenomena during the time of Jesus when the Jewish Sanhedrin were greatly intimidated. Their antipathy would eventually drive them to even kill Jesus. So great are bound mind circuits in humans!

"there is nothing new under the sun, all is vanity," Ecc 1

And so it is to this very day. But the voice of history can be instructive if we have an ear.

It is most disturbing to think we are on track with correct doctrine only to find we are not! Perhaps this is the reason why Paul said,

"I was with you in much fear and trembling." Ibid

God required Paul to live in the desert of Arabia so that he could learn the Great Story (aka the gospel) firsthand though the Holy Spirit by faith. At

149

the same time, he was learning about God's grace he was also being deprogrammed from his religious indoctrination as a Pharisee. He described himself as a Pharisee of Pharisees. Paul realized how deeply ingrained he had become due to his religious training. He recognized in himself that he needed to be set free from his monumental religious mindsets.

After a period of fourteen years living in Arabia he purposed to go up to Jerusalem. He was deeply concerned about the accuracy of his grasp of "the great story" of the gospel of Grace. He wondered if somehow, he had run in vain. He went to Jerusalem to submit what he knew to the brethren. Paul was not afraid to check himself out. Can we do the same?

Theological Wilderness

Is it remotely possible we may be trapped in traditional Christian theologies wandering around in a theological wilderness? Round and round and not even aware of it? Is history repeating itself in a way similar to Galileo who was butting up against the glass ceiling of his day. Has the Church hit a glass ceiling again and no longer progressing?

It is time to ask ourselves, are we able to kill Issac?

Issac was Abraham's most precious son. He was the son of promise. What an incredible issue it was for Abraham to offer his son up for sacrifice on the altar. Are we secure enough in Christ to offer on the altar what we think are our most cherished and sacred views of the Word?

Are we on the right track or on the wrong track? Remember, Mystery Babylon is a symbolic image representing religious deception. Even those who have learned to use Jesus' name and who can string together scripture, who can cite all the doctrines are still to fear, tremble and walk circumspectly. Paul did! Paul was fearless when it came to dealing with himself! Look at the frightful words directed at the Church of Ephesus warning of false Apostles. There really are issues at hand.

"I know your deeds, your labor, and your perseverance. I know that you cannot tolerate those who are evil, and you have tested and exposed as liars those who falsely claim to be apostles." Rev 2:2

Yet here it is! There are those who called themselves Apostles who were not. The term apostle means one sent (apo-from, stello-to send). There are so many that stand in pulpits who claim authenticity but are not apo-stello. They are not sent! And who needs a title? One is either sent or he is not. And so, we must listen intently and discern.

Even preaching can be a giant misstep. It can lead in the wrong direction wasting years and in the end those things can be rendered as dead works. We do not have time to waste building on a false foundation.

Our lives should be centered only on Jesus not the pastor nor congregation. The works that were prepared for all before the foundation of this world must be revealed through prayer and study.

We are to build on Christ Jesus and Him crucified. This was what Paul so clearly understood. Yet anyone who calls themselves Christian and seeks to serve may not be actually building on that foundation.

Paul said, "I determined to know nothing else than this one thing." Yet Paul knew many things. He was caught up to the third heaven and saw and knew many things. Why did He say this?

It was because the so-called leaders in Corinth and the people were following men rather than Jesus. Some were saying, "I am of Paul, others I am of Peter, others I am of Apollos etc." They were believers all right, yet they were following men. Paul had to correct them to the fact that it was Jesus who died for them and in following men they were walking as mere men. Not according to the death of Jesus. This meant they were walking according to the flesh and not on the "knife's edge."

This is exactly what men do today that profess themselves as Christians. They boast in their membership in the Baptist church, the Catholic church, the Lutheran church, the Pentecostal church etc., but they do not boast in the fact they are living the death of Jesus.

"For we who are alive are always consigned to death for Jesus' sake, so that the life of Jesus may also be revealed in our mortal bodies." 2 Cor 4:11

We cannot walk in the Spirit if we do not properly walk in the spiritual reality of Christ's death. They in Corinth were not walking in the Spirit. They had not endeavored to know Christ and Him crucified. Paul proved this fact as he pointed out their carnality. Instead of living by faith they were following men not Jesus. To the carnal believers in Corinth, men had become their rule and consequently their law. This is what men do!

Therefore, as we read earlier all men ought to pray and not lose heart. Prayer is what Jesus went into the temple to restore when He rode into town to the Father's house. He turned over tables that they had set in the temple. Those tables were set with religious items, but the reason for setting the tables with religious items was for commerce. Since we are the temple of God will we allow the Lord to overturn the tables we have set up in our heart of ideas, doctrines and traditions?

God's house (which is who we are) is a house of prayer. Praying is the operation of faith. If we are to grow, we must allow Him access to overturn the things we have set tables for. We must break out of our religious mind circuits and besetting sins. Are we truly willing to put Issac on the altar? Unless we can gather the inner resolve, we may well be locked up and are destined to ride the merry-go-round. It is high time we take a giant step of faith and really find out how real the Lord is. Is Jesus just notional or is He experiential?

I want to encourage you in how to ride the train. I want to help you to walk step by step. I want to help you to walk in the Spirit as we climb the mountain.

Chapter 35

Great Hindrances to Prayer

The actual context for asking the question, "will the son of man find faith," was put forth in a parable. Jesus taught in mind pictures presented as stories and that is what parables were, mind pictures. Here is the story.

"And he told them a parable to show that they must always pray and not be discouraged, saying, "There was a certain judge in a certain town who did not fear God and did not respect people. And there was a widow in that town, and she kept coming to him, saying, 'Grant me justice against my adversary!' And he was not willing for a time, but after these things he said to himself, 'Even if I do not fear God or respect people, yet because this widow is causing trouble for me, I will grant her justice, so that she does not wear me down in the end by her coming back!'" And the Lord said, "Listen to what the unrighteous judge is saying! And will not God surely see to it that justice is done to His chosen ones who cry out to Him day and night, and will He delay toward them? I tell you that He will see to it that justice is done for them soon! Nevertheless, <u>when the Son of Man comes, then will he find faith on earth</u>?" Lk 18:8

The story or parable was couched in the negative because most people project onto God ideas which are in absolute contradiction to His nature. The misconceptions lead to false conclusions!

God our heavenly Father is in no way like the unrighteous judge. Yet for many, they think He is. They project! Even for many of those who actually believe in Him they still think He is out to get them, or to treat them harshly.

Why would anyone feel this way? He never behaves in the way of the judge in the parable. He is altogether kind and just in His dealings with all mankind, because He is not a respecter of persons. Everyone has the same opportunity of access. And He shows great favor granting provisions of His divine promises as He has provided audience before His very throne in the heavens. The problem is that so many do not take advantage of His invitation. They tend to look at Him through the lens of the world. The world is full of chaos and evil. They blame God for earthquakes, famines, pestilence, wars, you name it from the outside world and God gets blamed.

Yet, He is a loving God, slow to anger and full of compassion. He is not in any way the picture of the "unrighteous judge." But fallen human beings characteristically do not see Him in the correct light! For the most part even those who seek to follow the Lord have a very flawed picture of the Lord. They tend to think of God as angry and always getting steamed! Watch out! They are just waiting for Him to drop a rock on them because their conscience argues against them.

They evaluate God's favor based on how they feel about their own worthiness. It is due to a guilty conscience! Through their own weaknesses they project their flawed calculations onto Him. So they think they must pray over and over again because He does not seem to answer. They see Him as the aloof unrighteous judge!

Yet with regard to these unanswered prayers people begin to think they have to wear God down bombing His throne with multiple prayers. Just like the women in the parable who repeatedly came back to the unrighteous judge.

Those that hold to the repetitious prayer syndrome do not understand how God answers prayer. Subconsciously they calculate, "since God is unapproachable, as the judge in the story, and only through much importunity will He answer, why pray? But the same prayer repeatedly is a prayer without faith. The woman in the story did not need to make requests repeatedly had she had a righteous judge!

The parable is couched from the point of view of this flawed perception. It is the predominantly errant view of God. It is because of this negative point of view that men become discouraged from praying.

As in the parable,

"so men ought often to pray and not be faint of heart." Lk 18:1

If the Lord God were an unrighteous judge, then it would be understandable that we would have to wear Him down with the same request over and over again. How can we pray with faith if our perception of God is thus flawed?

If we start with the wrong premise concerning the Lord's nature and the notion He is too far above it all, and He doesn't listen and does not care, we are defeated before we utter a word. The parable is a serious look at how people see and feel about God, but it is actually a reflection on how they feel about themselves. As a result, there comes the temptation to correct with human missteps.

Misconception of Two Temptations

Penance is the false attempt to earn God's approval and used as a rationale as to why God should hear our prayer. Perhaps had the women gone out and done a hundred hours of community service the unrighteous judge would have listened! This is how people falsely reason.

License is the polemic. It is the assumption we can do as we please, but the cavalier attitude nonetheless sullies the conscience making it difficult to lift our head before His throne in prayer.

Since we cannot live up to what seems to be a very high standard, we throw caution to the wind and just do as we please. But this attitude is a tremendous danger. And this is a condition of mind that hinders our ability to pray.

When we suffer a failure or misstep we simply must immediately ask for forgiveness and cleansing. This is what is meant by "the sprinkling of the blood." It is the application of the antidote which is "everlasting righteousness." His everlasting righteousness allows for us to abide in His presence and before His throne.

Nevertheless, as we let things go, the multiplied effect of sin in the course of even one day begins to weigh down, clouding our thinking and outlook. As undealt with transgressions build up and persist, we see God in a clouded light and find it most difficult to pray. He now becomes the unrighteous judge.

Now we assume He is sufficiently ticked off, and now has absolutely no time to consider our prayer. We have lost faith! The very thing Jesus is looking for when He returns. But faith can quickly be restored by the application of the sprinkling of the blood. Even when one commits the same sin numerous times in one day Jesus forgives "seventy times seven."

This kind of forgiveness is mind boggling almost incomprehensible, but it is written. It seems we cannot fathom the magnitude of an ever empathetic, forgiving loving God who eagerly waits for us to come into His presence making requests of Him. For the most part the average person does not believe in God this way. In many respects it is because they themselves live in a state of unforgiveness.

But God, on the other hand, is quick to forgive. And yet without recognizing His enormous empathy and compassion for our human predicament we see the Lord as an exacting Judge.

Nevertheless, the flawed subliminal logic is that now we must earn His audience again. We tend to see Him calling for hard labor to gain His ear. If we can just accumulate enough points! Thinking we must pile up points to have access is a horrible misconception. This is penance, but it is not the New Covenant. In fact, He is the opposite!

The misconception is due to being under a guilty conscience! We do not gain audience with God because we can earn it. We can never earn God's presence or privileges. God's favor is truly a gift, an unmerited gift!

Rather than taking responsibility for the sin we seek to adjust our conscience by trying to be good, or by doing good deeds, or the other extreme; we push the issue out of mind and just do as we please.

And people do the same thing with people. Rather than saying I'm sorry they go about trying to fix a personal problem by doing something good for the person they've offended. You know, just balance the scale! This is human penance!

God knows our predicament in this life and in this futile body. That is why He came to earth in the first place! And that is why Jesus taught about foot washing!

Prayer is the Fundamental Work of God!

Prayer is the fundamental use of faith. It is the exercise of our belief. How can one lift his head if one feels unworthy? But if the atonement in Jesus is not applied, we feel we must earn audience and favor. Then as we fail to comply with even self-imposed regulations there comes further, and deeper guilt and the cycle becomes repetitive. There truly is no condemnation! It has been removed!

*"When He said a New Covenant, <u>He has made the first obsolete.</u> Now what is becoming obsolete and growing old **(The Law)** is ready to vanish away." Heb 8:13*

But remember the grace of God, this amazing kindness of the Lord, does not give a license to sin. If we regard sin in our heart the Lord will not hear us. He cannot hear us because if we continue in sin we cannot lift our prayer with faith.

Cheap Grace

In the 16th century the Catholic Church and its leaders convinced the people that they could actually buy indulgences to sin even before they committed those sins.

For example, they would buy from the priests a certificate with the right to commit fornication before going out and doing the act. It was a get out of jail free card. These indulgences were one of the ways the Church was able to raise money.

The exercise and misuse of authority in the Church was also prevalent in the first century, it was characterized and called "licentiousness." The right to have a license for illicit behavior.

The idea was that since Jesus had forgiven sin it was now possible knowing that He had died and forgiven sins one could now go sin. So then in that line of twisted reason people would be free to sin whenever they pleased, since Jesus had already forgiven the sin.

The false doctrine had metastasized as the Church formally legitimized sinning into a written document called indulgences. This was a license, and it was and still is a heresy. But with the advent of indulgences sin became a refined legitimate and licensed behavior. More importantly for the Church it was a way of making money for the clergy. It was for this heresy that brought the reaction called the "Protestant Reformation." The indulgences became the ignition point, and "cause celebre." It was the reason and impetus for those who protested (Protestants) against the Catholic Church.

The followers of Jesus who subscribed to the heretical belief negated faith and thus prayer. The quicker to repentance via the sprinkled blood of Jesus, there comes the confidence to exercise faith and the return to the power of prayer. In fact, repentance is an act of faith.

"Will the son of man find faith?" Ibid

Chapter 36

The Art of Inversion

Needless to say the episode with my daughter in law caused great havoc and dismay in my family. The great anger and then sorrow of heart led to prayer but then came a tremendous fear. It came upon my whole family as we considered the terrible consequences awaiting her. But in a strange way it bolstered our own resolve in Christ Jesus.

If you are on the right track even terrible negatives can work in a positive way to faith. Horrible events can be "inverted." When it comes to prayer this is an important promise given as an inheritance granted to God's people.

"All things work together for good to them who love God and are called according to His purposes." Rom 8:28

But not for the offender if there is no repentance. If there is no repentance all things do not work together for good. Without repentance there is no restoration. So, then the untreated transgressions will actually halt the use and exercise of faith.

But faith works through love, God's love! So much success in prayer is grasping the "art of inversion." If our outlook is constantly negative and we always see the glass half empty rather than half full will tend to not pray with faith. When people worry or see the world outside with uncertainty they will not pray. Life outside is arranged to test our faith. It was meant by design to be uncertain. If we can learn to embrace the uncertainties as opportunities, we allow God our Father to demonstrate His love and reality affirming we are on the right track. This is the beginning of the art of Inversion.

So the focus on the end of the parable.

"And will not God surely see to it that justice is done to his chosen ones who cry out to him day and night, and will he delay toward them? I tell you that he will see to it that justice is done for <u>them soon!</u>" Ibid

Astonishing Answers to Prayer

There are other reasons why God delays. But every time there is a perceived delay to answers of prayer, it is because He has a timing. He has a better way of going about the answer then we do or what we assume is best. He is working on matters that we cannot see.

Years ago, I had two astonishing answers to prayer. I have had many many answers to prayer, but these two answers were standout mountain top answers. These answers to prayer have become beacons that continue to light the way when I find myself in a valley.

The first occurred when I had been in the office of pastor. Our church was not growing. In addition, we had been seeking the Lord for an answer to a terrible problem which was occurring on the other side of the country.

There was a serial murderer killing innocent black children in the state of Georgia. We as a congregation stood before the Lord seeking a remedy to the murder spirit operating in the killer. But we did not see an answer forthcoming. We had prayed, "but where are you Lord"? We did not see the horrific activity stop.

The murders continued unabated, and it was becoming daily headlines even on the west coast in Seattle. But we did notice that the killer was changing his behavior. We noticed that instead of picking on young children under ten he began to focus on older children in their teens. Nevertheless, the murder spirit was not stopped. We as a people were frustrated. I told the Lord that I did not want to continue as pastor.

Consequently, I took counsel with three other brothers and told them my perplexing concern. The brothers were the stalwarts and confidants in the church. They had actually come with me along with their wives to found the church in Kirkland Washington. This was in 1978.

Three years had gone by from the time we first founded the church, but now we had come to an impasse. I had to see the hand of God move or for me it was over. I told the brothers that we must fast and put some substance into our prayers. We could not just lift our voices we must enter a travail.

It was not to make our voices heard in heaven it was about binding Satan. God is not deaf, but when we fast we act as His proxies on earth. God works through His representatives. We were standing on earth locked into a deadly battle with Satan. In my heart it was him or us.

I asked the men to seek the Lord and asked each one how many days we should fast. I told them we would meet the next day and each would share his thoughts concerning how many days.

Three of us said twenty-one days and one said twenty. We all knew it was to be a twenty-one day fast. We sent our wives and children away so that we could have quiet until we had our appetite under control.

The Atlanta Murders

The **Atlanta murders of 1979–1981**, sometimes called the **Atlanta Child Murders** were a series of murders committed in Atlanta, Georgia, from the summer of 1979 until the spring of 1981. Over the two-year period, at least 28 African American children, adolescents and adults were murdered.

Wayne Williams, an Atlanta native who was twenty-three years old at the time of the last murder was arrested and convicted of two of the adult murders and sentenced to two consecutive life terms. Police subsequently have attributed several of the child murders to Williams and closed the cases.

We began the fast on May 1, 1981. Twenty-one days later on May 21, 1981 we finished the fast.

Wayne Williams was apprehended for the murders the very next day on May 22, after our fast ended.

In addition to the capture of Wayne Williams, it was also during the fast the Lord made it known to merge our congregation with a congregation that was meeting across town. They were to bring their entire congregation to our facility. Our church doubled overnight.

161

The two congregations came together and out of that merger the church grew exponentially. Over the next couple years not only did the membership grow into thousands, but as a result many churches were birthed in the greater Seattle area. God had mightily answered prayer.

But what is to be carefully noted is that there are times we must enter into travail and then be patient with waiting on high for the answers. God's timing is not the same as ours.

The second mountain top answer to prayer was a somewhat painful experience, but it is nonetheless important and worth telling.

After my third church planting in California, I took a sales job with a health insurance company. Then, after two years I was promoted to a regional sales management position. The company was a large company based in Rockford Illinois. But the marketing company fell into trouble and wanted to close my regional management office.

They offered me another management position in Orange County, but I decided against it. I wanted to move back to Oregon and pursue another direction. I had been working on a manuscript for a book and I was no longer interested in a so-called secular job.

I went in search of a house for my family. I had come across what I thought was a perfect house. I was certain it was one my wife and sons would enjoy. I put an offer in and waited for the bank to approve the loan.

In the meantime, I returned to San Diego and prepared to move my family and all our household items. After ten years in San Diego, it was time to go back to Oregon.

We packed, moved, and arrived in several weeks later, but the bank loan languished. Week after week went by. I had put all our household goods in a storage facility, and we camped out at my mother in law's two bedroom condo. We kept praying. A month went by, and I was still sleeping on the couch with the wife and three kids in the spare bedroom.

Two months had gone by and no word from the bank. We kept praying. Then after three months I gave up. It was now late November. The rains had returned, and the bad weather had set in. It was a nightmare. I totally gave up on the house and we rented a place on the north side of town.

We put the kids in school, and I returned to the manuscript I had been working on in San Diego. At that time, a friend who I had known for years heard about the book I was writing and offered to finance the publishing. It was going to happen. I was assured that the book was going to be published. To make a long story short concerning the book, it became a bestseller and it sold over 35,000 copies. We made a film out of the book that has been seen by millions of people all over the world.

When the effort of writing the book was completed my wife had stumbled upon a house which had just that day hit the market. I told her that if she really liked it then let's offer full price and get it. We put in the offer and won the house the next day.

How different that was compared to the house I had thought would be perfect but did not go through. God had a timing, and I was amazed to say the least.

The great Judge had our best interest in mind and kept us from a disaster. The first house was a house that had been partially burned in a fire and not suitable in terms of a soundness in its re-construction.

We moved into the house my wife found and fell in love with it. It could not have been more perfect in every way. I ended up building a film studio upstairs. And from that upstairs office I produced twenty documentary films. God had a plan! Don't be discouraged!

God loves us and even though we had to wait three months at my mother in law's house and another three months in a rental, He knew how much we would love and enjoy the house. He kept us from making a huge mistake that we could not see.

When He delayed, it was because the house He had in mind for us would not have hit the market for many months. It was not within our time frame. God loves us and has our very best interests in mind continually. Even though it was painful to wait until our house came on the market it was so well worth the wait. We lived in that house for twenty-two years.

When we are set into a time of waiting, we tend to think God has not heard our prayers, and sadly project the idea that He is like the unrighteous judge in the parable. But if we have faith in His goodness, if we have the correct premise, then we do not allow delays to swerve us from the truth of His true nature expressed in the parable. You have to invert the curse.

"how much more will God speedily answer His children who cry out to Him." Ibid

Our God is a righteous Judge! His timing is not ours. Invert the curse!

We sold our house several years ago, but that answer to prayer is a constant reminder of how the Lord watches over us. He is a good God and great Father, and a righteous Judge!

"So ought men to pray and not lose heart." Ibid

...but when we think God is not paying attention or does not care for men and is an unrighteous judge, we can and often do lose heart. But He is none of these things. We are told in the word that even the hairs of our head are numbered.

"But will the son of man find faith when He returns?" Ibid

This parable though, lays the basis for the reason why I would say to Jesus I hope so, but I am not sure.

Perhaps you would agree with me. But hopefully it will not engender a sense of guilt, but may it serve as an inspiration for the daily choice to ride on the right track.

But what is most often overlooked, when it comes to using faith is that we forget that faith comes by hearing. We fail to wait on the Lord for His word.

We simply must learn to invert.

164

Chapter 37

Are You On The Right Track?

The "City of God" obviously is where we want to go and is the correct track and the right choice. It is the place where we want to arrive. Who in their right mind would choose otherwise?

Yet astonishing as it may seem, many Christian people think whole heartedly they are on the right track but are actually on the wrong track. They are heading toward the city of Babylon. Perhaps there is recoil at the thought, but I am reminded of what Jesus said,

"whoever wants to be my disciple must take up his cross daily and follow me." Lk 9:23

And this is why He said, *"will the son of man find faith when He returns." Ibid*

These statements by Jesus are tough words! My answer to Jesus, "I am not sure" was not from an altruistic attitude. My response is from a lifetime of failure, failures of my own faith.

But our ride upon the contradictory railroad tracks is not to impose a guilt trip from past faith failures. It is the context of our daily contested journey. The understanding of which is the ticket to an incredible destination, the City of God. If your ticket has been punched, then I just want to help you stay on board and on track.

But as it is for the moment, I would have to say the answer is up for grabs! It is the reason why it is said,

"if the righteous are scarcely saved what will happen to the ungodly?" 1 Peter 4:18

By and large most people do not know how to find faith let alone use it. Faith is the victory that overcomes the world. So, then we had better find it and then learn how to use it!

Right Track Wrong Track

There are so many millions of people that have their ticket (believing in Jesus the Lord), and yet leaning on the wrong track. And why? Because they do not understand one cannot be on the right track when not using faith daily. And it is the exercise and using of faith that insures properly dressing for the grand party and entry into the City. And to be dressed properly there must be a clear understanding of what faith is and how to maintain the use of faith. If we are to put on the robe of righteousness faith is the key!

Faith is not a Formula-Use It or Lose It

It is remarkable to watch how there are those who begin to learn to use faith but end up turning faith into a formula. The use of faith is not to degenerate into formula!

There was a group of people that were mightily used by God in the 1800's. They became known as the Methodists. They were given the name because they began to use new methods in their service before God that were unique for that time. God used them mightily.

These were a people that began to use their faith and God honored them with inventive and unique ways of serving. In their successes however, they became so convinced by the new methods they began to focus on the methods rather than using faith. Their faith degenerated from faith to formula. Instead of continuing in faith they just followed the methods.

Then other people began to study their methods rather than seek God by faith. After all they were having great success. Why not copy?

Initially faith did yield those unique methods. But methods do not excite faith. One could say the methods were the fruit of faith and not the other way around. The Methodist movement degenerated into becoming another stuffy religious denomination just as so many others. It all degenerated into religious tradition and formulas void of faith. What began as faith became a form.

The Proper Use of Faith

Faith is like a drawbridge that must be used each day. It is an operational faith not a mere doctrine that intersects with God's glory. That is why "without faith it is impossible to please God." God is pleased when we are changed from glory to glory. It is not enough to know the doctrine of faith; it must be an action. It must be exercised. One must use it or lose it!

Here is a great and simple illustration which exemplifies faith as opposed to method. It comes from the life of King David of Israel. It is a very very simple example but easy to understand.

As King David began to move his headquarters from Hebron to Jerusalem his enemies caught wind of it. They must have felt that in his transition it would be a good time to attack. So, they marshaled their forces to come against David. When David was alerted to their attack, he sought God for how to deal with the impending urgent situation.

At the time Abiathar the high priest was with him, and they inquired of the Lord through the Urim and Thummim. The Urim and Thummim was the listening device carried over the breastplate of the high priest. It was used for important decisions as a device in which they could hear from God. (It would be nice to have one of those today) We do, but that is for later.

David was given direction to attack the Philistines head on and he would be granted victory over the vast hordes of the enemy. He did and he was successful.

Afterward the Philistines tried to attack again. So, David sought the Lord a second time. But this time the Lord said do not attack them head on. But go around behind them and when you hear their footsteps echo in the trees then you shall come against them from the rear, and you shall defeat them again.

Had David taken on the Philistines head on again with the frontal attack he used the first time he would have been defeated. Had he used the same method presuming God was with him again he would have had big trouble. He would have subverted faith defaulting to a method. While God may give a plan of attack in one instance it is presumption, not faith, to

167

use the same method in another instance. Faith is not a formula.

In addition, other people's successes should not be assumed to be the road map to take in pursuit of success either, because that too would be a method and not faith. This was the common fault of the Methodists, and for those that followed their methods. Faith is personal and dynamic. What works in one instance is no guarantee for another. It is easy to become lazy and live on methods and formulas and not faith.

But faith can be exercised when we worship and lift our hands to God or when we just sit quietly before the Lord. We are directed to "be still and know, He says, "that I am God." He leads us beside the still waters. The still waters are those moments in quietness when we can hear from our inner sanctuary. If we have filled our heart with His Logos (the collected sayings of God), then His rhema (the individual sayings of God) can be quickened to us by His Holy Spirit. Then we can hear His rhema/word. This is another activity of faith.

Faith Hindered

While we have briefly mentioned the danger of false doctrine, what follows is a more concrete example of how false doctrine can damage the use of faith. It is one thing to use Jesus' name fraudulently and in error, but it is quite another to create prophetic heresy.

And since most of the Christian world has embraced "a massive heresy" it is safe to say their faith has been greatly diminished, if not extinguished. It is because there is the clinging to the most notable false doctrine.

Any doctrine that mitigates against the completed work of Jesus is false and can damage faith. Such is the case with those who attempt to teach the, so called, "Golden Prophecy."

Chapter 38

Heretics of the Golden Prophecy Club

Of all the teachings that have come along in the past five hundred years the most destructive is the false-teaching of the so-called "Golden Prophecy." There are so many that teach the classic error that they are without number.

Jesus warned His people there would come many false prophets who would lead many astray. Yet even with His warning to "be not deceived," this is exactly what has happened. The whole world has fallen under the spell of this false doctrine. Could this have something to do with the reason why Christ would ask the rhetorical question "will the Son of man find faith when He returns"?

The doctrine of the Golden Prophecy so commonly miss-taught has become a veritable monkey wrench disengaging the exercise of faith. In a carefully crafted way, it was subtly thrown into the theological mix. The doctrine, for the most part, has slipped in undetected.

The majority of those who teach this portion of the Old Testament do not fully realize they claim that the Messiah only *partially completed* the work at Calvary when He died on the tree. The false doctrine comes from a terribly twisted misunderstanding of Daniel 9:24-27.

They teach that the Messiah did *not completely* accomplish all that He did accomplish!

According to the famous text the Messiah would and did clearly accomplish a number of things:

"He would finish the transgression, He would make an end of sin(s), He would make reconciliation for iniquity, He would bring in everlasting righteousness, He would seal up vision and prophecy, and He would anoint the most Holy." Dan 9:24-27

Jesus, the Messiah, accomplished all of these things in totality. He completely fulfilled the scripture. Yet, the widely held interpretative view is that He has not yet fully completed all these six matters.

The false teachers say, "what was indicated in the text of Daniel 9:24, was only partially completed by Messiah."

The enormous heresy has literally deceived nearly the entire Christian world. But worse than the deceit it has damaged people from properly using and exercising faith. It is because the faulty interpretation causes people to look outwardly for external signs thus neglecting the operational daily use of faith. The misstep is huge!

Faith is the daily exercise of seeking the Lord so that in purposefully reaching towards God we enter the Sabbath rest. In the Sabbath rest we are able to hear His voice. God set aside a Sabbath day and called it "Today."

In hearing His voice, we are touched and thus grow in his divine nature. This is the robe and the proper garment for the wedding celebration. We must understand the utter necessity of spiritual preparation, and if the use of faith is frustrated by false doctrine or heresy, then the divine nature waits hanging in the closet.

"Today, if you hear His voice harden not your heart." **Heb. 3:15**

Faith is not about pet theological theories falsely authenticated by jangling the Logos. It is about hearing the rhema. Faith comes by hearing.

How can we hear the rhema if we are locked up and following false interpretations?

If Jesus, the Messiah, forecast in Dan 9:24 had not fully completed all that was stated by the prophet Daniel then there are monumental implications. The false premise of the miss-teaching concerning the fully completed work of Christ creates serious hearing problems.

Not only monumental in terms of the frustration of the use of faith, but the heresy shuts up the kingdom and the access for God's redeemed to obtain proper spiritual light. Yet the heretics of the "golden prophecy" cult have carelessly created at least the partial reason for Jesus' rhetorical question.

The Call

The call is not for the wise and the learned, and certainly not for the smug and self-righteous, but for all who would come. He came into the world to seek and save that which was lost. The vulnerability of those not well versed in the Word/Logos is that they are easily manipulated and brainwashed by the so-called experts who make confident assertions. This is what Jesus warned against. Look at the scripture again.

"For many will come in My name, claiming, 'I am the Christ,' and will deceive many." Matt 24:5

This was His response when they had asked Him about the future and when He would return. They were asking Him to give an answer and it was in the context of prophecy. He was saying be forewarned about so-called prophets.

It is important, vitally important, to revisit what we have accepted from whom we have deemed respected teachers. Our working use of faith is at stake.

We do not enter the banquet on the coattails of other men's labor, i.e., their well-established doctrine. We enter by our own faith.

If we can recall the parable of the wedding feast, the King arrived to see the guests who wanted to be at the wedding feast for the Son. But he found a man who was not wearing the proper wedding clothes. The King addressed him as "friend", but do not be misled by this word in Jesus' teaching, for when he called someone friend (He called Judas friend) it was in some cases an irony. He made it clear they were not His friend even though He was theirs.

So we see this King who presided over the wedding feast who wanted to know how a man had gotten into the celebration without the proper attire, but the man could not answer and was speechless. It was a sign of his guilt.

We cannot put on another man's robe. When we follow on blindly in another man's doctrine are we not putting on another man's robe?

The robe of righteousness He has made, is specifically personally tailored for each individual. It can only be worn by faith. It can only be acquired by faith. What works by faith for one is not to be assumed by another. The man in the parable did not know how to use faith. Hence, he was not clothed properly. A person's robe is his righteous clothing derived from knowing Jesus personally. That robe can only be acquired by the proper use of his faith.

171

No one can wear your robe, and no one can wear mine. They are tailored. They have the same substance but are tailored by faith.

And as we acquire the divine nature by faith we overcome. We even overcome false doctrine. You yourself are responsible for what you hear and what you allow into your inner chamber.

"And this is the victory that overcomes the world-even our faith." 1 Jn 5:4

It is a clarion call to warn the unsuspecting of spiritual traps that shipwreck faith.

Chapter 39

The Robe You Wear?

When I was only one week old my aunt, who was an Eastern European Jew, baptized me in water. She had come to America and had given her life to Christ Jesus. My parents were furious with her influence upon me. They too were Jews, but neither my mother nor father had given themselves over to a belief in the Messiah.

My aunt had come to the Lord Jesus in Los Angeles. She in turn wanted her baby nephew to come to Christ, so she baptized me in water. My mother kept this secret from me until I was in my sixties. But as I look back over my life, I can see the Lord's hand and how He protected me in all my formative years

The baptism by my aunt was so profound that from the earliest moments of my life, I was always thinking about Jesus, even though His name was never mentioned in our house.

Nevertheless, I did not get on board the train until I was twenty-five years old. You must not only believe you must receive Jesus. Believing is the first step, but then there is the receiving! When I was younger, I did not realize that God was inviting me to board the train. It took twenty-five years to get my ticket, accepting His invitation to get on board and ride.

"A man believes in his heart unto righteousness and confession is made unto salvation." Rom 10:10

I finally confessed with my mouth that Jesus is Lord. I finally got on board, and was then sealed in Him at a later water baptism, but this time the baptism was of my own choosing. I entered into faith, not by my aunt's volition, but by my own. My water baptism, at twenty-five, was my public confession and submission to Christ. But my aunts dipping me when I was an infant had a profound effect from the beginning. It seemed to mark me out for God and set me apart from my Jewish culture and heritage. I never had a Jewish bar-mitzvah.

173

Later, after my decision to be water baptized again, I was permitted to experience the "powers of the ages" to come. Faith is not blind. God permits the experience of His Kingdom in degrees. Our human bodies cannot handle to any great surge of spiritual amps, so He allows incremental portions. This is what is meant when the scriptures describe the term from "glory to glory." The term glory to glory is not a superlative or hyperbole, but a description of the power He sends in portions. It is power He sends in degrees.

But there is one enormous initial surge. It is called the "Baptism of the Holy Spirit." It is accompanied and followed by the speaking in tongues. The speaking in tongues is an angelic language and is given to be exercised for the strengthening of one's inner self.

"The one who speaks in a tongue edifies himself, but the one who prophesies edifies the church." 1 Cor. 14:4

There are countless bible teachers who say this gift of tongues was done away with after the apostles died off. They often say the gift is not from God and try to dissuade by discouraging people from seeking the gift of tongues. They say it is selfish because it edifies self, therefore it is egocentric. But Paul said he spoke in tongues more than all. The reason he encouraged people to speak in tongues was that it edified self.

But the self Paul was referring to was the *inner self* or the inner sanctuary. The inner sanctuary is our spirit. It is who we are. The gift of tongues strengthens our spirit. Why does our spirit need to be strengthened? Because it conflicts with our outer self which is our flesh self. Our spirit is who we are. So, Paul encouraged all to be strengthened in the inner man by exercising in the gift of tongues.

"I wish that all of you would speak in tongues." 1 Cor 14:5

Those (Christians) who deny others from being strengthened in the inner man are not spiritual Christians they are of the natural man.

"But a __natural man__ does not accept the things of the Spirit of God, for they are foolishness to him." 1 Cor. 14:6

The Baptism of the Holy Spirit is the spiritual surge that brings with the Holy Spirit the gift of speaking in tongues. The gift is a lifelong companion and when exercised strengthens the inner man. That is why Paul would have all speak in tongues. It is also why he said,

"forbid not the speaking in tongues." 1 Cor 14:39

But there are Christian pastors today that teach their congregation to not speak in tongues. A direct opposite to the directive given by Paul. What is very strange is that these same people are most often those that further the false doctrine of the "golden prophecy cult."

Even during the time of Paul there was a problem with people teaching others not to speak in tongues. There are Christians, even Christian leaders who follow the inclinations of the natural man. They are not spiritual but mentally orientated intellectuals.

But again, confession and water baptism got me on board the train. I still did not clearly understand the day-by-day walk.

I have been on board now for some fifty years. Nevertheless, I have to admit at times it seemed as though the train had stopped. In those brief instances or lapses when nothing seemed to be happening, I was tempted to get off, but those moments were only momentary lapses of judgment.

Nevertheless, even momentary lapses can sully the garment. The keeping of our garment clean is a daily discipline which comes from the exercise using of faith.

Christian Heritage of No Use

There are so many people who know the name of Jesus that are born into a Christian family and heritage but are not riding the rails properly. They are falsely trusting that their family tradition qualifies them before God, but they are not actively learning to put on of the robe of righteousness. They run the risk they will be asked to leave the party. The same problem exists for anyone who trusts in yesterday's faith. Faith is today. It is not as though using faith becomes a work. Faith is a gift that allows communication and communion with our Father.

There are many who believe in Jesus but so do devils. We must understand the critical importance of allowing Him into our inner man, our inner sanctuary. If we want living faith and the reward of a clean heart and the possession of our soul, we must come to grips with the fact that Jesus calls us to faith today. He is alive and so must faith be alive. He wants to disclose Himself daily.

Yet to come to grips means a death. And that death is the death to the outer man which is the flesh. The death is to die daily. The flesh hates faith.

So then, even getting on board does not mean one is heading down the tracks properly. We can start out in the spirit and gravitate back to the fleshly man. We can get off the right track. There are multitudes of people who get on the Jesus train yet remain worldly. They fail to recognize they are heading toward Babylon. This is self deception. And the self I am speaking about this time is the lower self.

Nor does it mean you remain on board. There are numerous scriptures that speak of people who have gotten on board yet abandon Jesus and go back into the world. My daughter in law is a case in point, but there are others mentioned in the bible, who departed from Christ.

"It is written that in the last days many will depart from the faith giving heed to seducing spirits and doctrines of demons." 1 Tim 4:1

Here are a few specific instances:

Paul was speaking,

"for Demas, having loved this present world, has deserted me and gone to Thessalonica." 1 Tim 4:10

...and another

Hymenaeus is included in the "some" who had put away faith and a good conscience and who had come to shipwreck in their faith. The apostle adds that he had delivered Hymenaeus and Alexander to Satan that they might learn not to blaspheme. I Tim 1:20

Such was also the case in Corinth when a man in the church had given himself over to terrible sexual perversions so that Paul had to deliver him over to Satan for the destruction of his flesh, that his spirit might be saved in the day of the Lord.

Here is that report.

"It is reported commonly that there is fornication among you, and such fornication as is not so much as named among the Gentiles, that one should have his father's wife. And ye are puffed up, and have not rather mourned, that he that hath done this deed might be taken away from among you. For I verily, as absent in body, but present in spirit, have judged already, as though I were present, concerning him that hath so done this deed, In the name of our Lord Jesus Christ, when ye are gathered together, and my spirit, with the power of our Lord Jesus Christ, to deliver such a one unto Satan for the destruction of the flesh, that the spirit may be saved in the day of the Lord Jesus." 1 Cor 5:5

Sadly, this is what I had to do with my daughter. Should we not all fear? Is this not another reason for Paul expressing his attending fear when he said,

"I was with you in much fear and trembling?" 1 Cor 2:1-4

On Board but the Wrong Track

So even if one is on board, he may still be on the wrong track. In many ways I was on the wrong track even as a pastor.

We must know how to keep our garments. If you get on the wrong track, you may be dismissed from the wedding feast which takes place only in the City of God. How can one attend the wedding feast if the venue for the celebration is in the City of God, but he is on the wrong track? If one is headed for the city of Babylon guess what, you will miss the celebration because you will be in the wrong city. We should all be as Paul and fear.

Let's take a closer look at the two cities. The robe one wears indicates the proper destination.

177

Chapter 40

A Tale of Two Cities and a Robe

Remember the man at the wedding feast who was not dressed properly? This is serious stuff we must take to heart! Many will say Lord Lord didn't we do this in your name? The many seem to be Christians. After all they cast out demons and do miracles in His name. It is important to ask ourselves if I could be one of those many? How can we know for sure? This issue is the fulcrum point upon which the teeter totter of our faith sits.

In reality which track we lean toward is discerned by our perception of the world. And the way we see the world is critical to putting on the correct clothing. And the correct clothing guarantees you are on the right track and ensures arrival to the correct city. But how is it possible to be objective about ourselves?

A powerful checkpoint for examination begins with an honest objective understanding of life's context. What is meant by context here is how we see the world. This is our worldview. And how we see the world will help in determining and assaying if we are properly dressing.

It is through the strands of God's glory, which He imparts and dispenses to His elect. God's glory is not to be taken as a superlative. His glory is His divine nature which He desires to impart day by day. This is His robe. Just as an earthly garment is weaved thread by thread so are the stands of glory to be acquired and accumulated for a heavenly garment. We participate in the weaving as we connect with His presence. We enter His courts by thanksgiving, praise, worship and prayer.

Whether our progress is perceived by others or not, everyone is preparing a robe. But which robe? The man in the parable was somehow there but not dressed properly. Let us carefully examine ourselves.

That reminds me of the great story of the emperor who had no clothes. Everyone has heard the classic. The moral to the story is that it is possible to believe you are clothed properly and yet you are not. Hence the man at the wedding feast who was found without the proper garment.

Let us ask ourselves, is it Christ's robe of righteousness or our own we are putting on? There are two robes. One is spiritual and the other is carnal. So, to get on the right track to make sure we are on the right track, we must begin with *our world view.*

Context

A world view is the lens with which we look through as we process this life. The context we hold to is our world view. It is our lens!

Today, it seems that no matter who you talk to, most all seem to be consumed with politics. It is the new religion. In election years the conversation becomes deafening drowning out all other voices. But the whole notion of earthly politics is based on a misapprehension. Our default bias should rather be a "spiritual worldview." An undue cleaving to politics is an earthly view. Everyone has a worldview whether realized or not, but what is it? Nevertheless, the most important question to ask is do we have a spiritual worldview?

The worldview is the context or the framework for how to ride the rails and without the proper lens we invariably default to the wrong side. If our bias becomes purely political, we have mistakenly taken the track toward the city of Babylon. Obviously, it is important to distinguish one from the other.

The Pollyanna Principle

Is it "a wonderful world" as sung by the great Ray Charles? Well, there are some aspects of this world that are pretty wonderful. We see the beauty of creation, the animals, and then there are some pretty good people.

There are some wonderful things we can point to especially in the United States and other nations in the western world. But so much of this wonderful world isn't so wonderful. Nevertheless, there are those who refuse to see the world as it is. They are the Pollyannas. (A subconscious bias towards the positive is often described as the "Pollyanna Principle")

It is the faulty idealism hoped for and projected, but the truth is far different.

The world is filled with wars, starvation, disease, slavery, rape, murder, and horrible things that we would rather not look at. So how can this wonderful world have such tragic evils. There seems to be a great contradiction. Bing Crosby tried to reconcile the problem in his song, "You have to accentuate the positive and eliminate the negative." but since the release of that musical philosophy things have only gotten worse! How can the contradiction be reconciled? How do we sort these things out and come up with a believable and real-world view?

If we view the world through the lens of politics, then there is the assumption somehow through politics we can fix things to the positive side. But what is politics? A reasonable definition is that it is the process whereby men determine how they will be ruled. But in many parts of the world and from country to country there is no process where men can reasonably hope to affect the world. They do not get to vote or participate. And sometimes governments are hijacked by fraud!

So, at best "participatory" politics is only partial it is not universal, and even then it is at best a vague and remotely unattainable hope. And sometimes we only have a perception of participation.

The truth is even in countries where people are allowed to vote it can be a mere ruse. If the political climate does change for the better, it is at best only temporary. But even if hope is placed in the political process, it is only because we erroneously assume we can bring lasting change to the world. Idealistically we think we can fix the world and make it better. Hence the Beatles famous song "Imagine"!

Many tragically, as it were, hope to see politics as the great change agent that can fix the many sorrows of this life. People actually think the world can be fixed. There are even Christian books written such as "Out to Change My World" that have embraced this ultimate futile form of optimism. It is because they have a flawed world view. They are engaged in the Pollyanna Principle.

But if this misplaced optimism is fatally wrong, and there is a massive universal corporate delusion, what then is the proper worldview? How are we to comprehend our physical existence?

Foundational Reality

Sorry to burst the Pollyanna bubble but.... we must come to see that something terrible has happened to this world. That something we must come to grips with or we will not see why we are traveling down the two railroad tracks, and neither able to discern who we are.

What lies ahead and what we must look at may come off sounding surreal but hang in there!

Before there was the beginning, there actually was a before. Most people when they want to learn as much as they can from the Bible begin with the book of Genesis.

Even for those who have never ever picked up a Bible know what it says.

"In the beginning God created the heaven and the earth." Gen 1

Every single translation of the Bible begins this way. But is this where we should begin? Just as an aside for the moment, the word for God in the above text for "God" in Hebrew is strangely not Jehovah. It is Elohim. (You may say, "who cares what difference does it make?" It makes an enormous difference, but we will bear down on that matter in a later chapter) The point being made here is that the beginning of Genesis does not denote the beginning.

Hence before the beginning denoted in Genesis 1:1 there was a before and that before is noted in the book of Revelation chapter 12:7. There was a war in the heavens. In fact if you want to go way back to a description last book of the Bible gives a better understanding of the before the beginning. (Again, this we will deal with in more detail in a later chapter)

But on a closer look the heavens and earth denoted in the first sentence of Genesis actually did not occur until after God separated the waters. Separating the waters created "the expanse." The expanse is equivalent to the universe. Before there was a heaven and earth there had to come first a separation of the waters. Then after the waters were separated there was the expanse. The expanse is best visualized like a hamburger between two buns. I'm merely speaking in human terms! Just as the meat separates the bun on top from the bun below so did the expanse separate the waters above from the waters below. The expanse is the visible universe of stars and galaxies etc.

In the seven creative yom/days it says, "the evening and the morning" defining each day. It says this in all the translations. But these could not have been literal twenty-four hour days because the sun was not yet created until the fourth yom, or fourth day. How could there be a twenty-four hour day if there was not the setting of the sun and then rising in a twenty-four hour period? The term morning and evening is better understood as dawning and setting. The dawning and setting of a yom. A yom meaning an age.

Hence the dawning and setting of an age. The seven yoms were ages (long ages) not literal twenty-four hour days. Again, how could there be a twenty-four hour day when the sun was not created until the 4th day or yom?

And so, the beginning for most who read the Genesis account is only to the extent that we mark human time within an understanding of a visible material universe.

And this is critical in understanding and coming to grips for developing a proper worldview.

In dealing with the **was** (Revelation 12:7-"There was war in the heavens") (which was before, "In the beginning" of Genesis one), it will allow us to see what happened to our present world, and the ensuing horrific corruption.

It will enable us to see why we are presently on the train going down the two tracks and how to ride the train to its proper destination. We must implicitly gain a new objective perspective!

Then, the spiritual world view becomes the preferable lens from which we can view this world. The spiritual lens worldview will help keep us on the right track.

The Great Calamity

The book of Revelation for the most part is misunderstood. It is because those who seek to tackle the book do not first undertake to comprehend its proper context. The context for Revelation must be approached with spiritual vision which is Alpha Omega vision. And it is Alpha Omega vision which is the first order in which to understand the book of Revelation and world view. Again, once we obtain a proper worldview it helps immeasurably to better grasp the book of Revelation and stay on track.

Learn to Turn

In brief John heard a voice behind him and turned around to see the voice.

"On the Lord's day I was in the Spirit, and I heard behind me a loud voice like a trumpet." Rev 1:10

The voice was the voice of Jesus the Alpha and Omega. The meaning of Alpha and Omega is the beginning and the end. In other words we must turn (John turned to hear the voice) from the way we see things and learn to see things from God's perspective. We must turn! When John turned, He saw Jesus the Alpha and Omega. He saw from the perspective of the six days of creation. The six days or yoms of creation was before earth time. It was before human history commenced. Earth time commenced on the 7th day or Yom.

We must see from heaven to earth and not earth to heaven. We must learn to turn. We must learn the full art of inversion, because for the most part we see only from an earth-bound point of view. Six hundred years before Christ, in the book of Isaiah, people were instructed to look down from God's perspective.

"Lift up your eyes to the sky, <u>then look to "the earth beneath</u>;" For the sky will vanish like smoke, And the earth will wear out like a garment And its inhabitants will die in like manner; But My salvation will be forever, And My righteousness will not wane." Isa 51:6

184

When we stand on the earth and look up, we can see the sun and the moon. What is fascinating is that from our perspective on earth, they both look about the same size. But the fact of the matter is that it would take 50,000,000 moons to full up the sun. But from our point of view, they look the same size.

We must come up to a greater objectivity. This is Alpha Omega vision. So then let us return to painting the picture of a proper worldview, as we *learn to turn.*

In doing so we begin to move and stay on the correct track and the weaving of the robe of righteousness, the garment for the City of God. The robe to be worn at the wedding feast. As we understand the primary objective, of this life, it is to put on this His robe.

The Great and Terrible War

Initially, let us proceed with a cursory view and introduction to the mysterious chapter in the book of Revelation twelve; the war in the heaven(s).

Please Note: We will deal more fully with the war in Heaven in a later chapter.

"Then a war broke out in heaven: Michael and his angels fought against the dragon, and the dragon and his angels fought back." Rev 12:7

This war took place <u>not in heaven</u> as what is commonly understood, but rather it took place in the heavens. It was in the expanse or firmament. It took place among the stars in the heavens.

The word for heaven in scripture is a generic word (ouranos) and in this case in the 12th chapter it is to be interpreted and refers to the physical visible universe. This was in the expanse in between the waters above the firmament and the waters below the firmament. Waters above the firmament must be looked at as energies!

This war took place somewhere within the roll out of all the ages or yoms of the creation week of ages as indicated in Genesis one. The heavens and the earth were created before man's arrival on planet earth. So, the war it seems took place between the 6th yom/age and before the 7th yom.

Revelation makes clear in the 12th chapter, that the war in the heavens had a profoundly disastrous effect on planet earth.

The recorded event seems surreal because we are in human bodies, and it is hard to reflect on the spiritual world in our limited human capacities. Our flesh bodies act as veils over our spirit. We tend as humans, to compute within mortal calculations and not spiritual calculations. The reason we have trouble with connecting to the spiritual has also a great deal to do with the war that occurred before man was ever here on earth.

It was the war in the heavens which eventually came down bringing spiritual sickness, spiritual amnesia and a deluge of evils upon humans and even the animal kingdom. I know it sounds surreal. I told you in advance. Hang in there!

So, all the spiritual issues that we cannot seem to grasp were and are presently the effects due to the war in the heavens. So immediately it can be seen that "the something" that caused trouble here on earth happened from outside this world in the heavens. It happened due to what we can ascertain from Revelation twelve, which explains the war in the heavens.

Keep in mind as earthlings this is far out of reach for most humans. Even to Christians it tends to become surreal due to the natural mind inclinations. All who live in this human temporal body, which is wasting away, tend to conceptualize forming thought within our human mental grid logic which is normally affected by the outside material realm. And, that which is fixed within the frame of our own physical lifetime span of seventy or so years.

This, sadly, is the daily default bias. It is a work of faith to lift ourselves out of ourselves to the objectivity of Alpha Omega vision and see things from God's perspective. We must learn to turn! And unless we practice or exercise daily, we will default and reset to our natural mind bias and inclinations.

Remember what it says about the natural man.

"For anyone who is a hearer of the word and not a doer of the word is like <u>a natural man</u> who looks at his natural face in a mirror and goes his way <u>and forgets</u> who he is." James 1:24

"But a <u>natural man</u> does not accept the things of the Spirit of God, for they are foolishness to him, and he cannot understand them because they are spiritually discerned." 1 Cor 2:14

We are all beset in having to deal daily with our natural man. **Only** those who can rise to Alpha Omega vision will begin to function in the "spiritual man." But it is a daily discipline!

"The <u>spiritual man</u> judges all things, but he himself is not subject to any-one's judgment" Ibid

So then are we spiritual or natural? This is the daily question! And this is the issue of which garment we are putting on. It most clearly is the fulcrum of the teeter totter.

"Then war broke out in heaven. Michael and his angels fought against the dragon, and the dragon and his angels fought back. But he was not strong enough, and they lost their place in heaven. The great dragon was hurled down—that ancient serpent called the devil, or Satan, who leads the whole world astray. He was hurled to the earth, and his angels with him." Rev 12:

It is tantamount in forming a proper worldview to grasp the enormous impact and significance of the war. This was a war among God's very messengers or as they are called in the scripture angels. The war occurred before mankind appeared on earth. It was a great great transgression of sin by those heavenly beings when they went to war.

The Origination of Sin

Thus, the sin of the angels then came into our planet. Sin, original sin, happened from outside this world among angels. Everyone thinks sin originated with Adam and Eve, but that is not the case. Sin originated with the angels and came from outside and then into this world.

Even though, in traditional Christian theology they are blamed for the original sin, it is only in the sense that sin entered the world through them.

The origination of sin, according to Revelation twelve, occurred by the angels. Sin entered the world through Adam, yes, but it did not originate with Adam. Read it for yourself.

"Therefore, just as 'through' one man 'sin entered' into the world, **Rom 5:12**

Then as a result of this problem we find the coup d'grace.

Chapter 41

Grounded

Unless a man or woman is properly grounded, they will not be able to properly control their thought life. They will not be able to bring every thought captive to the obedience of the master rider; Christ. They will not be able to differentiate between what thoughts are out of the flesh and what thoughts are of the spirit. And that is because they will not be able to screen thoughts through the lens of the proper worldview. And yet we are called to this very thing. Remember the mind is the gateway the dark spirits use as they seek to penetrate and ultimately possess one's spirit, or the inner self. Satan (the opposing force(s) seeks to conquer the heart.

"We tear down arguments, and every presumption set up against the knowledge of God; and we take captive every thought to make it 'obedient to Christ'." 1 Cor 10:5

Thoughts that regularly occur in the mind are very much like viewing lightning in a bottle. The electrical flashes are wild and random. This is a good mind picture of a person's thought life. Wild and indiscriminate thoughts flash about without anything to ground them.

Grounded Thought

Electrical grounding originally began as a safety measure used to help prevent people from accidentally coming in contact with electrical hazards.

Think of a refrigerator. It is a metal box standing on rubber feet with electricity running in and out of it. You use magnets to hang your child's latest drawing on the metal exterior. The electricity running from the outlet and through the power cord to the electrical components inside the refrigerator are electrically isolated from the metal exterior or chassis of the refrigerator.

If for some reason the electricity would come in contact with the chassis, and if someone touched the refrigerator the electricity would flow from the chassis of the refrigerator and through the unlucky person. Perhaps causing injury or even death.

Grounding is used to protect that person. By connecting a green ground wire from the metal frame of the refrigerator the undesirable electricity would travel through the wire back to the electrical panel, thus tripping the circuit-breaker stopping the flow of electricity. Additionally, that wire must be connected to something that is in turn connected to the earth or the ground outside.

This is done by directing electricity into the ground through the wire. If there is an over abundance of electricity it will not flash but will flow safely into the ground.

The same idea is utilized for electrical storms. If wild lightning strikes in a storm it can be contained with a lightning rod. Instead of the lightning striking a house or car in the storm, the lightning is attracted to a lightning rod that is connected by a wire and into the ground. If the lightning hits the rod the energy of the electricity is harmlessly directed downward into the earth. Thus, the electricity is grounded!

Without a proper Biblical worldview, the human mind is not grounded. Hence the thought life can run wild the same as electricity that is not grounded. The source of most mental diseases is due to a lack of proper grounding. It is the thought life running wild.

A proper view of the world is the ground mechanism for a protected thought life. We need the Biblical lens to ground the wild thoughts that surge through the mind. In this way errant thoughts can be brought captive to the obedience of Christ.

The elephant in the room is how do we progress to the proper Biblical worldview?

Grounded Worldview

It is absolutely unconscionable that so little attention is given to the momentous issue. It is because of this waste land of ignorance; people cannot grasp why they think what they think. It is also why they cannot grasp what is going on with this planet.

If we do not come to grips with a clear understanding of the matter then we will become entangled with our errant thoughts and will not know how to process what is happening to ourselves and this confusing outside world.

Once a person is turned inside out by the dark spiritual forces he will unwittingly fall into the love of the world. The love of the world is not just the pursuit of money or things, or the futile pursuit of fame or popularity. One may actually hate the world because of the evil in politics or the greed of wall street, or becoming incensed with the human sex trafficking, or the disparity of wealth among people and nations, but it is still the love of the world. Even if we become obsessed with trying to fix it is still the love of the world.

It is not unusual to be troubled and alarmed at the horrific atrocities in the outside world, but without a proper lens the antipathy gives people a reason to turn against God. They say, "if God is really real and if He is there, why doesn't He do something about it? "Where are you God if you are real? If I can see evil why can't He?" And so it goes!

Altruism is a form of self righteousness, while assuming oneself to be wiser with a higher moral standard than even God Himself. This is where people step in and try to fix the problem(s). Unknowingly, they are involved in the love of self (self righteousness) and the love of the world.

Where Is God?

I once had a particularly good friend I cared deeply about. One day she called me on the phone.

We had met in college, but she moved away to another University for her junior and senior years. Her parents could not afford the out of state tuition, so she moved back to California. We kept in touch. But one day when she called it was not to be a happy conversation. She called to tell me that her father had just been killed in a terrible plane accident. It was devastating news!

He was a colonel in the air force, a pilot who had flown numerous combat missions during World War Two and then also in the Korean War. I later found out that he was present at the Japanese attack on Pearl harbor. He was a great man and war hero.

When she began to relate what had happened, I was terribly shaken. Later that day I decided to fly down to California to comfort her and her mother. She was literally beside herself.

The day after I arrived at her home was the day of the memorial service. I will never forget what she said after the service. She said. "Where is God?" She was a Lutheran girl. In other words, how is it that God would allow for this to happen. "Where is God now"?

As a person not being brought up in church, there was no way I could give an answer. I didn't know what to say. She simply could not sort out how this could have happened to her father and why.

It is the same rationale that people come to when they cannot make sense of greed, murder, kidnapping, disparity among nations, slavery, you name it. People in general cannot sort out why God not only allows such things, but then does nothing about it. Even the greatest Bible teachers do not have an adequate answer.

Her words, "Where is God" is the same common thought that surges in people's minds when it seems there are no answers. It is also why in certain instances they take things into their own hands. It doesn't even matter if they are religious or not.

They reason, "If God is not going to do anything, I'll do it myself," and off they go. These are thoughts not grounded! And why a proper worldview is essential to process the meaning from what seems to be the vacuum of silence.

So where is God? Why does He seem impotent and not caring in the affairs of men? What are we to make of such circumstances, and how are we to explain the great conundrum? How do we process?

What I am about to say will no doubt stretch credulity to the breaking point. It may sound outlandish and almost mythological, but it is the most important aspect of what one must come to terms with if they are to begin to form a proper world view lens.

If I could have known then what I know now, perhaps I could have brought some comfort with understanding to my friend. I would have been able to answer with knowledge and wisdom. But at that time, I was dumbfounded!

After all she was the Christian!

The Shocking Answer

The stark answer is that God Himself purposefully set up all the chaos and the emptiness. That's right! It was God! I know. "This guy is out of his mind and is absolutely crazy!" No, I am not crazy! God purposely set it up this way.

There is only one clear vis-a-vis passage in the bible which explains with clear certainty this conclusion. But once the astonishing biblical fact is recognized and underscored it all clicks into place.

Chapter 42

The Crystal Window

Here is the amazing window into this remarkable revelation of existent reality.

As a result of the problem of the war in the Heavens, **_God then subjected_** the world to "vanity" or corruption. Here it is.

"For <u>the creation was subjected to futility</u>, not willingly, but because of <u>Him</u> who subjected it, in hope" Rom 8:20

This is it! This is the critical beginning for the proper worldview. It was God who set up the present chaotic conditions on planet earth. It cannot be changed. It cannot be fixed!

There it is in plain black and white. It is right there in Romans 8:20

It is God who subjected the creation to futility or vanity. Another sense and meaning for the word vanity can also mean a temporary time and condition. He set up a spiritual void, an emptiness. So, God Himself turned the whole creation over to corruption!

He set the whole world into a convolution of vanity. Solomon of course makes this the central theme in his book of Ecclesiastes, and this was why he wrote the book.

"Vanity of Vanity", he writes in a capitulating tone to what he perceived as the world being in utter futility. "All is vanity," and he was correct because it was God Himself who subjected the creation to this present condition.

Of course, amid the tragedy, as with my friend, you do not want to be insensitive and say, "well God turned the whole creation over to vanity and that is why your father died." Of course not! Who would do such a thing? But at that time, I didn't know what to make of the terribly tragic situation.

The fact of the matter is this outer world including our human bodies, which is also part of the outer world, was given over to vanity.

It is important to notice that when Jesus was on earth, He did not heal every leper, nor every blindness, nor did he always feed everyone. Even more clear is He did not come to overthrow the Roman Empire. At the time of Christ's earthly presence there was slavery, which He did not come to change or deal with. Nor did He try to fix the political world. He did not come to fix this outer world.

The Romans controlled the world in those days and Jesus did nothing to overthrow the Roman empire. He did nothing for two reasons. His Kingdom is not of this world and two, He uses the present conditions as goads, so that we would learn to turn to Him and not ourselves for answers in the midst of calamities. As we look to Him in hope we can grow in faith. In the growth process we acquire the divine nature. The outer world which includes our bodies, is the mighty antagonist to our inner man's growth.

He is saying in this life's experience, in light of this mighty void, "What do you think about the fact that I have recused myself and my glory from this present world?" This is the great lesson we must learn here on planet earth. It may take your whole life to hear this from the heavens, but this is what He is saying.

Faith is the Substance of Hope

Yet, while He subjected the creation in vanity, He has also subjected the creation to hope. There will come a time when the vanity over the creation is repaired and lifted, but that is when He returns not for now. For now we must live with the polemic of the inner Kingdom of Jesus in contradiction with the outer world and our ball and chain bodies. All of which have been subjected to vanity. There is no growth without the conflict.

So, then we find...

"that the creation itself also will be set free from its slavery to corruption into the freedom of the glory of the children of God...the whole creation groans and travails in pain together until now." Rom 8: 22-23

Here, in these passages, come the startling picture for the proper and correct worldview.

Once we begin to grasp the perplexing conundrum of human existence, we can begin to make sense of our predicament here on earth. We now have the proper context. The antidote is, of course, to know the Lord Jesus Christ personally which is an everyday matter.   And yet given even one day apart from the Lord God there comes a dampening and diminishing of this spiritual fact. Unless we die daily, we will quickly lose sight slipping back to sleep into our natural man, and the confusion of the vanity of this present world!

It cannot be fixed! The world outside and our bodies cannot be fixed! It is not meant to be fixed! It is the counterweight to the inner man. It is the antagonist opposed to the protagonist. The futility of men is their scream for social justice and political change, but they are pushing in the wrong direction.

Christianity was never intended to change the world nor was certainly not designed to be institutionalized. It was meant to be understood as the "process of transformation" for God's elect.

God is not focused on fixing the outer world. God is deeply concerned with fixing His people. The Kingdom of heaven is at hand, and it is to be within, but do we have eyes to see?

The World is Kryptonite to Our Real Self

The whole world was subjected by God to a temporary condition that is rendered as futility or called vanity. It is a spiritual vacuum void of God's presence. That is why His Kingdom, and His presence is to be within. It is an inner Kingdom. And our real self is our spirit!

This one scripture is the **absolute key** for understanding the world in which we live. Without this KEY no one will develop properly. It is this very issue which is the foundational reality for a proper worldview and the context for weaving His garment. If you do not get this right, you will waste years and possibly a lifetime.

It began with the war in the heavens and resulted in a world sentenced to vanity. Earth is a prison planet!

Until God lifts the sanction nothing can change the present earth condition. We humans have been placed in a world of vanity that leaves us helpless. It is a furnace of affliction! The only thing we have power to change is ourselves, and that only through faith in Jesus. Because it is through faith, we can appropriate God's grace, and why this is the victory that overcomes this world of vanity. Earth life is the kryptonite to our spirit!

The Antidote is Grace

Grace is not just a concept. People say grace is God's unmerited favor. They think that grace is merely a concept that only needs a definition, but grace is far more than a concept. It is God's very power that keeps us, not only as a preservative, but as an accelerator for ever increasing dimensions of His own likeness within ourselves. Grace imparted grows within. It is His divine nature.

Once eyes are open to the effect of the "angel war" only then can we gain a proper understanding of this world and our place in it. Apart from this understanding we are tossed about by every wind and wave of doctrine, and the massive calamities and lies from the world outside.

We are on a train heading for a city! The question is which City?

How else are we to understand the meaning of human life on this earth? Why are we here? What is going on and what to do about my present existence here and now? The profound answer to these questions is riding on the train going down the tracks. Remember, this is your life! You cannot depend on anyone else. The ball is exclusively in your court. It is between you and God. We must wake up!

We get seventy years, maybe eighty. Some are allowed ninety, but few today attain one hundred years. What should our lives be about? What is the focus?

I tell you without equivocation it is about the train going down the track. God calls this life a vapor and a light and momentary affliction. Seventy years is considered light and momentary, but it is exceedingly critical because if we apprehend it correctly it can work an exceeding weight of glory. The weight of glory is the magnitude of His divine nature.

The word glory was not meant to be understood as a superlative. It actually designates an actual real weight, but not as understood in this world. The weight that is promised is an inner weight for the inner man. It is an eternal weight!

We are not presently weighty, because we are trapped in earthen vessels of the human body and cannot see far beyond into any range of spiritual distance or time. Nevertheless, we can begin to extend our grasp of total and comprehensive existence if we can just learn a few things because the weight begins here and now.

In order to begin to grasp the supernatural we must take hold of this proper spiritual worldview. It is our lens.

Chapter 43

The Poison of Human Logic

Human logic is the default mechanism people use as the primary means in calculating for decisions. It is not all together wrong but wisdom is not always confined to mere human calculations! Please take note.

"Trust in the LORD with all your heart And <u>do not lean on your own understanding.</u>" Prov 3:5-6

Did you get that? Do **_not lean_** on your own understanding!

Our bodies, described as earthen vessels in the Bible, are temporary and we tend to calculate daily existence through our body's finite nature. Yet, if we will allow ourselves to be instructed from a source outside of our physical selves, through the Holy Spirit, we can transcend our human self's bias, and become spiritually enlightened making superior decisions. This ability is the power of grace. It comes into our spirit when we learn to lean not to our own understanding, but rather reach to our Father and learn from the Holy Spirit.

We know now why God turned the world into a convolution. But we must remember, He also subjected the world in hope! The hope is the abiding promise that we can be transformed from being more than mere men, and then finally to when the vanity is lifted off the earth. And in the redefinition of who we are, have access to superior knowledge and wisdom.

Let's take a closer look at that scripture in the book of Romans chapter 8.

The Dilemma

"For the creation was subjected to futility, not willingly, but because of Him who subjected it, in hope that <u>the creation</u> itself also <u>will be set free</u> from its slavery to corruption into the freedom of the glory of the children of God. For we know that <u>the whole creation groans</u> and suffers the pains of childbirth together until now. And not only this, but also we ourselves, having the first fruits of the Spirit, even we ourselves groan within ourselves, waiting eagerly for our adoption as sons, the redemption of our

body." Rom 8:20-23

We also see a conjunction with this verse in Psalm 51:5-6

"Behold, I was shapen in iniquity; and in sin did my mother conceive me. But then.... Behold, thou desire truth in the inward parts: and in the hidden part thou shalt make me to know wisdom." Psa 51:6

When the world was set into the convolution, or as noted, subjected to vanity, so also was the human body. The body can and does affect the shaping of the inner man if we allow. Yet, this seems to be the case and even Christians fall into the pit. This should be seriously recognized and guarded against.

Nevertheless, this is the dangerous fact. If the earthly bodily instinctive impulses are not monitored, they will form and take hold of the inner person.

The inner man is the hidden man. We choose who we are. We chose what spirit we are!

As we read from the Psalms, God desires that we acquire truth in the <u>inner parts</u> to circumvent and counter the effect of the vanity that comes from our bodies and the world outside. The bodies that were born in iniquity and were vexed and subjected to vanity must be overcome. This is "the mastery"!

The body as it was established by God in vanity has a counter effect on the inner man. It is as though we have been set in a prison cell for life. Our body life span is characterized as a vapor. Again, it is a light momentary affliction. In other places it is called a phantom. It is because of this condition we must learn to overcome our natural inclinations and impulses (inclinations of the body) since they are in contradiction to God's nature.

Nevertheless, the natural bias for all our present mental calculations for the most part, is based upon our physical body lattice. The Apostle Paul firmly grasped this horrific conundrum.

"Oh wretched man that I am who shall save me from the BODY of this death" Rom 7:24

We do not apprehend the degree, and the magnitude, to which our human logic is subject and infected by our lifelong prison incarceration. Most of the time we are held hostage and chained to our human appetites for food, sex, and the need for shelter. These ever-present physical demands dominate most all human thinking.

The body's affect is so pervasive to our daily thoughts and calculations that even when we do have a spiritual thought the body acts like a gyroscope setting us back to square one. We think in fleshly terms and earthly time. So, then the body is the enemy of our inner man. We literally wear an enemy.

Look what the scriptures say about war as it pertains to the body.

"What is the source of quarrels and conflicts among you? Is not the source of your pleasures that wage war in your members? You lust and do not have; so you commit murder. You are envious and cannot obtain; so you fight and quarrel." James 4:1

Even wars, since the beginning, can be traced to the human body. When the Apostle Paul wrote to the Church at Corinth, he noted that he was there with much fear and trembling.

"For I determined to know nothing among you except Jesus Christ, and Him crucified. I was with you in weakness and in fear and in much trembling." I Cor 2:3

Why? Why was he there at Corinth in weakness and fear and much trembling? Could it have been that he was so aware of his carnal appetites of his human self/man that he was fearful that he too could fall into the flesh and thus be disqualified and become a castaway?

Is this not a warning to all that we should be very very careful how we walk out our terrestrial life?

Consequently, he wrote....

"He that seeks "the mastery" is temperate in all things." 1 Cor 9:25

"Do you not know that those who run in a race all run, but only one receives the prize? Run in such a way that you may win. Everyone who competes in the games exercises self-control in all things. They then do it to receive a perishable wreath, but we an imperishable...

Therefore, I run in such a way as not beating the air; but I discipline my body and make it my slave, so that, after I have preached to others, I myself will not be disqualified." 1 Cor 9:24-27

So, then the mastery is about controlling the human bodily nature which is a prison equipped with chains.

Not only is the body a prison, but all its angers, lusts, emotional outbursts, fractional impulsive thoughts, and negative reasoning are chains that bind us while we are in this present state, Paul called it the "body of death."

The battle is never ending with our flesh until the body is put back into the earth. It is the implacable foe we carry all the days of our sojourn here on earth. Just as politics cannot fix the world neither can our earthly bodies be fixed.

Yet there is good news. Particularly good news. Our true eternal bodies wait for our return.

The Eternal Body

Eternal bodies wait in suspension. Look again at Romans 8

"Because the creature itself also shall be delivered from the bondage of corruption into the glorious liberty of the children of God. For we know that the whole creation groaneth and travaileth in pain together until now. And not only they, but ourselves also, which have the first fruits of the Spirit, even we ourselves groan within ourselves, waiting for the adoption, to wit, <u>the redemption of our body</u>." Rom 8:23

Chapter 44

The Redemption of the Body

When the scripture speaks of the redemption of the body it is not speaking of the redemption of our present human body! There is nothing redemptive about the human "body of death." It is so entirely ruined it must be buried in the earth. There is nothing, nada, redeemable about our temporary human bodies.

The redemption of our body cited in Romans pertains to our "heavenly body."

We groan within ourselves because we long to be set free from this damnable prison and put on the eternal body that waits for our return.

Paul was able to see clearly, we must be prepared to live in the City of God along with the myriad of God's celestial beings, so that in our **re-acquired** heavenly body we can take our place in the Fathers House

What must be clearly understood is that righteousness, and its ongoing acquisition, can be misconstrued unless we keep the understanding of its acquisition within the context of the duality of our being. Righteousness should be seen as the ongoing pursuit and strengthening and expansion of the inner man.

"Not that I have obtained all this or have already been made perfect but I press on to take hold of that which Christ Jesus took hold of me." Phil 3:12

When one stops to consider the heavenly body, which has existed for eternity as opposed to the earthly body that lasts only temporarily, the comparison is not worthy of consideration.

We simply must count the real cost while here and now and build our inner man in preparation for re-entry into our real body which is waiting in suspension and reserved in the heavens.

The Redemption

"Now I say this, brethren, that flesh and blood cannot inherit the kingdom of God; nor does the perishable inherit the imperishable." 1 Cor 15:51

The preparation for re-entry into our real bodies can be however, very difficult. There are many dangerous moments recorded in the Bible that point out this fact, because the re-entry requires growing in our inner man from glory to glory, but this growth can only occur through much conflict. Nevertheless, we simply must be advancing in glory. We are either growing in God's glory or shrinking back into our old self.

If we look backward all our former life in the flesh memory is recorded. And if we do look back the recordings of our old self and all that we have lived in the flesh can be recollected! It's very much like the trash that can be brought back when you discard unwanted stuff in your computer.

"Like a dog that returns to its vomit so is a fool who repeats his folly." Prov 26:11

This is the meaning of the message of Lot's wife who when turning back to look at Sodom became a pillar of salt. (She turned back toward Sodom which was destroyed by fire and brimstone which most likely fell upon her as well).

Inwardly We Groan

We groan inwardly, which is our inner man, because we live in a body that is temporary. We want to be clothed with a different body that is not subject to earth time and decay as we presently know time and is free from the many maladies of pain and sickness that accompany human life. But look carefully and the text says,

"waiting for the redemption of our bodies." Ibid

If the human body is mere dust and must therefore go back into the ground from whence, it was derived, then how can it be redeemed? In what sense will it be redeemed? The answer is it cannot be redeemed. Then why does the text speak about a body to be redeemed?

This is where I will get into trouble with the many Christians, because they are locked up in a religious tradition which will not allow them to consider what I am about to say. But if you are secure in Jesus and are not afraid to step out of the boat onto the water like Peter did when he saw Jesus walking on the sea, then come on.

Let us look to Jesus who perfectly lived the divine nature, for He is the author and finisher of our faith not traditional church doctrine.

So please let me press the point!

"Now we know that if the earthly tent we live in is dismantled, we have a building from God, an eternal house in heaven, not built by human hands. For in this tent we groan, longing to be clothed with <u>our heavenly dwelling</u>." 1 Cor 5:1-2

Other translations say it more clearly as *"eternal in the heavens"* as opposed to a heavenly dwelling. *2 Cor 5:1-2*

It says eternal in the **heavens.** Why the heavens and not heaven? The heavens is plural. That is because heavens is a reference to the universal construction or the expanse and not heaven above the heavens. The heavens, as previously noted, is the expanse or the physical visible universe.

Our new bodies must be able to travel in the heavens or within the universe. Flesh and blood bodies cannot inherit the Kingdom (the Father's House) because they have been made subject to vanity or a temporary condition, we call time. So then the Kingdom of God must begin within ourselves and eventually we obtain the new body that can travel the star ways. We do not go at first to heaven, we must first go into the heavens, and to do that we must put on the eternal body.

What is astonishing about this scripture in 2nd Corinthians is that when it is connected with the Romans 8:23 scripture we learn more about our new body. It is not the old body that is buried and decays in the grave. The scripture says it is dismantled. This simply means it disintegrates. The scripture explains the physical body as a tent. A tent is a temporary dwelling. It is also to recall and look backward to the temporary "tent of meeting" in the wilderness wanderings of the Hebrews after they escaped from Egypt.

"Now that if the earthly tent we live in is dismantled, we have a building from God, an eternal house in heaven, not built by human hands." 2 Cor 5:2

The redemption of the body then, is not about our earthly body. It is the redemption of our heavenly body. It is an entirely new body and most importantly it is eternal in the heavens. But wait a minute. How can it be new if it is eternal? And how can it be redeemed if it wasn't first possessed? You cannot redeem something unless you first once possessed it.

It is new only in the sense and in comparison, with the body we now dwell in, but if it is to be redeemed and is eternal this suggests something more far reaching; something far different.

God foreknows from His side what it will be, but we do not. That is why we must supply all diligence to our faith in pursuit of the divine nature. We are directed to redeem the time because the days are evil. This is not some nice suggestion as though a whimsical idea from God. This is a calling to prepare for our new bodies.

The reason it does not yet appear what we shall be is because we cannot fathom nor imagine what our former celestial body will be like. But what is astonishing is the celestial body is eternal. How can it be eternal unless it had existed before we had even existed as humans? When did eternity begin? Eternity does not begin when our physical bodies die! Eternity is eternity. It has been before there were humans on the earth.

The reason it must be redeemed is because it is waiting for us "to repossess." We must have possessed it before and for a specific reason, as we shall see, had to vacate. That is why our eternal bodies must be redeemed. They have eternally existed, and we are now coming back to reclaim them.

Why would God promise mankind eternal life before the world began? But this is exactly what was spoken by Paul to Titus.

"In hope of eternal life which God, who cannot lie promised, before the world began." Titus 1:2

These bodies that are eternal were once ours. As I said, many people are going to freak out and accuse me of heresy, but all I am doing is pointing out scriptures, and asking a bunch of questions. If this is true, then why can't we remember? This is the conundrum and perplexity of the new assertion. In the succeeding chapters, we will deal in greater detail with this momentous question.

If you have the intellectual courage, the rescue mission of the Father coming to earth in the person of Jesus takes on a much greater magnitude with regard to the redemption of the human race.

It does not negate, in any way, Jesus as the Son of God. Not at all! In fact not even the slightest! God forbid! It affirms and broadens the enormity of His love and the utter awesomeness of His merciful rescue mission. He didn't just come to redeem a bunch of lost sinners, that is true of course, but it was something far far more significant!

Chapter 45

The Danger of God's Glory

The most spectacular occurrence of the manifestation of God's glory, apart from the Mt. of Transfiguration, occurred on Mt Sinai. This was of course some thirteen hundred years before Jesus came to earth.

It was at Mt. Sinai where ten thousand chariots descended, as it was described in the psalms. It seems so surreal and beyond human comprehension! But nothing like this had ever happened on earth before or since. It was at that time when the Law, the Ten Commandments, was given to Moses. One can only speculate as to the meaning of the ten thousand chariots! The book of psalms described the chariots of God in terms of myriads and myriads.

"The chariots of God are myriads, thousands upon thousands; the Lord is among them as at Sinai, in holiness" Psa 68

As we try to imagine that moment in time there can be no doubt that God's Law came down to the Earth accompanied by a great entourage.

The description of the event makes the giving of the Law a most fearful and dangerous moment in human history. It is told that if anyone even came close to the mountain, or if an animal even so much as touched the mountain, they would perish. So terrible was the sight and the sound that the people begged for it to cease.

There was something about the great holiness of the glory that prevented men, except for Moses, from coming near.

It was similar to how the high Levitical priest was prevented from coming near to the ark of the covenant inside the veil of the temple. It was only through animal sacrifices, intensive purification through washings and then the anointing of precious oil, that he alone was allowed to enter. Once the preparation was completed, he was to make entreaties for the people, but that was only permissible once a year. The glory was so intense the high priest could only handle very little.

Even then a rope was tied around his ankle, in the event that if the preparation was not performed correctly, had he died inside they could pull him out by the rope.

When the ark of the covenant was carried into the Jordan river the divine presence actually caused the river to retreat backward. The river went into reverse flowing contrary to gravity retreating upstream to the city of Adam. Such was the awesome power of the glory.

Even more incomprehensible is that God desires to place His glory within our being.

The Waters Retreated

If we take a closer look at that moment recorded in the book of Exodus, there is something exceptionally deep and powerful to be learned. It was the moment when God's people were about to take the promised land, but this event signaled not just a moment for them at that time but a moment universal.

After they entered "the Promised Land," the Promised Land became a symbol and a metaphor of the Kingdom of God. The waters of Dan had to be cut off and backed up to the city of Adam.

The Jordan river waters that flowed from the city of Adam were a vivid picture of genetic waters that flow down through humanity from generation to generation beginning with Adam. All human beings inherit their genetics from Adam. Hence the genetic waters within all humans must be backed up to our father Adam.

We must overcome Adam's likeness which is transmitted by genetics. The power in the ark of the covenant, which was the glory of God, caused the waters of Dan to back up to Adam. "Jor" means waters, and "Dan" means the tribe of Dan which was to the north and encompassed the area of the sea of Galilee. It was the land of the headwaters of the Jordan river. We must understand that to overcome our genetics it must be achieved through God's glory.

One of the great prophets of the Old Testament, was the prophet Daniel but there is an interesting prophecy in Genesis that is about the tribe of Dan, and it is not favorable.

"Dan shall judge his people, as one of the tribes of Israel. Dan shall be a serpent in the way, A horned snake in the path, that bites the horse's heels, so that his rider falls backward." Gen 49:17

A judge is one who uses the Law. The Law was given by God to Moses as a restraint on human behavior. It also was a curse though, because no one was capable of living the Law nor keeping it. The snake Satan uses the Law to condemn and cause all to fall backward because in our flesh there is no good thing.

The waters of Dan signify the human flesh which is condemned for its unruly behavior. The Law condemns the flesh. Human bodies are all derived from Adam and his genes. The only way to overcome these waters and cause them to retreat is by the glory of God. The glory of God causes the genetic waters of Adam to flow backward.

Many times, it is said by God

"I will visit the iniquity of the fathers unto the third and fourth generation." Deut 5:9

In other words, God would visit the sins of the fathers unto the third and fourth generation on the children. Many of our besetting sins are inherited genetically from our fathers. These waters of genetics are then best described as in the metaphor and historic picture of the Jordan river.

There is information that is passed onto us from our fathers via the genes. It originates from Adam and is passed down through each successive generation. It is the Adamic nature, and it must be cut off and backed up to the point of its origin which, in this incredible illustration, is the city of Adam.

But when God's glorious presence enters the stream of our being even our genes are transformed as we accumulate God's divine nature from glory to glory. And the genetic waters descending from our fathers and our father's fathers and so on and so on, till all the way back to Adam they are cut off. So then we are ultimately transformed in the inner man and become purified and capable of reentry into our celestial bodies.

This is the necessary and ordained process which allows for the subsequent redemption and reentry into our heavenly bodies. Remember true Christianity is not contained nor understood in the institutions, it is a process!

The Glory

In those days there was something about the glory which was powerful and real. God is the same yesterday today and forever and the glory of

God is not a theoretical force, it is a real force! It causes the natural or nature to give way to the supernatural. In those days it manifested externally but today primarily it is inwardly manifested.

In the New Testament era men and women are warned not to take the sacraments of communion unworthily as they will become sick, because they represent the body and blood of Christ and there is glory attached.

The human body mitigates against the spirit and coming to recognize this polemic in our own being is paramount to the overcoming that is described extensively in the book of Revelation. We can observe this terrible negative side in the demise of the seven churches in the book of Revelation. If we seek escape velocity from the gravitational pull of the flesh and the world, we must come to grips daily with this reality. All the churches in the book of Revelation failed and their light was extinguished.

"Dear friends, I urge you, as foreigners and exiles, to abstain from sinful desires, which wage war against your soul." 1 Pet 2:11

Yet we are to know there is a changing that is to take place in our inner man. We are to be changed in the inner man from glory to glory. The glory is a dynamic force that is to be an ever increasing and expanding spiritual reality. But the outer man is a fading glory. Yet look at the emphasis today. When all attention should be on the divine force of glory to glory, we place our primary focus on the outer man and the world outside. Today the focus is on politics and our preoccupation with our physical body which is fading away. It is the opposite to what it should be!

Contacting Gods' Glory

The glory of God cannot be contacted without faith. That is why without faith it is impossible to please Him. God is pleased when we touch His glory because it changes us into His likeness inwardly.

We are all on this conveyor belt process working out the things that must be fixed!

"... But we all, with unveiled face, beholding as in a mirror the glory of the Lord, are being transformed <u>into the same image</u> from glory to glory, just as from the Lord, the Spirit." 2 Cor 3:18

As the anticipation grows by seeking His glory, we must learn how to operate in the kind of faith that can appropriate His glory. The glory of God is in seeking His face.

Chapter 46

The Shadow World

"Now if He were on earth, He would not be a priest at all, since there are those who offer the gifts according to the Law; who serve <u>a copy and shadow</u> of the <u>heavenly things</u>, just as Moses was warned by God when he was about to erect the tabernacle; for, see, He says, That you make all things according to the pattern which was shown you on the mountain."
Heb 8:5

In another passage it is stated,

"Therefore no one is to act as your judge in regard to food or drink or in respect to a festival or a new moon or a Sabbath day-- things which are <u>a mere shadow</u> of what is to come; but the substance belongs to Christ." Col 2:16

Here we are taught that this world in which we presently find ourselves is a shadow world. And that even the food and drink and supposed sabbaths are mere shadows of the real. Real substance is spiritual not material!

When people, religious people, argue over which day is the appropriate and correct day of the week for the Sabbath, the scripture is saying it should not even be part of the conversation. These sabbath days they fight over are only a shadow of the real sabbath day.

The book of Hebrews explains the Sabbath day as "Today."

The Real Sabbath Day

When John was exiled on the Isle of Patmos he wrote. "I was in the spirit on <u>the Lord's day</u>." And he was told to write.

Are we supposed to believe the whole book of Revelation was written in one session? No! It was written on the Lord's day which is "today." John knew how to get back to the Lord's day, which is today! The true Sabbath!

Would it have been possible for him to write all twenty-two chapters of this astonishing revelation, and in just one earth day and in just one session? No! Not a chance. He had to write it on the Lord's day. And the

Lord's day is described in the book of Genesis 2:1-2.

"Thus, the heavens and the earth were completed and all their hosts. By the 7th day God completed His work which He has done, and He rested on the seventh day from all His work which he had done." Gen 2:1

The Lord's day, the 7th day is eternal.

But take note. All the other days in Genesis 1 end with the statement "and the morning and the evening", but the 7th day has no such accompanying conclusion of morning and evening. The seventh day never begins or ends.

That is why in the book of Hebrews the Sabbath day is "Today." Because every day can be today for those of faith. John knew how to enter the 7th day. Hence, he could hear the voice of God.

"As it has been said: 'Today, if you hear His voice, do not harden your hearts, as you did in the rebellion'." Heb 3:15

Let's be clear as to what it says in the book of Hebrews,

*"there remains a Sabbath day of rest for God's people." **Ibid***

Those that argue and fight over a specific Sabbath have failed to enter His rest, because they are still living in the shadow world. They are living according to the flesh or the natural man.

But the Apostle John demonstrated by receiving the momentous Revelation that he knew how to enter on the Lord's real Sabbath day.

Here is another reference to the shadow world. It is in the psalms. Here is the excerpt.

"Yea, though I walk through the valley of the shadow of death, I fear no evil: for thou art with me; thy rod and thy staff they comfort me." Psa 23:4

We as humans are living in a place called the "valley of the shadow of death." It is not our permanent place of residence, but the psalmist characterizes it as a valley of the shadow, and in the text incorporates the word death. "The valley of the shadow of death." We have more to say about this valley, but just for the moment notice it is called a valley of the shadow. The world we currently live in is a mere valley and just a shadow of reality. As a result, we tend to live out our lives following shadows.

The book of Hebrews tells us that all the implements of the physical temple and the temple itself were mere copies or shadows of the real tabernacle which is in the heavens.

The physical temple of the Jews was referred to as the outer temple. The outer temple, as it was called, was in the outer world, or the shadow world. Everything outside of our inner man is the outer world including our bodies. We currently reside in a shadow world!

Even the linen ephod worn by the priest was a copy and shadow of the heavenly. If they are shadows, then how do we see the reality?

Let us look at the shadow purpose of the ephod and seek to come to grips with its heavenly meaning. It is a meaning that pertains to our approach to God and the proper use of faith and prayer. In this way we can connect with the glory of God. The glory is spiritual reality.

Here again just to underscore and give emphasis is Hebrews.

"Now if He (Jesus) were on earth, He would not be a priest at all, since there are those who offer the gifts according to the Law, who serve a copy and shadow of the heavenly things, just as Moses was warned by God." Heb 8:4

But ....

"by this arrangement, the Holy Spirit was showing that the way into the Most Holy Place had not yet been disclosed as long as the first or outer tabernacle was still standing." Heb 9:8

Just as an aside. This scripture proves that the book of Hebrews was written before the fall of Jerusalem because the outer temple according to this portion of scripture was still standing which is noted in this text. But for the Jews to have any chance with faith in attending and entering the true Most Holy Place which is in the heavens, the outer temple had to be removed.

God used the Romans to do that very thing as they destroyed the physical outer temple in 70AD. With the outer temple gone the Levitical priesthood became totally obsolete. There could be no more sacrifices for sin according to the requirements of the Law. By the destruction of the outer temple, the shadow, sacrifices and offerings ceased.

So then when Jesus ascended and went into the heavens through His own blood, He entered the heavenly eternal sanctuary. The cleansing of the heavens by Christ's own blood is what paved the way for Him to send the

Holy Spirit to the earth. The Holy Spirit was sent once the heavenly sanctuary was cleansed. It had to be cleansed due to the defilement from the angel war in the heavens.

When the Holy Spirit was sent it broke forth on the day which came to be known as the day of Pentecost. It was the beginning of the advent of the Kingdom of Heavens coming to earth, but not for the external world. The Kingdom came only into the hearts of believing men and women. It was the fulfillment of what the prophet Joel had predicted.

Now it is through the Holy Spirit we have access to the heavenly tabernacle through faith. We now have access into the Most Holy Place before the very throne of God in the Heavens.

Yet the natural man (even most Christians) looks for an external Kingdom. But Jesus made it clear that there would be no external presence nor should external signs of wars, rumors of wars, or famines or earthquakes, or pestilence etc. be unduly looked upon as indicators. In light of these things Christ Himself said "but the end is not yet"! Most everyone today is focused on the outer world. Most all Christians are focused on looking for external signs.

But back into the shadow world we observe this.

Not only did the priests have to wash extensively and make animal sacrifices to be worthy to approach God they had to put on the garment of the linen ephod. The ephod had to be made of fine linen that was almost as fine as silk. It had to be made by skilled craftsmen.

The linen ephod of those days was also a shadow. In the Old Testament or the Old Covenant, the linen ephod was of course real, but now in the New Covenant era it serves as a shadow. It was a shadow of the ultimate call to spiritual reality which is the inward robe of righteousness. The robe of righteousness is not a garment as to what we understand on earth as clothing. It is the aura and the very righteousness of God. It is the divine nature we must put on. It is an inner ephod. In the book of Revelation, it is called white linen. But in order to attain to that robe of divine nature we must begin to put it on today. We must put on today's inner linen ephod.

"You are a royal priesthood, a holy nation a people for God's own posses-sion who has called you out of darkness (shadows) into His marvelous light." 1 Pet 2:9

We are a priesthood, and just like the shadow of the Jewish priesthood we must wear the ephod.

And through the putting on of the ephod by exercising faith in Christ we can assume our priestly office.

Remember, a king stands before men and a priest stands before God. The Jewish priest bore the nation of Israel on his breast. Our greatest position as God's people is not as one who stands before men but one who stands and faces God. In order to fulfill our greatest office, we must wear the at-tire of a priest. When we assume this position then will come the burden of prayer on our heart for His people,

Once the high priest had prepared properly, he could seek the Lord. But only the high priest could carry the Urim and Thummim which was a breastplate which had twelve precious stones on it. Each stone repre-sented one of the tribes of Israel. Thus, the high priest would carry on his heart the burden of all Israel. The regular priest had the ephod but only the high priest could go into the inner holy of holies once a year to make atonement for the sins of the people.

The Urim and Thummim was a device that was also used as an oracle wherein the priest could make inquiry to God for direction for the nation for whatever and whenever they needed answers from God. Then one stone or another on the breastplate would light up as the Lord was indicat-ing which tribe should do what and such. This was the primitive way they would hear from the Lord. Remember it was a shadow of the real.

That was then, but what about today? Most people today cannot hear the Lord because they have hardened their heart. Hardening one's heart oc-curs when one hears God's voice and ignores and turns away not listening. It can be so very subtle, or it can be deliberately rebellious

The second we turn away we harden. The hardening is actual muting of the voice of God. He never stops speaking but we cannot hear. It is very much like when the sun goes behind a cloud. The sun is still shining but the cloud hides the light. When we turn from His voice, we go behind the cloud. Thus, "today (the Sabbath) if you hear His voice harden not your heart."

Remember in those days they had an outer breast plate today we have our inner breastplate hearing device called our heart or our spirit.

We are instructed that we must put on the breastplate of righteousness and protect our heart and to keep our heart with all diligence for out of the heart comes the issues of life.

But if we are not taught how to put on the spiritual linen ephod of a priest, we are vulnerable to many forces. If we have hardened our heart because of not listening to the voice of God, it can still be remedied by turning back and receiving the sprinkling of the blood of Jesus in prayer.

Chapter 47

The Duality-You Cannot Escape!

The issue is paramount to master. The complication to hearing from God can be exacerbated if we do not understand "the duality."

In my early days as a believer in Jesus there was a man in our church organization who was a highly respected itinerant speaker. He was regarded as a prophet of God. His son was our pastor. This man was in the higher echelons of our church denominational hierarchy. As I said, he was greatly revered and esteemed. He was a good man!

Yet the deep spirituality in one of his messages I have come to take with great issue! It is an issue that is so significant that to master its meaning is tantamount in applying to our everyday temporal lives.

This came to light when he was teaching from Romans the 7th chapter. He was making a point concerning the conflict Paul was describing.

The chapter, he maintained, was for the unsaved. In other words, he was saying the chapter was about all those people who were not yet Christians. He clearly asserted the chapter did not apply to those who had become Christians. But unbeknownst to me he was teaching a false doctrine. At the time I had no idea how disastrous his misunderstanding was, and the remarkable error he was spreading. You will see for yourself!

This is the text he was referring to and one of the issue why so many people have difficulty hearing the voice of the Lord.

"For we know that the law (Ten Commandments) is spiritual, but I am of the flesh, sold under sin. For I do not understand my own actions. For I do not do what I want, but I do the very thing I hate. Now if I do what I do not want, I agree with the law, that it is good. So now it is no longer I who do it, but sin that dwells within me. For I know that nothing good dwells in me, that is, in my flesh." Rom 7:13

"For I have the desire to do what is right, but not the ability to carry it out. For I do not do the good I want, but the evil I do not want is what I

keep on doing. Now if I do what I do not want, it is no longer I who do it, but sin that dwells within me." Ibid

What this man was saying by his explanation was in total error. He taught that the dilemma Paul was describing was actually before he came to Jesus Christ. But now that he had come to Christ things were different. In other words what was being said in chapter seven no longer applied once a person had become a believer in Jesus.

Now, if one were listening to his teaching it would have condemned the listener. It would have made one think as though something were terribly wrong with themselves! Particularly, since one might still be having troubles with sin. To them it would seem as though he was not really saved and redeemed. It is because of this terrible misapprehension many people would think their salvation did not take. Often these same folks would go back up to the altar and ask to be saved again.

Just to be clear what the man of God was saying was, "If you are really saved you are totally free from what Paul was describing."

But no one is free from the conflict! The opposite is true. The reason no one is free from the daily conflict is because we are still in a human body; that is the flesh. The human body is still sinful even after having come to accept Christ. It is a restless evil that must be mastered because the body is not the real you!

Paul was not teaching what this well-respected man was teaching. In fact, it was the contrary. Paul was saying that as long as you live in this human body there will be this conflict between the two natures. Salvation is not some altruistic idealism. Salvation is "the process" of recognizing and dealing with the everyday conflict.

We only begin to become aware of the conflict when our inner man is touched by the Holy Spirit. The new inner man is who we really are, and henceforth we must fight against the outer old man who is who we were.

The outer man is the shadow. It is our lower self, and it remains until we leave it behind. This reality must be understood in order to grasp why we must strive to enter His rest. We have on our hands a titanic battle with our lower outer self. We literally walk in the valley of the shadow of death living in a body of death!

Each day is likened unto a rocket ship trying to break free from earth's gravity. There is a negative pull, and that negative pull is our body. Each day we must break free from the influence of the flesh. Even people who believe in Jesus do not fully grasp and understand the power of the flesh. That is why they do not pray or read the Word. The flesh is repulsed at the thought. Yet we must use our faith as the rocket fuel to break free.

Look at it this way. When you stand facing the sun you do not see your shadow, but if you turn around immediately you see that the sun is casting a shadow, the shadow of your body. If you do not turn back to the sun, you will follow the shadow of yourself. Following the shadow self is walking in the flesh. People that constantly take selfies with their phones are looking at their shadow self.

In my formative years as a follower of Jesus, I believed almost any and everything that came out of the mouths of these leaders, but I came to see that many times they were in tremendous error. So many of their teachings were simply wrong. They were not able to teach about "the duality." In fact, not even once had I ever heard a message on the matter!

Paul goes on to say,

"who will save me from the body of this death?" Rom 7:24

But let us return to the shadows for a moment.

"Yeah, though I walk through the valley of the shadow of death I fear no evil for thou art with me" Psa 23:4

As we live out the remainder of our days, we must truly come to grips with the fact we live in a valley. Earth life and earth time is a shadow valley set in vanity or subjected to futility and our bodies are part of the futility and why they must die and that is why Paul said,

"I die daily." Ibid

The meaning of this statement was in recognition that each day he must put down the influence of the body on his mind and spirit. He knew each day he must put to death the effect of the outer man.

Mystery of Dualism

Are we to have a flesh identity or spiritual identity? It is we who choose who we are and who we will be. If we can get a handle on this, we can grow spiritually and exponentially.

Have you ever noticed how easily it is to find fault with others? I mean if I focused my mind, I could make an enormous case on anyone. It is easy to find fault and point the finger at others and the reason is because they too are in a human body and full of faults. Finding fault is easy.

Those who willfully or even inadvertently walk in the motions of the lower self will function in fault finding. It is because they do not recognize that everyone, including themselves, also has a lower nature, and everyone is struggling at some level with coming to grips with the dualism.

It is the same for every human being.

The inner man is in perpetual conflict with the outer man. Which side prevails and wins the war hangs in the balance. This unalterable fact is why we must fight the good fight. This is why he who seeks the mastery over the flesh, the outer man, must clearly understand the battle. And he must also see the remedy. But the war is not won by the human will fighting against the flesh desires. The 8th chapter of Romans explains that the war is won through the Spirit.

"For the "law of the Spirit" of life in Christ Jesus has set us free from the law of sin and death." Rom 8:2

This is the very key to living out the victory. It is the "law of the Spirit."

This is so critical to grasp because most Christians are utterly defeated because they are not properly trained in dealing with their bodies. When they do fight, they try winning by their will power. Will power is not the answer.

The only way to come out on top is to learn and live the "law of the Spirit."

Chapter 48

The Law of the Spirit

Now we must learn how to walk. We must learn to turn and face the sun, so that our shadow self is not in control. We must learn to walk according to the "law of the spirit."

The law of the spirit is not to be understood in the same way as the external law of the Ten Commandments. The Ten Commandments written on stone were external laws applying to the outer man. The law of the spirit is for the inner man, and it is an inner guidance GPS. But the guidance is not a feeling. It is not of the emotions. It is a conviction, and a sense. It comes from our spirit.

As we learn to walk in the spirit, we find ourselves living righteously. Nevertheless, because we are in constant conflict with our body we must continually correct to our inner self. This is why Christ taught us to take communion often. Communion brings a remembrance of Jesus' death.

*"We know that from the time of Adam until Moses **(i.e., the coming of the Law at Mount Sinai)**, sin was in the world, but where there is no Law sin is not imputed." Rom 5:13*

God is just and He does not hold people accountable for sin, which is lawlessness, <u>when there is no Law</u>. And there was no Law written until Moses which was around 1300 BC. So, all the people who lived and died from the time of Adam (around 4000 to 5000 BC) until Moses did not have their sin imputed. Imputed means charged to their record.

The Remarkable Death of Jesus

When we take communion, we call to our remembrance this spiritual reality in the Lord's death. So, in effect He took away the Law by His death. And just as it was at the time between Adam and Moses, where there was no Law, in like manner there is no Law to the believers.

So then, sin is not charged to our account!

*"He took away the handwriting and ordinances against us (**The Law**) which was hostile to us and nailed them to the cross." Col 2:14*

(The Law remains for the unbeliever who does not accept the New Covenant in Christ's death)

Will Power or Faith

It is at this point we may get confused about how we go about the use of our will. God's power must be enjoined! Grace is not merely a concept. The grace of God is a gift, but it is an ongoing administration and accumulation of power. It must be entered into using our faith, and that is daily!

When we actively put our heart upon the Lord in prayer and recognition of His Word ongoing, minute by minute, day by day, year in and year out, we enjoin and are assisted by the Holy Spirit. We learn to surrender our will to His. This causes our spirit to merge with God's Spirit.

A person can be strong willed as a believer but be weak in the use of his faith. Being strong willed is not to be misconstrued as strong faith. Paul, the apostle said, "when I am weak then I am strong." (Paul actually had a strong will) What he meant was not strong in will power but strong in faith. There is a brokenness when we realize we cannot, but God can. As we subject ourselves in every department of our lives, our house can be filled with His glory.

The fulfillment of the righteousness evidenced in the Law, becomes the by-product of following the "law of the spirit." The Holy Spirit connected with our spirit fulfills what the Law could not through our human will power.

"But now apart from the Law the righteousness of God has been made known to which the Law and the prophets testify." Rom 3:21

We must learn to engage ourselves with the spirit. This is the meaning of the "law of the spirit."

Think of it this way. If you have a car and start it running it is not yet moving. Until you put the car into gear it just idles. This is a good picture of the need to engage in the Spirit. Until one engages in the Spirit the success of living in the Lord is in idle.

People who fail to learn to walk by the Spirit fall into condemnation or guilt because they are not practiced to engage in the Spirit. Thus comes the tendency to add Law to grace as Peter did. It was the appeal and seduction to will worship.

"But all those led by the spirit are the sons of God." Rom 8:14

We Stumble

That isn't to say there still won't be times to trip and fall, we all do, but when he or she stumbles there is also the remedy to be cleansed and to return to uprightness. We can be restored immediately. Yet the common temptation is to adjust oneself by rationalizing the imperfection, and resorting to a form of penance, i.e., gutting it up for Jesus. This is will worship. Instead of applying God's remedy of the sprinkling of the Blood, people tend to rather justify themselves, or make excuses or put themselves under a program or a set of rules and regulations. They do not understand the walk in the spirit nor how to be restored after stumbling. Restoration is by the sprinkling of Christ's blood.

The failure to use God's remedy in His blood there remains the propensity to resort to will worship. The assumption is "I will do better next time and just suck it up." So, there is the cover up. Instead of repentance it is a form of penance.

There is no need to justify the flesh. No one walks perfectly by the spirit. But when we falter, we can quickly be restored by Jesus and His sacrifice. This is what it means to be crucified with Christ daily. When we fail we cannot be corrected by the flesh.

If we learn the efficacy of the sprinkling of His blood we can walk in the spirit. We are restored to our true selves by using our faith in His everlasting righteousness. Everlasting righteousness is the New Covenant.

The life of the Spirit consequently flows out from our inner man affecting the outer man. Then, we strangely find, perhaps not perfectly, but living more and more in accord with God's nature which we find expressed in the Law. Thus, the meaning, "He writes His Law in our hearts." There is a righteousness apart from the Law and it comes from the law of the Spirit.

If we live accordingly and increasingly in our spiritual identity, we grow away from whom we used to be. We find ourselves not desiring to be likened unto our outer identity. The identity of the outer man which is who I was is no longer who I am. I am a new person; therefore I do not desire to be like the old person.

So, our standard is not some moral code of regulations, but an inner strength that continues to grow from glory to glory. Thank God for the provision He has made to deal with the problem of our current existence! Most folks today give no thought to the predicament.

"if we endure until the end we shall be saved." Ibid

It is impossible to walk in the "law of the Spirit" unless we understand the duality. And it is impossible to understand the duality unless one first comes to grips with the great war in the heavens which explains how sin entered this world.

Chapter 49

Sherpa at the Top

What might be the greatest wisdom one could ask for?

While there are many many revelations to behold and many mysteries which remain untold, the most important insight one could receive is the revelation at the top of Mount Zion. It is from the mountain top that the panoramic vista of spiritual clarity can be viewed and experienced.

Take a very close look at the two monumental physical locations that are used as metaphors to describe the most important revelation concerning the predicament of human existence. If we allow the insight to be riveted into our psyche it will enter the heart. Then it will always be a reliable lens to assay and evaluate every perplexing episode of life. For all our present life is based upon what you are about to hear from the mountain top.

The Two Mountains are Two Metaphors

In the cryptic book of Hebrews there are laid out the images of two mountains. One mountain is Mount Sinai. The other is Mount Zion. These mountains pertain to two real mountains, but they are used as metaphors to represent two covenants. The two mountains are in contradiction to each other or to be understood as polemic. They are polar opposites!

Mount Sinai is in Arabia and Mount Zion which once existed in Jerusalem. (It no longer exists because it was excavated and removed in the 2nd century BC by Simon the Hasmonean). But the fact remains they are both mentioned in the book of Hebrews, and both represent covenants.

Mt. Sinai represents the Ten Commandments, and Mount Zion represents that which has replaced the Ten Commandments, which is the New Covenant. The New Covenant provides connection with God through the Holy Spirit.

Each mountain clearly describes the incredible difference between these two covenants. In order to come to grips with our human existence it is critically important to see the two images of the two mountains.

The reason is because every human is living out one or the other covenants. While most Christians would claim they are living under the new covenant, the truth is they may inadvertently be living under the covenant of Mt Sinai.

Remember the two tracks, because the two tracks are also the two covenants, and the two covenants are the two robes. And the two robes pertain to the two mountains, which represent the two covenants.

Let's take a closer look at both mountains so we can get the visuals firmly implanted into our chamber of imagery.

Be Holy for I Am Holy

This call by God to be Holy is a very powerful compelling directive. Just how is holy to be accomplished? By what means? Just how is holiness achieved? For anyone who wants to see God's face when he/she awakes from this life on the other side then being holy is the prerequisite.

"be ye holy for I am holy without which (holiness) no one will see God."
Heb 12:4

So, when this life is over and we wake up on the other side, the question is am I holy? If we attempt to examine ourselves, in the here and now, the answer for most would be no, and that self evaluation creates a real conflict.

It is at this crisis point that we can miscalculate and default to the Mt Sinai remedy, and try to become holy or more holy by the human will. This is exactly what happened to Peter and why he was sharply rebuked by Paul.

So then if we are to be holy how do we achieve holiness?

The answer lies in the living and present tense working of the two mountains. In our human condition on this side of eternity we must master the knowledge of the two mountains because the acquisition of holiness hangs in the balance. There will always be, as we live out our mortal lives in the present world, crisis points which test our resolve in which covenant.

The Fear Covenant of Mt. Sinai

This is how the book of Hebrews characterizes the covenant of Mt Sinai.

"Now Mount Sinai was all in smoke because the LORD descended upon it in fire; and its smoke ascended like the smoke of a furnace, and the whole mountain quaked violently." Heb 12:18

When this covenant came to earth it was a fearful sight. The entourage that accompanied the handing down of the Law to Moses was myriads and myriads of angels. It was a holy convocation of God's dignitaries bringing into this world a testimony of God's holiness. The holiness of God in his angelic representatives, and in the expressed Law on stone, shook the Mountain. The people feared greatly at the sight and the sound. This is a picture of the Old Covenant. No flesh could stand in the presence because it was holy.

Keep in mind the directive to "be ye Holy for I am Holy," because this is the point where people get confused and default to the wrong covenant of Mt. Sinai.

As we live out our human lives, we tend to fall back to the Old Covenant way of trying to be better or more holy by reverting to the keeping of rules and regulations i.e., the Law. After all it says to be holy. So instead of living in the Spirit we revert to rules and regulations; a vain attempt to be holy.

The issue of our lives is to become holy. But the wherewithal in seeking to accomplish this directive is what daily hangs in the balance scale. The truth is we are tested concerning this matter many times during each day and that is why we must get the clarity worked out in our chamber of imagery. None can escape or circumvent the test. It is one mountain or the other every day.

Mount Zion is the Holy Mount

The other mount is Mt. Zion. This mount which existed literally at the southern end of the city of David, was physically excavated and removed. But it was not removed from the standpoint of representing the Holy Mount as a metaphor. Notice that Mt. Zion is a holy mount. Here is what it says about Mt. Zion.

"But you have come to Mount Zion, to the city of the living God, the heavenly Jerusalem. You have come to thousands upon thousands of angels in joyful assembly, to the church of the firstborn, whose names are written in heaven. You have come to God, the Judge of all, to the spirits of the righteous <u>made perfect</u>, to Jesus the mediator of a new covenant, and to the sprinkled blood that speaks a better word than the blood of Abel." Heb 12:18-24

Did you notice that it is at Mt. Zion where our spirit is made perfect? A spirit made perfect is a spirit that is becoming holy and has been made holy. The spirit refers to the heart. Our heart has to be made perfect. This is holiness! A heart that is made perfect is one that has <u>achieved</u> holiness. It is the process that occurs and is achieved on Mt. Zion.

This Mt. Zion formerly in the city of David was replaced with the Mount of Transfiguration. The Mount of Transfiguration was Mt. Hermon, and the physical location of Mt. Hermon was where the Kingdom of God came down on earth. Mt. Zion was kept as the metaphor, but the kingdom came down on Mt. Hermon. It was the mountain of the Transfiguration!

It was there on that holy mount of Mt. Hermon where Peter, James and John witnessed the transfiguration of Jesus. The holy mount became synonymous as the spiritual symbol with Mt. Zion.

"For we have not followed cunningly devised fables when we made known unto you the power and coming of our Lord Jesus Christ but were eyewitnesses of his majesty....

For he received from God the Father honor and glory, when there came such a voice to him from the excellent glory, this is my beloved Son, in whom I am well pleased.

And this voice which came from heaven we heard, when we were with him in the <u>holy mount</u>." 2 Pet 1:16

This is the mountain for obtaining holiness. But this figure of speech in the two metaphors is to be an everyday working spiritual reality for each and every person. But the fact is that for most it is not, and that is why even Jesus had to ask the sad rhetorical question.

The Great Default

People tend to default to the wrong mountain, symbolically speaking, because the Law does not require faith. But because this testing of the New Covenant is tested everyday, look what happens.

The holiness that people seek is actually put in reverse and the provisions of the holy mount are cut off and negated.

"<u>We have</u> <u>an altar from</u> <u>which those who</u> <u>serve</u> <u>at the tabernacle have no right to eat.</u>" Heb 13:10

231

The meaning of this scripture is that if one tries to achieve even a measure of holiness, as Peter in the Galatians fiasco, the provisions of the altar (the altar meaning Jesus crucified and hanging from the tree) which flows from Mt. Zion is interrupted.

The holy mount of Mt. Hermon/Zion is a living kingdom that imparts holiness. It imparts holiness by perfecting our spirit. But when people, as did Peter, revert back to Mt. Sinai the kingdom's new altar provision provides nothing. It is because, if you keep one part of the Law you must keep all.

I ran into a good Christian friend some time ago and he was telling me that he was trying to balance out his life. He was a believer and was for some time. He was not a newbie. He was telling me that he was spending a great deal of time watching TV. But, in an attempt to balance himself he decided, that for every hour of TV watching he would spend an hour in the scriptures.

I love the guy and always had. I had known him for over forty years, and he had a very lovable personality. So, I had to chuckle inwardly, but his mistake was a serious one. Yet this is what people do to themselves. He had inadvertently placed himself back under the Law, or a regulation, in this case one of his own making. His was a common and vain attempt to achieve a measure of holiness. It is a common problem with God's people. You cannot perfect the inner man by attempting to regulate the outer man. The outer man is ruined beyond repair. His case was a classic example of identity crisis and reverting to a legalism in a futile attempt to holiness.

Paul knew this separation and it is why he said,

"I buffet my body and make it my slave so that after preaching to others I might not find myself to be a castaway." 1 Cor 9:27

Buffeting his body did not make him more holy; it only indicated how well he understood the predicament between his body and his spirit. In that light we can see why the statement in Romans becomes so noticeably clear.

"There is therefore no condemnation (It is the Law that condemns) to those who are in Christ Jesus who walk not after the flesh but the spirit." Rom 8:1

When we find ourselves committing sin we either seek remedy from Mt. Sinai or Mt Zion.

The altar of Jesus is the everlasting fountain for the perfecting of our spirit.

The fact of the matter is that the provisions of the altar of Jesus are every day present and even work (providing greater provision and dimension of holiness) while we sleep.

"I will bless the LORD who has counseled me; Indeed, my mind <u>in</u>structs.... me in the night." Psa 16:7

and again ...

"You have tried my heart; You have visited me by night; You have tested me and You find nothing;" Psa 17:3

Even while we sleep God is working His holiness into our spirit as long as we have not cut off His altar, by trying to become more holy through the old altar of rules and regulations.

This is why angels are sent to the heirs of salvation, and their ingress into our spirit is not based on being good.

Just as Nehemiah (Nehemiah means comforter) surveyed the ruined city of Jerusalem at night so does God investigate the brokenness of our being (our spirit) to restore and rebuild even at night.

Read it again.

"<u>We have</u> <u>an altar</u> (the Tree i.e. or the Cross) <u>from</u> <u>which</u> <u>those who</u> <u>serve</u> <u>at the</u> <u>tabernacle</u> (old altar of the Law) <u>have</u> <u>no right</u> <u>to eat.</u>" Heb 13:10

That is what it means when those alternatively serve the tabernacle. The tabernacle was a representation of Mt. Sinai or the Law. The tabernacle was where the Law was housed.

Those who listened to the persuasion of the Judaizers who sought to bring Law into grace and who are still trying to commingle the Law into the New Covenant still happens today.

Legalism may be the greatest affront to God because it mitigates against what Jesus accomplished by His death. His death opened the door to Mt. Zion. If we turn back from the holy mount, we will not see the face of God. But so many of God's people do not realize they have turned back and put themselves under the Law. They have swerved onto the wrong track. How do multitudes of Christians get off the track?

Paul was focused on knowing the reality of Jesus Christ and Him crucified. Why? It wasn't because of false doctrine; it was because he knew unless he applied the death of Jesus to his everyday life and even throughout each day he too would become a casualty to his flesh. The flesh is an unruly evil. We are at war with it.

He was fearful he might diminish his consecration and thus his ministry because of the inability to have control over his body. Paul knew the power of the flesh and what a tremendous threat it was to his ongoing spiritual calling.

This is where the rubber meets the road. And it is thus in chapter seven of the book of Romans where we get our greatest understanding into the insight for why we live in constant jeopardy.

Paul became known as the apostle of grace because being a devout Jew he knew full well there was no other way home without a thorough grounding in the blood of Jesus and the law of the spirit. He was fully equipped to teach and preach God's way to holiness.

Chapter 50

The Way To Holiness

He died to forgive our sins, but <u>He also became sin</u>. If you ask the modern Christian why did Christ die on the tree they would say, "He died for our sins." That would be correct of course, but there is more to it but is greatly overlooked.

It is of a very serious nature because it pertains to the acquisition of the holiness that enables us to see God's face.

"For he hath made him <u>to be sin for us</u>, who knew no sin; that we might be made the righteousness of God in Him." 2 Cor 5:21

Jesus not only forgave our sin(s) He became sin. This is fundamentally critical! There are strongholds in our inner man that must be placed on the One who became sin.

"You have come to myriads of angels in joyful assembly, to the congregation of the firstborn, enrolled in heaven. You have come to God the judge of all men, <u>to the spirits of the righteous made perfect</u>." Heb 12:23

What does this mean in practical terms? Look closely what happens on Mt. Zion. Specifically, the word where it says, "to the spirits of the righteous <u>made</u> perfect." The spirits or hearts have to be made perfect. Underscore this because spirits are made perfect on Mt. Zion! For certain it begins when one accepts Christ Jesus as savior, but there is <u>the process of being made perfect.</u>

Strongholds in Our Spirit

As we come into the initial knowing of Jesus, we do not comprehend that in former days we set up idols in our heart. These idols became strongholds and places within our inner sanctuary; or within our heart/spirit. These strongholds from those former days can persist in our spirit. Many times, we are not even cognizant of these existing dark pockets within our inner man. While Christ forgives of former sins these are areas He seeks to cure.

For our spirit to be made perfect, we too should desire to remove those strongholds in our hearts. They cannot be removed by the strength of our own will power! Legalism is not holiness. New year's resolutions do not work! This is what my good old friend was laying on himself.

When the outside world, which is the circumstances of this mortal life are heated up, those circumstances test the nature of the inner man. When outer circumstances are stirred up it tests the inner condition of our spirit. We find the degree of our sanctification and where we stand in the process of being made holy. The strongholds that exist will come to the surface and then we must determine how we will deal with them. Do we revert to self imposed sanctions of Mt. Sinai, or will we stand on Mt. Zion?

It is in this process that we discover whether we stand on Mt. Zion or Mt. Sinai. But it is our discernment that determines which mountain. It is not hard to tell which is the one or the other in how we respond to difficult circumstances.

For there to be deliverance from the strongholds there must be the understanding that Jesus did forgive our sins but that He also became sin.

He Became Sin

What does this mean He became sin? Here is the magnitude of His kind intention, His incredible salvation, and how He would save us to the uttermost. It is the fundamental process of holiness.

This becoming sin means Jesus, for those who cast their care upon Him, became the thief. He became the adulterer. He became the whore monger, and the whore. He became the blasphemer. He became the one who has any kind of addiction. He became all that.

So, when we find ourselves as one of these and are vexed by besetting sins we must put all of those conditions or strongholds onto Jesus, because He became all that when He became sin. He not only forgives sin He became sin. We become holy by putting all our inner problems on Him who became sin. This is accomplished in prayer.

That is how our spirit, our true self, is perfected and how we are made holy.

There is no other way to have a clean spirit, or heart. There is no other way to become holy. All other ways such as ten steps of Alcoholic anonymous or gamblers anonymous or self-imposed restrictions and regulations may work temporarily, but it is only working to restrain the outer man or the flesh. It does not deal with the heart or provide holiness. Nor do other religions, nor does going to church on Sunday or whatever day, nor any other regulations provide the means to holiness. When we place our sin on the one who became sin, we exchange who we are for who He is. God alone is Holy. This is how we become holy. So then, all the issues we discern within ourselves as issues of darkness must be put on Jesus.

And then can we say as Paul,

"I am persuaded that he is able to keep <u>what I have committed</u> unto Him against that Day," 2 Tim 1:12

and also,

"He who began a good work in you will perform until the Day of Jesus." Phil 1:6

As we recognize the strongholds and place them on Christ Jesus then it becomes His work to will and to do His good pleasure in us.

That is why no man will be able to boast as to what he has attained to. Neither can one boast in external good works. If we pursue that course correctly, we are putting on His robe. All other robes are robes of the flesh and self righteousness.

"Create in me a clean heart (a clean spirit) O' God and renew a right spirit within me." Psa 51:10

Chapter 51

The End is the Beginning

Now that we have come to the top of the mountain it is time to see into what Solomon could not. Solomon wrote that there was nothing new under the sun. He could not see beyond earth time. But now that we have come to Mt. Zion, it is time to look beyond earth time.

Ordinarily when a story reaches its ending segment there is a resolution portion. This is how the masters teach when it comes to dynamic structure. If one were to study dynamic structure most all movies and books, follow the same pattern. There is, the setup, the complication, and the resolution to a story.

At the beginning of every movie script or book they all commence with establishing the story world. In the case of the movie the Hunt for Red October, the movie begins with a submarine in the middle of the Arctic Sea. We know then by the establishing scene that the story is going to take place within that story world which is the Arctic Sea.

The establishing scene sets the context for the movie. In the case of this book, we have left the context, or the story world, for the end of the book.

This is unusual. This had to be done purposefully and the reason is not to be novel or clever. The end portion is so powerful that the impression it leaves will become the default mechanism and lens for returning again and again to the meaning and purpose for this entire book and more importantly our lives.

Since much of the setup in the book concerned Solomon, we will pick up again, from one of his classic statements.

"This is an evil in all that is done under the sun, that there is one fate for all men. Furthermore, the hearts of the sons of men are full of evil and insanity is in their hearts throughout their lives. Afterwards they go to the dead." Ecc 19:3

Carefully note these words of Solomon.

238

He is perhaps the most enigmatic man in human history. He seemingly had it all! He had one thousand women at his pleasure with seven hundred wives and three hundred concubines. Compared to the Muslim idea of heaven Solomon's idea makes Islam's reward look minuscule. Islam allows only four wives. But the faithful followers of Allah are promised an after-life of seventy virgins when they get to heaven. This is not even one-tenth of what Solomon was working with when he was king.

Solomon was beyond imagination wealthy with land, cattle, gold and sil-ver. He had untold numbers of soldiers that he could command at will. As a king he wielded political authority unilaterally. And then he was consid-ered the wisest man who ever lived. At least up until that time. The whole world came to him.

It is hard to argue against the fact that in this world he had it all. But the statement he made concerning what was the end for all men brought him to an interesting conclusion.

"All of life is vanity and futility." "We all end up the same!" Ecc.1:16

What a commentary on his perception of existence! Men are all insane and no matter what they achieve here on earth, they all end up at the same place.

So, what is the point of life?

If we take a cue from the 2nd of the Ten Commandments, we can begin to erase barriers to earth bound thinking. I know, why skip the first com-mandment? Which is,

"Thou shalt have no other Elohim, or gods, before me!" Ex 20:3

Yes, we will deal with the 1st Commandment soon, but first look at the sec-ond commandment.

"You shall not make for yourself a graven image, nor any manner of like-ness of anything that is in heaven above, that is in the earth beneath, or that is in the water under the earth." Ex 20:3-5

Why would God not allow images of anything in heaven on earth or under the earth? What was so inherently odious about images?

Image is a Context

The fact of the matter is image is a context. We know that when Solomon built the temple with its interior he made images of angels, palm trees, and flowers. So how do we reconcile the fact that Solomon made images which seems contrary and in contradiction to the Law. What is the deal?

The idea for the second commandment was to explain that no one can ever achieve any understanding of God if he tries to put Him into a context. He does not want anyone to try to define Him. God does not have an ego problem as men do. God is limitless there is none like Him. He is beyond definitions and forms. God is so great that He is beyond description and cannot be defined. And for Him to be defined is tremendously disadvantageous for humankind. It really is an insult and disrespect. A definition is a context. He was saying in essence,

"I do not want you to make images because I do not want you to get the idea that I can be put into a box." Creating boxes also constricts human creativity.

This is why the great I AM is invisible. If He had a context, He would have a border and thus be defined. This would be a limitation.

Nevertheless, at the initial beginnings of God's revelation of Himself to mankind, He had Moses create the Ark of the Covenant, which was a box. His presence would be limited to within a box. The reason for this was because of the massive limitations of men in their mental capacities to begin to comprehend the utter greatness of God. God reveals Himself progressively within man's enormously limited capacity of understanding. Eventually it was why He came to earth in human form. We humans could not have begun to grasp God unless He came to earth in human form. Hence, Jesus came as the Son of Man.

Yet men are infirm and strive to put God back in a context or a box. We simply cannot stand the idea that God cannot be defined. This is why men try to make God into their own image. We must find a way to wrap our minds around what some call the Deity. See what I mean? We even stoop to call Him the deity in a vain attempt to define Him. Doctrines and theologies and denominations are men trying to put God in a context and thus back into a box. These are but futile attempts to capture this elusive God who remains at large. Yet we want to tame Him by corralling Him into our own categories and theologies. So short sighted!

But all is not morose in following Solomon's depressing statement. What is our destiny? It is true that under the sun it is chaos. And the idealism of so many in thinking earth life can be changed is futile, but there is hope and a great hope! There is more, a great deal more, <u>above the sun</u>. In fact it was also Solomon who said,

"I have seen the task which God has given the sons of men with which to occupy themselves." "He has made everything appropriate in its time. He has also "set eternity" in their heart, yet so that man will not find out the work which God has done from the beginning even to the end." Ecc 3:11

What stands out in this passage is,

"He has set eternity in the hearts of men," Ibid

yet there remains a limited capacity to see.

All men, even those who are totally blind and deaf to God, still have eternity set in their heart. So, Solomon was not totally negative. Solomon still had hope, but admitted he was not blessed with three hundred and sixty degree vision. In fact, who does? Yet the theologians persist and insist they know from beginning to the end. One other thing we find in this passage...

"He has made everything appropriate in its time." Ibid

Today, we see the advancing of Islam globally and at the same time thousands upon thousands of people leaving the Church. What is going on?

Why are people leaving the Church? Is it because we have put God in a box? Are people getting fed up with what seems to be an irreconcilable feeling there has got to be more?

Are we so wrapped up with doctrine and theologies fighting to defend the faith we cannot face the fact that perhaps we have put God in a box? No doubt ministers, today, would defend themselves by saying, "No, people who are leaving the church is because it is the great falling away that was prophesied."

But what if present theologies and doctrines are short sighted? What if there is more to it then what we can presently wrap our minds around? When God formerly lived in a box, in the Ark of the Covenant, there came a time when He broke out of that box. In fact, it was prophesied that He would.

"In those days when your numbers have increased greatly in the land declares the Lord, people will no longer say, the ark of the covenant of the Lord, it will never enter their minds or be remembered, it will not be missed, nor will another one be made." Jer 3:16

Since He had made everything appropriate in His time, perhaps He wants out of the box(es) in which we have imprisoned Him. Maybe we have made God after our own image. Doctrines can become the new Law and when people do not agree or conform to those doctrines and theologies, they fall under condemnation from the people that do. Honest questions should not be avoided! Those who ask the hard questions should not be dealt with by rejection. Yet this is the case. There must be more. Jesus even said,

"I have much to tell you but right now "you cannot bear it." Jn 16:12

Look also at this scripture in Hebrews.

"About Him we have much to say, and it is hard to explain, since you have become dull of hearing. For though by this time, you ought to be teachers, you need someone to teach you again the basic principles of the oracles of God. You need milk, not solid food, for everyone who lives on milk is unskilled in the word of righteousness, since he is a child." Heb 5:11-13

The religious world is a sad story and dull of hearing, but there is hope on

242

the horizon. It is time to pull out the tent pegs and lengthen the cords. The blessing coming is an awesome revelation of the incomprehensible. We are on the mountain top!

We know there is more because the Apostle Paul was caught up to the third heaven and saw things that according to him were unlawful to even talk about. What did he see? And if God is not a respecter of persons, then why can't we see as well?

I think it is instructive that Paul was caught up to the third heaven. It was not the first heaven or the second heaven. It was the third heaven. So according to Paul there are three heavens.

Why is it we cannot see very far off? This is an important question to ponder. Why is our mental vision so dull and so limited? Why can't our ears hear? Let that thought simmer in the back of your mind as we move forward.

According to this very obscure passage in 1st Corinthians the idea of eternity in the heart of every man is corroborated by other passages, but when looked at carefully it will challenge the scholars of traditional doctrines.

Chapter 52

Annoyed Scholars

"There are many voices in the world and not without significance." 1 Cor 14:10

According to this very obscure passage in 1st Corinthians, the idea of eternity in the heart of every man is corroborated by other passages and when looked at together they will annoy traditional biblical scholars.

Wherever you go in this world people are thinking about God. We know that Solomon's word is true. When one looks at that word along with the message in the gospel of John,

"He is the light that lights every man that comes into the world" Jn 1:9

it becomes even more intriguing.

We know that the spirit of man is the candle of the Lord! Yet traditional Christian doctrine does not allow that God would be lighting every man that comes into the world. Christian doctrine demands He only lights people after they accept God's Son Jesus.

That isn't to say that every man is redeemed, it means that every man has some measure of light. And that is why all over the world in every country men have God on their mind. The point of this exercise is that we all have limited light even those who think they have it all figured out.

The Three Heavens

Let's get back to Paul and his three heavens. What is so fascinating about these three heavens is that King Solomon alluded to them as he was contemplating the building of the first Jewish temple. This is what he said.

"Now therefore, O God of Israel, let Your word, I pray, be confirmed which You have spoken to Your servant, my father David. But will God dwell on the earth? Behold, <u>heaven</u> and the highest <u>heaven cannot contain You, how much less this house which I have built!"</u> 1 Kn 8:26

And not only Solomon but Moses said,

"Behold, to the LORD your God, heaven<u>s</u> and the highest <u>heavens</u>, the earth and all that is in it." Deut 10:14

Then Nehemiah,

"You alone are the LORD. You have made the heavens, the heaven of heavens" with all their host, The earth and all that is on it, the seas and all that is in them. You give life to all of them and the heavenly host bows down before You." Neh 9:6

And it is in the Psalms as well.

"To Him who rides upon the "highest heavens," which are from ancient times; Behold, He speaks forth with His voice, a mighty voice." Psa 68:33

So we have numerous references to the "heaven above the heavens." It was the heaven above the heavens, that the Apostle Paul was caught up into. So then if Paul was caught up into the third heaven what is the 2nd heaven?

Look at this verse.

The Second Heaven

*"In beginning God created the <u>heavens</u> **(it is plural)** and the earth."* Gen 1

But also notice it goes on to say...

"...and the earth was without form." Ibid

Now when we think of the earth without form it is because the theologians have told us that there just was nothing on the earth it was a desolation.

This is the unfortunate picture that has been conveyed and is the common interpretative picture. When it says the earth was without form it means exactly that, it was not a globe. A globe is a sphere. A sphere is a form. But here we find that the earth had <u>no</u> form. It was in a different state then a sphere. It had no form!

When it was in a state of no form, it existed in a compaction with all the other matter we now see out there. The stars and galaxies once were all within the compaction, as well as all the debris out there and other objects we presently see in the heavens. All the galaxies, stars, planets were all in one place. So then before the present it was a mass of matter.

When the mass of matter was then released from its compaction it expanded and stretched out into celestial objects of galaxies. As it expanded it set up distances. It would take time to travel from star to star and galaxy to galaxy. Distance created time.

There was no time before there was distance. When distance was set it established the creation of universal time.

Universal time is presently measured by the speed of light, or light years. Universal time is different from earth time. That is for another discussion, but the point is there was time and before distance there was no time.

The scripture teaches that there will come a time when,

"time is no more." Rev 10:6

That is because the heavens or the universe will fold back up into a compaction. They will be rolled up like a scroll!

When we look up at the stars at night we are looking into eternity. Eternity is the term used to express universal time, but the reality is that there is an end and there will be a conclusion to universal time. So, eternity is a word that has to be redefined. Jesus Himself explained and predicted that the present universe (the 2nd heavens) would come to an end when He said,

"heaven(s) and earth 'will pass away' but my words will never pass away." Matt 24:35

And not only did Jesus say so, but we also find in the epistle of Peter, *"the heavens shall melt with fervent heat." 1 Pet 3:10*

Then again in psalms,

"the heavens are the work of your hands, 'they shall perish', but thou shalt endure: yea, all of them shall wax old like a garment; as a vestiture thou change them, and they shall be changed:" Psa 102:26

So, Genesis chapter one is pointing to the beginning point of the birth of a universe. The heavens are finite. Eternity has an ending, and the lifetime of a universe is an eternity. Most people use the term eternity as though there is no end, but eternity does end. It ends when the universe closes, or rather rolls up like a scroll.

The verse in Genesis...

"And Elohim created the heavens and the earth" Gen 1

is pointing to the 2nd heavens, or the universal construction.

Then look at this scripture in Isaiah 51.

"I have put My words in your mouth and have covered you with the shadow of My hand, to "establish the heavens" (the universal construction)....to found the earth, and to say to Zion, you are My people." Ibid

Once again, we see the word in plural, the heavens. This also, in Isaiah 51, is speaking of the 2nd heavens. Contrary to common Christian thought we do not go to the third heaven when we pass from this life. We go into the heavens. The second heaven!

While Paul went to the third heaven our flight initially is into the 2nd heaven. The second heaven as we have been saying is the universe. We go into the galaxies and the stars and the planets to establish the heavens.

Eventually we go to the third heaven above the heavens, but first into the 2nd heavens. This step is virtually unknown and unheard of in Christian circles, but look for yourself it is in the bible, and we have provided the scriptures for your own study.

We also get glimpses into the activity in the 2nd heaven when we investigate the book of Daniel as concerning God. We see an image of Him as the ancient of Days.

"I kept looking in the night visions, and behold, with the clouds of heaven(s) One like a Son of Man was coming, And He came up to the Ancient of Days And was presented before Him." Dan 7:13

The ability to see the Son of Man and the Ancient of Days suggests they have form. This is corroborated in the book of Revelation.

"… and among the lamp stands was One like the Son of Man, dressed in a long robe, with a golden sash around His chest. The hair of His head was white like wool, as white as snow, and His eyes were like a blazing fire. His feet were like polished bronze refined in a furnace, and His voice was like the roar of many waters." Rev 1:13-15

So, we have here, a vision of God with a clear definition of Him in a form. Here He is explained as having a form, and He is explained in some detail. But how can this be? If God almighty has a form, He would have a limitation. In this treatment with Him now having form would not that be putting Him back into a definition. As we observe Him in this snippet He is defined. But if God is infinite, God cannot have a form, and He cannot be defined!

So then, in following along consider this. When Jesus was confronted by the Jews He said this about Himself,

"for they had asked Him are you greater than Abraham our father?" Jn 8:53

Jesus answered,

"Before Abraham was I AM." Ibid

In saying this He was identifying with the revelation by the angels to Moses. When Moses said to them concerning Pharaoh, who shall I say sent me, the angels as proxies for God said,

"tell Pharaoh 'I AM that I AM' sent you." Ex 6:29

So Jesus was making an enormous statement to the Sanhedrin when He said this, but notice Jesus did not say before Abraham was I AM that I AM. He only said before Abraham was I AM. Why only one I AM? Why not two I AM's? In fact why were there not three I AMs? One for the Father, one for the Son and one for the Holy Spirit? Why only one I AM?

This important question in light of the second and third heavens is a critical consideration and a question to ask because it helps establish the story world or the enormous context for this whole book and why we have left it for last.

Chapter 53

There Are Two I AM's

If there is a second and third heaven, there must be three heavens! The first heaven is the realm of birds and clouds and planes etc. The second heaven is the expanse or the universe. It is the realm of stars and galaxies etc. The third heaven, as mentioned by King David, is the heaven above the heavens. The three heavens have in degrees the presence of God. God is all and in all!

In the second heaven, He has form as noted in both the books of Daniel and Revelation. But in the 3rd heaven He has no form because He is God and can have no limitation. He is the great I AM. He is God, in the heaven above the heavens, and He is invisible. That is to say He cannot have form. A form would mean a limitation. God I AM in the third heaven is infinite and has no form. Please note in the second heaven He is called I AM as well.

Yet at the same time in the second heaven where He is referred to as I AM He is one with the I AM of the third heaven. The I AM of the second heavens has form. To be clear the Great I AM of the third heavens is One with the I AM of the second heavens, or lower heavens. They are One and of the same essence which is Love.

Thus we have God I AM in the third heaven invisible, and God I AM in the second heaven visible with form. They are One, but in two different places. There is God who exists in both heaven and the heavens thus the name given by the angel to Moses was I AM and I AM or Jehovah.

Jesus called Himself I AM, because He is the physical human image on earth of the I AM in the 2nd heavens. Again, I AM and I AM are One. The I AM in the lower heavens is our heavenly Father who manifested Himself on the earth in the person of Jesus. I AM is God of the universe, but He is also One with God I AM in Heaven above the heavens. Thus, Jesus referred to Himself as the I AM of the Universe by identifying with our heavenly Father of the 2nd heavens. This is the secret meaning of the name Jehovah.

Remember we are dealing with mindsets that have persisted for hundreds of years as theologies and doctrines, but if we are to get God out of the box(s) we have made for Him then we must allow ourselves to grow and be enlarged.

No doubt we will catch hell from the religious sorts who will refuse to grow and look at the Bible again, because they are convinced and so deeply invested in their boxes. They will refuse to come into the light. But just remember God started out in a box. Don't stay boxed in with the old. If we are to put on the robe of righteousness, then we must become like a lobster molt. Can we shed our shell? How difficult it is to rid oneself of what one is so accustomed!

Remember we are setting up the context or story world for this entire treatise, even though it comes at the end. No doubt the entire revelation may have to be re-read in its entirety, but once having learned the astonishing conclusion the whole will come into greater mountain top objective clarity! We are on the mountain top of Zion!

Now if one were the critical and cynical type given to sarcasm it might be said, "so what?" "What difference does it make and who cares? How does this work for me anyway? These are just facts but there is no application!"

I honestly do not have a problem with that attitude if that were the response, but if you can work with me, as I lay more of the foundation there really is a tremendous payoff. Hang in there. Just be a little more patient.

OK Bible thumpers who want to argue and fight. Have we said anything that is not in the scripture? It may seem odd having never thought in these terms before, but remember over the centuries have we not put God in boxes? He would like to get out, but if we keep Him imprisoned in bankrupted doctrines and theologies then it frustrates the Holy Spirit from bringing fresh revelation. Consequently, it thwarts spiritual growth.

Peter asked, when Jesus walked on water, is that you Lord? Then Peter, contrary to the others, got out of the boat and began to walk on water. Do not be afraid to walk supernaturally. Satan will not like the idea that you may be leaving the boat of religious traditionalism. So don't be afraid. Ask, is this you Lord?

Great Deceiver

Lucifer's tactics are to first conquer a person's mind. Once he is able to convince a person with twisted logic he can accomplish his aim, which is to gain control of the heart. The heart, as you know, is our spirit. Our spirit is who we are.

Inaccurate stunted biblical doctrine, world philosophies, and ideological traditions are intended to capture the mind and then capture the heart. Look how Eve was seduced. It was because of the weakness of her mind. The mental confusions are weaknesses that Lucifer uses to capture the unsuspecting. The snake asked her,

"has God really said?" Gen 3:1

Lucifer attacked and questioned her mind. She was not schooled with enough depth to fend off the attack on her mind. One of the main defensive armaments provided by God is the helmet of salvation. Why is this? Because we are relentlessly attacked in our minds by the adversary Lucifer/Satan. He fires what are called fiery darts aimed at our mind.

If we are not able to shoot down the flaming arrows, the errant thoughts in our mind can enter our spirit. Once a doctrine; albeit even false doctrine, enters the heart it is almost impossible to root out and extinguish. But it is not just mental matters that can take the unwary. Lucifer is the master in manipulating emotions. Feelings, such as anger, rage, fear, the passion of human love, or even misplaced devotion to a people or a country. Once deep into the heart can turn into obsessions. These matters can totally dominate a human being. Heil Hitler was an obsession.

But when we begin to expand our thinking into fresh new vistas of thought, grounded of course in scripture, we can escape our mental limits and reset our mental horizons and put off the emotional chains that easily bind us. We put on the helmet of salvation.

But the first step in that direction is to honestly accept the truth that we are born in iniquity and are thus bound with many vanishing points in our limited human mind. The mental roadblocks must be cleared away so that our inner chamber of imagery in the inner sanctuary of our spirit can embrace true revelation.

God wants His people to get out of the boat and walk, so to speak, on supernatural waters. Most of the followers of Jesus could not get out of their comfort zones relying on so called conventional wisdom. They stayed in the safe confines of the boat. That was their box! But if you can make the application in the Lord this way, there must come a willingness to brave the challenge of stepping out of the boat. It is time to walk on the waters above the expanse, the waters above from the waters below.

There are clues all over the bible that cannot be collected by mere mortal men. There is so much more, but the provincial views held by the majority today forbid even the slightest thought of fresh and insightful revelation into the scripture. And those that brave those waters will be condemned as outrageous heretics. Therefore, if choosing to go forward be prepared. There is a price to pay, and it will be the branding of being called heretic. In fact, count on it! The insults will fly so be prepared. This treatment by the religious world was what Christ Himself had to endure. This will be the accusations that will be flung by professing Christians. Never would they stop to consider that they are the ones who are blind. They will accuse the very thing they are bound by. But it is the entry into the fellowship of His suffering.

That is why it is so important that once being introduced to these insights to do your own study. It must become one's own conviction. You must affirm your own views and be responsible for yourself.

"Study to shew thyself approved unto God, a workman that needeth not to be ashamed, rightly dividing the word of truth." 2 Tim 2:15

Study these things to make sure they are so. When you do then they will fortify your heart.

"Lord teach me to number my days so that I might present to you a heart of wisdom." Psa 90:12

Remember the heart is the inner sanctuary and the putting on of the divine nature is the objective and what is to fill the sanctuary. This is what is meant to be transformed and this is the robe of righteous.
Study!

The Beginning

The most critical factor is to recognize that the Kingdom of Jesus is not of this world. If we love the world, we will utterly fall far short in the pursuit of the development of His divine nature!

Loving the world means that all that is in the world, the lust of the flesh, the lust of the eyes and the pride of life is not of the Father but is of the world and the world is passing away. Even to be engrossed and immersed in the bitterness of the world in its political acrimony is a form of the love of the world. Yes, obsessing in politics is the love of the world!

"The heart knows its own bitterness, And a stranger does not share its joy." Prov 14:10

Now we cannot go into a deep study of the full extent of the meaning of the passage, but the intent of this section is for one to decide how much and to what extent the world has a grip on them.

To focus on the world's grip and the measure thereof is pivotal. It can frustrate the development of the proper world view and the acquisition of the divine nature.

Chapter 54

Greek Odyssey or Spiritual Reality

What is about to be shared will come off as surreal! To most it will appear as a Greek odyssey, but it is not a mythological story! Nevertheless, there are the many who will regard it as such. Please open the gates, and exercise intellectual courage. Please put on your best spiritual discernment filter.

The magnetic nature of the hostile outside world tends to draw one back and turn everything inside out and upside down. Consequently, spiritual equilibrium can be easily upset. It is a daily discipline to stay right side up and spiritually minded. Keeping a spiritual mind by understanding the need for constant watering is the work and discipline of faith. If the plantation is not watered by constant attention weeds grow choking off the good plants and the garden dies!

A prime example of this terrible consequence can be seen in the life, of all people, Martin Luther. Luther, as most people know, was the spearhead of the Protestant Reformation. And while he was in many circles considered the most brilliant theologian in all history, he nevertheless had a monumental decline in spirituality.

His great convictions which ignited the conflict with the Catholic Church became his own inner downfall. Let us all be warned! Here was one of the greatest champions of Christ and the gospel succumbing to the pride of the intellect. Here was a man who began to worship at the shrine of his own reason. If it could happen to Martin Luther it can happen to anyone!

Martin wanted to expunge the book of Revelation from the canon. Canon means measure or rule. Thus, the whole Bible is the Canon.

Let us consider this quote by Martin Luther when he said, "to my mind, it [the book of the Apocalypse/Revelation] bears upon it **no marks** of an apostolic or prophetic character. Everyone may form his own judgment of this book; as for myself, I feel an aversion to it, and to me this is sufficient reason for rejecting it." (Sammtliche Werke, 63, pp169-170, 'The Facts

About Luther', O'Hare, TAN Books, 1987, p203)
Imagine that! The great Martin Luther rejected the book of Revelation.

Yet, he was not the only one. Like so many others he had a problem conceptualizing and reconciling the supernatural with linear thought and human time. It is a common temptation to default to the mental rather than spiritual.

This is a huge mistake because it is part and parcel why people lose sight of and lay aside the book of Revelation. But the promise of the book itself is "blessed is he who reads and <u>keeps</u>."

Here is the actual text saying with the blessing attached.

"Blessed is the one who reads aloud the words of this prophecy, and <u>blessed</u> are those who hear it and <u>take to heart</u> what is written in it, because the time is near." Rev 1:3

Remember taking something to heart is to put it into one's spirit. The spirit is the real you. We put things in our heart/spirit by meditating and hearing within our inner sanctuary or our inner chamber of imagery.

Notice that it says **take to heart**. You hear it and it goes into your mind but then it must be taken to the heart of the inner sanctuary. Unfortunately, the great Martin Luther would not allow the book of Revelation out of the mental reasoning of his mind (psyche) and into his heart (pneuma). He did not comprehend the difference between mind and spirit. Taking something from mind to the heart is the willful activity of meditation and hearing.

When a thought is taken to the heart it can become subject to the Holy Spirit which is joined with our spirit. At that point of submission, it can come under the scrutiny of God because it is being brought to the Lordship of Christ and concentrated upon or meditated upon. This is what Jesus meant when He prayed to the Father,

"Father I would that they be one even as we are one." Jn 17:21

The Spiritual Man

"The spiritual man judges all things, but he himself is not subject to anyone's judgment. For who has known the mind of the Lord, so as to instruct Him? But we have the mind of Christ." 1 Cor 2:14-16

Did Martin Luther have the mind of Christ concerning the book of Revelation? No! This historic matter demonstrates that there is a contrast between the natural mind and the spiritual mind.

When we are able to bring such lofty matters into the heart we are allowing the Holy Spirit to appraise all things.

Meditation is the radiation of thought, and this is how an issue is taken to heart. It is all about focus. Just reading will not necessarily take a matter to heart we must hear.

Not every matter you think about is taken to heart. Not every matter should be! Remember, to never forget to....

"keep your heart with all diligence for out of it come forth the issues of life." Ibid

This should never be forgotten. The determination for what one brings to the heart from the mind is the critical matter. How do we pick and choose what to mediate on?

I have an old friend who tells me that he meditates every day. Ah yes, but what is he is meditating on? How is one to discriminate? How do we decide on what to program ourselves with? What do we allow to go and fix into our heart?

"The word of God is quick and sharp piercing even to the dividing asunder of soul and spirit and the joints and marrow and is a discerner of the thoughts and intent of the heart." Heb 4:12

The passage describes how to determine the information we allow into our heart. The word of God cuts asunder and separates between the soul and spirit. The word again for soul is **psyche**, and the word for spirit is **pneuma**.

257

It is critically important to distinguish between the two. As we have brought to light earlier.

Academia very well can be the overuse of the mind/psyche (the laptop) and those who pursue a mere mental approach to God (theological) are not spiritually minded. That is why secular academia and Christian theologians suffer from the same problem/condition.

This was exactly Martin Luther's problem. I am not picking on Luther as though to be superior. I am using him as an example to point out the difference between a soulish mental orientation to God as opposed to a spiritual. Luther refused to allow the book of Revelation into his spirit. The book of Revelation is beyond mere human understanding. A natural mind cannot grasp the book, but it is not beyond the spiritual apprehensions.

The spirit, our supercomputer, can be affected by the laptop. And those decisions, based upon our selection of thought, we allow to appear on our laptop (psyche) can frustrate the spirit (pneuma). This is what happened to Martin Luther!

When we compare our thoughts against the Logos, we have a lens and can make discerning and wise decisions.

"The mind of the flesh (the natural mind) is death, but the mind of the Spirit is life and peace, because the mind of the flesh is hostile to God: It does not submit to God's Law, nor can it do so." Rom 8:7

Hence....

"Keep thine heart/spirit with all diligence for out of the spirit/heart flow all the issues of life." Prov 4:23

We must learn to bring every thought in the natural mind, into the obedience of Christ who is one with our spirit. Our psyche (i.e. our soul) is swallowed up by growing the inner man/spirit and the outcome as we endure to the end, is the possession of our psyche or souls.

The sealing affirmative is then what we confess.

258

We must pay attention to how we talk. Is our conversation earthly or heavenly?

"Let the <u>words of my mouth</u> and the meditations of my heart be acceptable to thee." Psa 19:14

Our mouth will guide and affirm our heart. How we talk and what we say is critical to how our heart is affirmed. Is our word out of heaven or earthly?

Let each man understand the robe of righteousness is the fabric we weave by faith, and it is the work of weaving that garment which will be judged. We all tend to think that serving God is primarily done in the outside world, but the work of God commences with believing.

"The word of God is near you even in the mouth and in the heart that is the word of faith we preach!" *Rom 10:8*

And now onto the big picture......

Chapter 55

Returning to the Incomprehensible War

There are many things to be learned from the book of Revelation, but within the subject of the convolution, and its cause, we must return to focus on Revelation twelve. It is a daunting chore to try to sink our hearts into this incredible portion of the book of Revelation! But the big picture of the predicament of human existence cannot be grasped without beginning in the book of Revelation! We will soon see the utter magnitude of Jesus's rescue mission in coming to earth.

The nature of human beings is the tendency to focus on minutia. This is what Jesus taught when He said,

"they strain at a gnat and swallow a camel" Matt 23:24

This tendency is due to men's fallen condition. There is a lockup on the spiritual mind that can only be opened when one accepts Jesus and receives the fullness of the Holy Spirit. Nonetheless, once someone is spiritually set free, he may default back to the natural mind. So then let us return to underscore the momentous calamity of that war, because it is the key to grasping the bigger picture. It is time beyond the provincialism of myopic theologies and traditions that strain at the gnat and swallow the camel to press onto the big picture.

Put aside everything and focus on chapter twelve of Revelation. For unless we get this clearly implanted in our spirit the entire Bible will not be understood in its proper context. And neither will the world outside become understandable.

Here is what was written. We pick up the action in the 7ᵗʰ verse...

"Then war broke out in heaven. Michael and his angels fought against the dragon, and the dragon and his angels fought back. But he was not strong enough, and they lost their place in heaven" Rev 12:7

This powerful passage is the beginning understanding for the whole of human existence. It was this very war that impacted our present existence. It

260

must be fully grasped in order to comprehend the greatness of God's redemptive mission and the absolute imperative reason for Jesus having to come to earth.

Furthermore, without a clear understanding of the passage there will be an obscured understanding of the Bible. But once we take the message from a mere thought and radiate, (or meditate) on the teaching within our inner chamber of imagery by visualizing the war, it becomes the most major factor in grinding the new lens. This is what it means to read and keep. This is where the blessing takes place because we will begin to see with open far reaching spiritual eyes and hearing ears.

Spirituality is Far Sighted

Before the Hubble spacecraft was sent up with a new more powerful telescope men could only see so far. But with the Hubble the long-range vision into space was enormously enhanced. Now men could look far deeply into the physical universe.

So too will the spiritual vision be greatly magnified with the understanding of the war in the heaven(s). It is the enhanced spiritual lens.

Firstly, it must be understood that the war mentioned here did not take place in heaven. It took place in the heavens. It took place in the second heavens.

We have already laid out the difference in previous chapters. But to make sure, for clarity's sake, it is important to underscore. The war in Revelation chapter twelve took place in the second heavens. To be more precise it took place in our present galaxy we call the Milky Way.

Our galaxy is one of trillions of mansions in the Father's house. Jesus declared in the record of the gospel of John.

"In my Father's house there are many mansions." Jn 14:2

In other translations it says dwelling places. It goes on to say...

"If it were not so I would have told you." Ibid

261

So the universal construction is the Father's house.

Jesus also tells us that

"if my kingdom, (the Father's house) were of this world then would my servants fight." Jn 18:36

As has been previously noted. There are wars going on in the universal construction even presently. So then is this a way of sanctioning war on earth? No! We are not to wrestle or go to war with flesh and blood. The battle that we fight is a spiritual war which means a war against spirits. Mankind is blind to this fact being tricked into going to war against himself.

Nevertheless, when a segment of the human race becomes so imbibed with demonic power then a war among men is inevitable. Nevertheless, we are at war with spirits.

When the scripture instructs to "put on the whole armor of God" it is in preparation for battle against spiritual forces operating on earth, and afterward when we arrive in the Father's house.

In the book of Timothy, he is exhorted,

"Thou, therefore, son Timothy, endure hardness as a good soldier of Jesus Christ that thou may please Him who called you to be a soldier." 2 Tim 2:3-4

Again, recall the words from the book the prophet Isaiah.

"I have put My words in your mouth and have covered you with the shadow of My hand, to 'establish the heavens', to found the earth, and to say to Zion, 'You are My people.'" Isa 51:16

We are reminded that we go into the heaven(s) not heaven, and our destiny is to establish and plant the heavens. We go into the Father's house where there are many dwelling places and we will be engaged in conflicts and wars, but invariably we shall establish the heavens. It is right there in the prophets!

The question for the moment is why hasn't this been seen before? The answer is we did not have the spiritual Hubble telescope. We had vanishing points in spiritual vision. There was no ability to see far off. We needed a new lens.

There is another part of the scripture that perhaps hadn't been noticed and that is, not only the heavens are to be established, but also to found the earth.

So, we have a great panorama of the universe, and there is yet much to be settled in space, but then also to found the earth. For it goes on to say in the classic scripture in Isaiah.

"And to say unto Zion you are my people." Ibid

This all will become very clear as we keep looking with our new spiritual Hubble vision. This so-called Hubble vision is Alpha Omega vision. But for now, we must go back to the war between Michael and the dragon, and his angels.

War Among the Angels

Notice that the dragon had devotees or followers who were called angels. Angels actually means messengers, but Lucifer/Satan was also called the anointed Cherub. Anointed means Christ!

We also know that when Solomon built the inner sanctuary, he filled the cube with two enormous Cherubim angels. These Cherubim angels are also seen over the ark of the Covenant but in smaller renderings.

There are also references to angels in the book of Ezekiel connected with wheels. So, there is something amazing in the correlation of Cherubim to Lucifer. He was somehow also called the Morning Star, but so was Jesus referred to as the Morning Star.

Chapter 56

The Morning Star Revelation

The Mormons erroneously believe that Jesus and Lucifer, both called the "Morning Star," were brothers, but that is not true. Jesus and Lucifer were never brothers. But the connection and miscalculation of the Mormon's doctrine was due to the misunderstanding of the Morning Star. The Morning Star revelation is another key in understanding the divine nature. In order to see this matter clearly, we must look at the entire context to grasp the meaning of the Morning Star. Notice this admonition in 2nd Peter.

"And you will do well to pay attention to this message, as to a lamp shining in a dark place, until the day dawns and <u>the morning star</u> rises in your hearts." 2 Peter 1:19

What we do know about the Morning Star is that it is mentioned again in Revelation Chapter Two. It is the reward to those who overcome. Here is what it says about the Morning Star in Revelation Two.

"And he that overcometh, and keepeth my works unto the end, to him will I give power over the nations: And he shall rule them with a rod of iron; as the vessels of a potter shall they be broken to shivers: even as I received of my Father. And I will give him <u>the Morning Star</u>." Rev 2:26

While we have to look at the whole context, there are additional references to grasp the meaning of the Morning Star. Initially it can be seen that it is not a person but something to be given.

"I will give him the Morning Star." Rev 2:28

Notice too that the giving of the Morning Star is based upon a condition which is overcoming. It is conditional! It is only given to the overcomers! And what must the recipient overcome? In this directive it is based upon something God has against the elders of those in Thyatira, who were called the angel of the church of Thyatira. And what was God against? It was the "spirit of Jezebel." Her spirit was corrupting the congregation.

So, to him who overcomes the "spirit of Jezebel" I will give "authority" over the nations (ethnos) and I will give him the Morning Star. The giving of the Morning Star by Jesus is to the overcomers, and the Morning Star office comes with ruling the ethnos with a rod of iron. Hence, the Morning Star was and is an office. It was an office that was once chaired by Jesus who was called the Morning Star and then also by Lucifer also called the Morning Star.

A good metaphor in understanding the matter would be to look at the president of the United States, the one who chairs the presidency. There are times when the man in office is addressed as Mr. President. There is no separation from the actual name of the president; say George Bush, from the term Mr. President. We do not say Mr. Bush or Mr. Clinton or Mr. Obama we say Mr. President. That is a reference and the respect afforded to the office and the man who sits in the office.

Likewise, Jesus was called after the office, the Morning Star. But sadly, just as there were bad presidents, we called Mr. President, there was one who sat in the office of the Morning Star, i.e., Lucifer.

It was he who corrupted the office. And in that office, just as the President is the commander and chief commanding the entire military of the United States, Lucifer in the office of Morning Star commanded many angels/messengers. It was while in that office of the Morning Star that he corrupted the office.

And so, in the war among the angels, no place was found for him, and he was thrown out of office.

"How you have fallen from heaven, 'O star of the morning,' son of the dawn! You have been cut down to the earth, you who have weakened the nations!" Isa 14:12

In human parlance and in human affairs he was impeached and thrown out of the office of the Morning Star. The office was vacated. It still is, therefore, it is open and waiting to be filled. The promise of the office is granted to those of the church of Thyatira, which represents all who overcome Jezebel.

The Thyatira plague of the Jezebel spirit is a spiritual condition that persists throughout the ages. The promise of the Morning Star reward is to all who overcome her rule.

"I will give you the office of the Morning Star, and then you will rule with a rod of iron." Ibid

There will be no blurring of lines. The rulership will be with a rod of iron.

When Lucifer lost his office those who remained loyal to him were also cast out, and banished from occupying their position in his administration, under the office of the Morning Star.

It would be likened to a presidential administration with all the non-elected officials being kicked out along with the chairman. In this case we are using the allegory of the presidency of the United States as an example to illustrate the matter. If a president were found to be treasonous, and he had many elected officials they would be kicked out with him. This is what happened to Lucifer called the great dragon along with his angels.

So, then the Morning Star was an office that was once chaired by both Jesus and then subsequently by Lucifer. Lucifer lost the office of the Morning Star and then came the great war.

It was an office that was vacated and why the scripture indicates there came silence in heaven(s) for one half an hour. (Please keep in mind that one half hour in the heavens is not the same as one half hour on Earth)

"When the Lamb opened the seventh seal, "there was silence" in heaven for about half an hour." Rev 8:1

The office is waiting to be conferred upon those who overcome the Jezebel spirit. The true Church of Jesus Christ is currently in training to enter the office of the Morning Star. The Jezebel spirit surfaces continually throughout human time, so the church of Thyatira was experiencing a universal condition.

The church of Thyatira is representative of all who throughout time recognize the evil spirit and overcome Jezebel.

Those who overcome that spirit of Jezebel will be rewarded with the authority that comes with the office of the Morning Star.

But before we get into Jezebel, we must have additional information concerning the fall of Lucifer because the two are related.

Chapter 57

Lucifer Dragon

But why was Lucifer called the dragon? There is a location in the heavens of our Milky Way galaxy called Draco. The shape of the stars in that celestial construction are configured similar to a snake or dragon. This view can be argued as a subjective observation, but nevertheless, Draco defines Satan's nature. He is a snake! But it also may serve as a clue as to the location where this angel war battle took place in our Milky Way galaxy.

One of the most amazing prophetic scriptures that points to the location is in Isaiah nineteen. This is epic!

"In that day there will be <u>an altar to the Lord</u> in the midst of the land of Egypt and a pillar to the Lord at its border and it will be <u>a sign</u> and a witness to the Lord of hosts in the land of Egypt." Isa 19:19

The prophet Isaiah wrote that a monument would be built in Egypt that would contain important information. He said the pillar would be at the border and in the midst. Is it possible for a landmark (a pillar) to be at a border but at the same time in the midst?

Is it a mere coincidence that there was an upper Egypt and a lower Egypt which would require a border between? It would be this border that would define upper Egypt from lower Egypt. Is it a mere coincidence that where the two halves of upper and lower Egypt meet is separated by a line that goes right through the top of the Great Pyramid?

This means that the Great Pyramid is both at the border and in the midst. This is an exact pinpointed indicator that the Great Pyramid answers to Isaiah's prophecy.

A Prophecy Hidden in Stone

It has been proven that the great pyramid was not a tomb of the pharaoh Khufu, but rather as a prophecy hidden in stone. It was defined as a repository with hidden knowledge by the great historian Flavius Josephus.

Inside the Great pyramid, in the King's chamber there are two air ducts. One points upward toward the north and toward the constellation Draco. The other points to the south at the constellation of Orion.

In the light of that knowledge the air duct that points to the constellation Draco may be more than just a happenstance of engineering design. After all, the prophecy states that the monument in Egypt would be a witness unto the Lord of Hosts. Hosts mean angels, and angels mean messengers.

While it is important in seeking to substantiate the war in the heavens by using information from the stonework of the Great Pyramid, there is the unmistakable fact that even here on earth there are plentiful indicators of Lucifer's fall.

Along with Lucifer's fall is the disturbing reality of the multitudes of angels, yet under Lucifer/dragon authority. It is the fallen angelic intelligence which instigates chaos in this world. Lucifer is the god of chaos. There is no denying that the world today and throughout time itself has been in gross spiritual darkness and chaos.

The persisting violence and chaos has had to come from somewhere! And that alone is a witness and testimony to the terrible reality that the great dragon and his followers have come here to earth. In that respect the Great Pyramid is a witness unto the Lord of Hosts.

And the greatest corruption and chaos that has come into the world is through the Satanic effect which principally is channeled through Jezebel, and those individuals seduced by her.

When Lucifer/Satan was thrown down from his Morning Star office he swept away one-third of the angels with him. Those angels served under him in the office of the Morning Star.

"His tail swept a third of the stars from the sky, tossing them to the earth." Rev 12:4

Those that accompanied him to earth currently serve under him in this present world. The symbolism of the text shows that out of the mouth of the dragon along with his proxies, the fallen angels, poured forth a torrent.

"Then from the mouth of the serpent spewed water like a river to overtake the woman and sweep her away in the torrent." Rev 12:15

These filthy waters (waters in this case equate to energies) from the mouth of the dragon and his minions are principally directed at the Jews and the Christians.

Certainly, the filthy waters out of the dragon's mouth today literally can be witnessed as they manifest in the radical Islamic outbreak of hatred against Jews and Christians all over the world. And most certainly as evidenced in political extremism. It is the same evil waters that subtlety flow out from the United Nations.

It is not difficult to make many applications to the dark waters.. But the dragon effect has been present throughout human time. The dragon on earth is Satan (Satan means the opposing force) and was even there when Jesus was born and well before from the earliest of times.

The dark waters found a specific open vessel to work through a woman whose name will live in infamy. Her name was Jezebel. She and her name have become synonymous with extreme evil.

The Overcomers

What is Jezebel today? In order to overcome Jezebel, we must first identify her.

Jezebel, and the spirit of Jezebel, can become personified in either **man** or **woman**!

"Thou tolerates the women Jezebel." Rev 2:20

Have you ever noticed there are far more women who are attending churches? Why is that? It is not to indict women but perhaps the message coming forth from the churches does not appeal to men because the church has become feminized. Could this have been what was happening in Thyatira? Were the men in the church subtly being emasculated?

If the Morning Star is to be given to the overcomers what exactly is it they must overcome, and how has the spirit of Jezebel come into the churches?

The spirit of Jezebel in fact comes not only into the churches but it leaks into the whole world. How is this related to the fall of Lucifer? Jezebel is the manifestation of lawlessness personified.

But the promise of restoration to clear lines of definition concerning God's intended design will be restored through the Morning Star office.

Yet today the lines that define borders of nations, morality, husband and wife, and even male and female are being blurred. There is a comprehensive assault on all lines of order which is clearly presented in Revelation chapter two. It was presented to the church of Thyatira as the effect of the person historically known as Jezebel. She is a destroyer. Jezebel is a spirit and a force in the world.

Lucifer/Satan is a destroyer. Satan is at work seeking to destroy God's creation. Principal, in Satan's weaponry, is the use of the "effeminate spirit." Again, the effeminate spirit of Jezebel can manifest in both men and women!

It is a powerful spirit. But the condemnation of those entwined with the evil presence is woefully stated in that "no effeminate" will enter the Kingdom of God."

"Know ye not that the unrighteous shall not inherit the kingdom of God? Be not deceived: neither fornicators, nor idolaters, nor adulterers, nor effeminate, nor abusers of themselves with mankind," 1 Cor 6:9

The effeminate spirit becomes observable in the explanation of homosexuality. Homosexuality is unmistakably the blurring of the lines of a man and a woman. It is the alteration of God's principal design. But it extends far beyond sexual confusion. It is evidenced when a woman is allowed by weak men to take authority. Men must become priests of God! But it manifests because weak men allow themselves to become feminized.

Perhaps the clearest example of Jezebel is manifest in Genesis, where Satan confused Eve by saying, "has God said?" This is exactly the challenge by the Jewish Sanhedrin when they confronted Jesus. Jesus rebuked them by saying "you strain at a gnat and swallow a camel." In other words, they were focusing on small things and not the big picture. This is a classic example of Jezebel. She is hopelessly focused on minutia. She is blind and cannot see the big picture. And this is what the devil/Satan uses to usurp God appointed authority. This is what was happening in the church at Thyatira.

Jezebel is a clear example of the personification of the usurper. It is the alteration of God's principal design for men and women run to excess.

"He created them male and female, and He blessed them and named them Man in the day when they were created." Gen 5:2

Lucifer seeks to blur the lines and corrupt God's creation and His plan. Those who are the overcomers must come to grips with the confusion which is chaos. The blurring of lines is of a dark spiritual origin. The dark waters out of the dragon mouth seeks to find expression through open human vessels.

The mental and spiritual castration of men by the church is pointed out in the church of Thyatira. It is because men have lost their way with God and then go on to blame the woman. It is not women out of order though! As Adam said...

"It is the woman thou gavest me" Gen 3:12

It is not women out of order it is men! This excuse by Adam is sadly the same refrain of weak men today. Weak men are those who surrender to willful sinning and refuse the call to the priesthood. They ignore the calling to become priests as the sons of God.

It is the guilt from their own conscience and the hardened heart which disqualifies them from the leadership of priesthood. Women are forced to fill the void. While there are exceptions women for the most part were not designed, designated, nor equipped for the task. That is why ...

"The creation waits in eager expectation for the revelation of the sons of God." Rom 8:19

The acquisition of the divine nature begins the restoration to the proper order and the wholesome relationship between men and women. It will eventuate in fullness with the coming authority of the Morning Star office. But until then, as it is written, the condition persists. And that is ...

"she will have a desire to rule over you." Gen 3:16

And this is the current state of affairs, but it was pointed out in the letter to the church of Thyatira of the 1st century. The condition has been in the world since Adam and Eve. Jezebel is Eve run wild because Adam surrendered. Jezebel is Eve on steroids.

Yet men are called to love and cover their wives from Satan's purposeful and pinpointed attack. In fact, when men function in God's proper order they are to love and cover all women. (Note: It is paradoxical that Islam functions in the opposite toward women) Satan has targeted women as a principal point of attack.

"Husbands, in the same way, treat your wives with consideration as a "delicate vessel" and with honor as fellow heirs of the gift of life, so that your prayers will not be hindered." 1 Pet 3:7

Chapter 58

Painting The Narrative

We are painting a picture of the big picture which is the broader context. It is a broad panorama of our present human existence, our spiritual identity and our destiny. It is imperative that we see the big picture, because once the vision is firmly planted in our inner sanctuary it becomes a default mechanism. It is the lens to which we can constantly adjust to.

In order to paint that panorama, we must come to grips with this war in the heavens. Remember the war took place in the heavens not heaven!

It was principally the war among the angels that has created all the spiritual chaotic conditions on earth, and yet for the most part it is very much neglected nor even discussed in the organized Church or anywhere else for that matter. But if we are to understand our perilous predicament on earth this is where it all began. It only entered this world through Adam and Eve.

It is into the very throne of our inner sanctuary that the image must be implanted and riveted. When the Apostle Paul wrote to the Ephesians, he wrote to them the deepest revelation of God that they could bear.

"That in the dispensation of the fullness of times he might gather together in one all things in Christ, both which are in heaven, and which are on earth; even in Him" Eph 1:10

We who dwell on earth exist in a condition and disposition of futility or vanity. It is incumbent to wake up from any present delusion and understand the immutable truth. The whole present existence has gas lighted our natural mind.

The key is to learn to choose to yield to the will of God. God does everything according to the council of His own will. So, we must learn to surrender to Him in all things because the fall of Lucifer/Satan, and the fall of those who accompanied the evil one, dismissed God's will for their own. That is why we must forever learn from that catastrophic error.

The angels also have free will as do humans. Yet they were enchanted and enticed, and it was for that reason they chose to stray from their first love.

It is also for this cause the subsequent war in the heavens ensued. It was the result of falsely assuming that exercising free will apart from God's will would be non-consequential. This same delusional mistake is reoccurring among humans continually even to this day. It is the very same miscalculation.

The result of the angels' choice from the point of view of the Father was that it would cause Him to withhold, to great degree, His Spirit.

He would bring about an emptiness. It is not as though His creative design cannot be seen. It is obvious! He also draws us by His messengers. But the lesson is without Him we are nothing. This is the critical lesson! This is why we are presently on earth and what we must learn!

We have a lifetime to wake up and learn it. On earth we live in a world almost exclusively without God. God must withdraw from sin because He is Holy. This lifetime is to learn one single thing. The horrors of sin and the resultant calamity and emptiness caused by God's withdrawal.

He is present here principally within humans who are filled with His Spirit. His people are His temple, and God resides in His temple.

We must recognize, if we are to be conformed to His likeness, that we must surrender our lives. By using faith, we can be immersed in His will and re-connected to Him through His Holy Spirit. This is what Paul recognized and why he would refer to himself as a bond slave of Jesus.

Paul saw no other purpose!

The recognition of the fault of the angels and how their miscalculation eventuated into a war must remain tantamount in our consciousness. This is the principal lesson we must learn while still here on earth. The will of God is the principal thing. And because of this we must deal with all the areas of our lives that are not aligned in accordance with His will. We are called to re-establish His presence within ourselves.

"The kingdom of heaven will be within you." Lk 17:21

Do not look for it outside of yourself. This is what Jesus taught when He said,

"At that time if anyone says to you, 'Look, here is the Christ! or 'There' He is! Do not believe it. For false Christs and false prophets will appear and perform signs and wonders that would deceive even the elect, if that were possible." Matt 24:23

and

"And when he was demanded of by the Pharisees, as to when the kingdom of God should come, He answered and said, 'The Kingdom of God cometh not with observation.'" Lk 17:20

This statement by Jesus was to indicate the Kingdom is a hidden Kingdom. It would not be seen by the outside world. It is a Kingdom within!

Many today are focused on the outside world looking for signs of His coming Kingdom, but Jesus taught not to look for His Kingdom outside for signs. It was to be evidenced by a Kingdom within. This is why we must make the way within clear for greater infilling(s) and room for His Presence.

The Holy Spirit makes manifest the impediments that are not in accord with His will. He is not angry with our impeditions. He desires to remove them, and He wants to make us whole with a clean spirit. Therefore, we must crucify the old man which wounds our inner man. It is a lifetime of healing for our spirit. This is the pathos of our lives in our present condition and in this dispensation of time.

In each and every life there is just this breath of time to rid ourselves of the impeditions that so easily cause us to come behind in who we really are.

Summing Up of All Things

But in the big picture, which includes both the heavens and the earth, there is to be the <u>summing up</u> of all things. This means a reunion of angels. If there is to be a reunion and the summing up of all things into one, then what does this say about we humans?

"That in the dispensation of the fullness of times <u>He might gather together in one</u> all things in Christ, both which are <u>in the heavens</u>, and which are <u>on earth</u>; even in Him:" Eph 1:10

The Reconciliation of the Angels

Throughout the whole of the Bible in both Old and New Testament there is unmistakably the presence of angels. It doesn't matter where you look you find angels. In the reconciliation of all things there is something very significant about the angels.

It is not as though we are exalting the angels or trying to replace the Son of God by subverting His preeminence and Lordship in deference to angel worship. Not at all! God forbid! But in accordance with the summing up of all things in the heavens with the earth we must become wise in what the great apostle was saying.

"In the gathering together into one" Eph 1:10

...it must be first assumed that there was a scattering.

Why else would there be the necessity for gathering, if it is not the gathering into one that which had been scattered? Certainly, the answer must be the regathering back into the one. There is going to be a great reunion!

We also find that those who overcome will be announced or confessed by Jesus to whom?

"Like them, the one who is victorious will be clothed in white garments. And I will never blot out his name from the book of life, but I will confess his name before 'My Father and His <u>angels</u>.'" Rev 3:5

The announcement is before the Father but also before the angels. Why both? This again is not a superlative or hyperbole it is a spiritual reality.

"In whom also we have obtained an inheritance, being predestined according to the purpose of him who works all things after the counsel of his own will:" Eph 1:11

The condition for this spectacular moment, if you can call it a moment is conditional. But how can it be conditional if it is predetermined? If we were predetermined before the foundation of the world then how is it even remotely possible that one can be blotted out of the book of life?

"In whom obtained an <u>inheritance</u>, being predestined according to the purpose of Him who works all things after the counsel of His own will."
Eph 1:11

The inheritance is obtained and secured only if we walk according to the counsel of His will. And yet while it is conditional it is predestined.

Chapter 59

Picture of Predestination (Angel vision)

Look at it this way. Let us suppose there are two freeways. Both are paved. One freeway which goes west to east represents God's will. There is another freeway that goes south to north. These two freeways represent the opportunity of your will. You can choose either freeway. Each is paved and ready to use. If you take the west to east freeway, it is paved all the way to New York. It is predetermined or predestined that if you stay on that paved road you will arrive in New York. Staying on the freeway means you are predestined by God to arrive in New York. Done deal!

In other words, it is predetermined that if you get on the freeway you will inevitably end up going from the west coast to the east coast. It is predetermined even before you choose which road you take. Get on the west to east freeway you will certainly arrive in New York. But you do not have to choose that roadway. You can choose the alternative which is south to north.

If you take that route you will end up in Alaska. Each freeway represents a predetermined destination. God's will or your will and each roadway has a predictable predetermined end. But you must make a decision. Yet, it is only predetermined if you stay on the freeway. But you must remember that each new day you must stay on that road. It is predetermined yet remains conditional.

The freeway to New York has many off ramps, but if you refuse to take those sidetracks and stay on the road to New York you will end up where you ought to be in New York. But God never rescinds His gift of choice.

The question must be responded to daily. Do I want to stay on the freeway or take an off ramp? Paul said it this way, "I die daily." I can choose to get off, which may be a fun thing to do, or I can die to that idea and stay on the freeway. This is what Paul meant when he said I die daily.

This is why the scriptures wisely direct us to lay aside every weight of sin that so easily encumbers us considering Jesus the author and finisher of our faith.

The outcome of our faith in this sense is arriving in New York. Many will assume New York represents heaven and that's OK, but the passage reads, *"having as an outcome of our faith the possession of your souls." **Ibid***

The reward for our wise daily decisions to stay consistently on the freeway is the possession of our soul. It is the daily use of faith that aligns us with God's predetermined plan.

But in the big picture commencing with the fall of the angels due to the war, there is also the gathering together from the scattering of all things on earth. This means there is a gathering of humans with the inhabitants in the heavens, namely angels.

Once there is the re-convening there is the testimony or announcing to the angels and the Father the success of the overcomers and hence the combining of all things into one.

Predestined for the Great Reunion

I don't know about you, but I love reunions. I even love reunions when I see a pet dog reunited with his master. I love to see husbands and wives reunited after long stretches of separation. I love when friends from the long past come back together again.

But there is a reunion coming that is far beyond what we can imagine, and it is the reunion for all the overcomers with their celestial brethren; the angels. That the angels are our brethren is made clear in the book of Revelation.

" Then the angel told me to write, blessed are those who are invited to the marriage supper of the Lamb. And he said to me, these are the true words of God. So, I fell at his feet to worship him. But he told me, "Do not do that! I <u>am a "fellow servant"</u> with you and of '<u>your brothers</u>' who rely on the testimony of Jesus. Worship God!" Rev 19:10-11

When I attended my 50th high school reunion I had to prepare. I bought a new sports coat, made plane reservations and then a hotel reservation. I got all decked out.

In the preparation for the reunion in the heavens we must also prepare and what follows is one of the major considerations in preparation.

Let us first look at an amazing scripture from the book of Genesis that is often misunderstood. When one truly looks at the expanse of the heavens in comparison with other celestial objects, we are incredibly small in comparison. There are even stars out there that dwarf our sun. And then there are galaxies that make our own milky way seem like a toy. But it says of our God that He spans the heavens with the palm of His hand. So, we need to get a grip on how small we really are because God wants to enlarge us.

"Your eyes will shine, and your heart will thrill with joy, for merchants from around... Then thou shalt see and be radiant, and thy heart shall thrill and be <u>enlarged</u>." Isa. 60:5

It must be remembered that when Lucifer/Satan was thrown down on the earth, he was micronized and shrunken. Nevertheless, his horrific effect on humankind has weakened the human race.

When we arrived in this world we were sold into sin. We were conceived and born in iniquity. Thus, we were born blind spiritually and terribly afflicted. As a result, our far sighted vision was greatly wounded and reduced to superficiality. We simply must be healed and restored.

This is what it says about our entry into this world.

"The wicked are estranged from the womb; These who speak lies go astray from birth." Psa 58

We are all born with the same problem. We go astray from birth because we were conceived in iniquity. This we must face if we are to get on the pathway to overcoming and restoration.

"A highway will be there, a roadway, and it will be called the Highway of Holiness. The unclean will not travel on it, but it will be for him who walks that way, And fools will not wander on it." Isa 35:8

Once we get on the proper freeway which is through Christ Jesus who is the toll gate keeper, we must expand our inner horizons and see God in a much greater and greater light and capacity. In preparation for the great reunion we must see as the angels see.

Angel Vision and the Little Book

It may be paradoxical, but when Paul was writing to the Galatians he said,

"you welcomed me as if I were 'an angel' of God, as if I were Christ Jesus himself. What then has become of your blessing? For I can testify that, if it were possible, you would have torn out your eyes and given them to me." Gal 4:15

Was Paul's expression hyperbole or was there something deeply hidden in his discourse with the Galatians?

In the tenth chapter of the book of Revelation there is an obscure passage concerning a "little book." The Apostle John in this scene was before an angel of the Lord. In most circles this passage of scripture is regarded as of small importance. Even to this day it remains an obscure mystery and though it is a little book, it is of enormous importance, because it is key in the restoration of angel vision.

The Time Machine

"Then I saw another mighty angel coming down from heaven. He was robed in a cloud, with a rainbow above his head; his face was like the sun, and his legs were like fiery pillars. He was holding <u>a little scroll</u>, which lay open in his hand. He planted his right foot on the sea and his left foot on the land, and he gave a loud shout like the roar of a lion. When he shouted, the voices of the seven thunders spoke. And when the seven thunders spoke, I was about to write; but I heard a voice from heaven say, 'Seal up what the seven thunders have said and do not write it down.'" Rev 10: 1-11

Why this section of scripture is so important is so that we can see as the angels see. We must learn to wrap our minds around the war of the angels and the monumental words of Jesus when He said...

"heaven and earth will pass away but my word shall never pass away." Lk 21:33

These words were not a superlative as though He was making a grandiose statement about His Word. These words are actualities that have occurred and are occurring as I speak. We must come to see what He meant concerning the heaven(s) and earth passing away and how this relates to the seven thunders of Revelation chapter ten.

The Seven Thunders

When we were born into this world, we lost our ability to see spiritually. We had no ability to see as the angels. Paul in his letter to the Galatians said, you received me as an angel of God. Why did he say this in his letter to them? Why did the Galatians feel this way about him?

Paul, was the one who approved of Stephen's murder and even persecuted the church, nevertheless after his conversion he developed "angel vision."

We know he could see far off because he had traveled into the third heaven and saw things that at that time he was not permitted to speak of. Paul had angel eyes. We too, can ascend to "far away eyes" as did Paul and our vision can be restored to angel vision.

And this portion of scripture in Revelation ten will enlarge the eyes of our heart and restore a grasp on what heretofore has been weakness and limitations of our spiritual vision.

Revelation chapter ten will prove just how blind and short sighted we are.

Yet far more importantly, the text will open our spiritual eyes and expand our ability to see the greatness of God. In addition, it will lead us to a new understanding of who we really are.

It is in the "little book" where we discover the ability to see great things. In this "little book" we are being permitted to see not only far away into the future, but also far back into the ancient past. In fact, so far backwards even before the time of Genesis.

The little book is a time machine. This is angel eyes. This is Alpha and Omega vision.

Chapter 60

The Little Book

In this section we discover the meaning of the seven thunders coming out of the little book. The book was sealed and so the knowledge of what it meant was shut up. But as we carefully study the events of the war in the heavens, we are given a greater view into the meaning of the seven thunders revelation.

There are numerous indicators in the Old Testament that shed light on this locked up revelation. It was not allowed, at that time, to write down its meaning, but that was then. Let us look at some of the keys that allow us to peer into the past which is represented in this classic mysterious window of Revelation ten.

Here are key scriptures that reference the same thing.

"He that sitteth upon the circle of the earth, and the inhabitants thereof [are] as grasshoppers; that stretches out the heavens as a curtain and spreads them out as a tent to dwell in" Isa 40:22

The focus is to recognize that the heavens were 'stretched' out and spread as a tent.

"Who commands the sun not to shine, And sets a seal upon the stars; Who alone <u>stretches out the heavens</u>" Job 9:8

"Thus says the LORD, your Redeemer, and the one who formed you from the womb, 'I, the LORD, am the maker of all things, <u>Stretching out the heavens</u> by Myself and spreading out the earth all alone.'" Isa 44:24

When we consider Genesis one in light of these scriptures, we begin to get an altogether new and different picture of the creation. Look again at Genesis one,

"Elohim had created the heavens and its matter, and the matter called earth was without form." Gen 1

What does this mean without form? Today, we understand the earth as a sphere which is a form. So then if the earth had no form, it was not in the shape of a sphere. It had not and was not yet formed. The earth was without form.

Genesis is giving a picture of a non-spherical description of earth. It existed only in the mass and collection of all matter. It had no form. It existed within all the collective matter before there were galaxies and stars.

All matter previously existed in a mass of compaction. What we see today in the observable universe consisting of galaxies and stars and planets was formerly a compaction of matter with no form. The earth was formerly part of that compaction, albeit a very small part. Then there was a great thunder, and then the matter stretched forth. What we see today is the result of a big bang or as the Bible puts it a thunder. In viewing the galaxies and stars, planets and gases etc., what is observable is the debris from a great thunder. The scientists are right! There was a big bang! But scripture calls it a great thunder!

The result of the great thunder resulted in what the scripture calls the "expanse." The expanse is the enormous universe!

The Six Days of Creation

Please keep in mind that Genesis one, regarding the six days of creation, is a record of the design stages of creation. It is very much likened unto a screenwriter who first writes the movie in a script form. This is how a movie comes about before the actual filming portion takes place. It is produced initially in a written form.

The script in this case is God's book. After the script is completed, as in Genesis one, then comes the actual physical production which is the filming of the script. Genesis two would be the actual production of the script.

Jehovah Elohim rested on the 7th day from the writing stage. So, then it is to be understood that after the writing side of creation was completed it was time for the production side to commence. This began on the 7th day when He was at work in the outer world. On that 7th day He created Adam and Eve, and He planted a garden as well.

In that He rested on the 7th day, it was only in the sense that He rested from the script writing stage of the creation work.

Just as a builder must make blueprints before he actually goes to the building phase so was the actual external creation preceded by a blueprint. The first chapter of Genesis was a record of the blueprint design phase.

The actual language of Genesis 2:2 says it this way.

"And Jehovah Elohim rested from everything He created <u>to make</u>. (the 'to make' was the actual external production stage)" Gen 2:2

Let's go back to the design blueprint phase just for a moment of emphasis.

The Waters Above and the Waters Below

The term waters can be misleading in that waters above expresses energies, not waters simply as we understand the term water.

Jesus made this clear when He met the woman at the well. He asked her to give Him a drink of water from the well.

The Samaritan woman said to him,

*"You are a Jew, and I am a Samaritan woman. How can you ask me for a drink? **(For Jews do not associate with Samaritans.)**"* Jn 4:9

Jesus answered her, "If you knew the gift of God and who it is that asks you for a drink, you would have asked him and he would have given you **"living water."**

Jesus went on to say,

"Everyone who drinks this water will be thirsty again, but whoever drinks the water I give them will never thirst. Indeed, the water I give them will become in them a spring of water welling up to eternal life." Ibid

So, there are waters above the firmament and waters below the firmament and they are different. They are not the same in substance.

How did this separation occur?

It happened simultaneously with the thunder which caused the creation of time. Before there was an earth there was only matter in the compaction. Earth, as we have noted, was part of the massive compaction of matter. In that compaction there was no form. No stars, no planets, no sun, no galaxies, no universe, no time. When the thunder took place, it created distance as the matter stretched forth. Distance created time!

The Bible records just as the scientists have discovered there was a big bang. Don't forget Galileo! The Church did not believe him either. There was a great thunder or explosion and God stretched forth the heavens.

Now look at this.

God will *"**fold up**"* the heavens like a garment. The heavens will retreat into the mass which was formerly without form.

"Of old You founded the earth, And the heavens are the work of Your hands. Even they will perish, like clothing but You endure; And all of them will wear out like a garment; you will change them, and they will be changed." Psa 102

"In the beginning, Lord, you laid the foundations of the earth, and the heavens are the work of Your hands. They will perish, but You remain; They will all wear out like a garment." Heb. 1:11

"And all the host of heaven will wear away, And the sky will be rolled up like a scroll; All their hosts will also wither away As a leaf withers from the vine, Or as one withers from the fig tree." Is 34:4

"The sky receded like a scroll being rolled up, and every mountain and island was moved from its place." Rev 6:14

These scriptures point to the coming end to the physical universe. But wait a minute.

Look at this scripture in 2 Pet.3:10

"But the day of the Lord will come like a thief. The heavens will disappear but the elements will be dissolved in the fire, and the earth and its works will not be found"

Yet....

"For, look! I create "new heavens and a new earth; past things will not be remembered, they will no more come to mind." Isa 65:17

Also, again in the book of Revelation.

"Then I saw 'a new heaven and a new earth', for the first heaven and earth had passed away, and the sea was no more." Rev 21:1

So, what we see from these numerous biblical references is a portrait of the universe(s) in circuitry. It begins as a mass of matter. Then it explodes (i.e., a thunder) it expands as we see in numerous scriptures indicating as a stretching forth. Then returning toward matter again, described as the rolling up like a scroll. The later stages of the returning to matter is described vividly in the book of second Peter as the elements melting with fervent heat.

"But the day of the Lord will come as a thief in the night; in which the heavens shall pass away with a great noise, and the elements shall melt with fervent heat." 2 Pet 3:10

287

So, we see a circuitous design to the creation(s) from matter to the expense, thus the creation of time. And then back to matter compacted "when time is no more" as the universe collapses back to its original state. There are no distances hence nor more time.

Then out of the original matter a new heaven, i.e., expanse, or universe is created with also a new earth. So, what we see in the first chapter of the book of Genesis is a snapshot of the cycle of creation of universes. While Revelation ten shows the roar of thunder it is also showing additionally how seven previous universes existed and also commenced. God makes universes because in them He creates life. God loves life!

How 's your angel vision coming?

In every translation of the Bible it says, In the beginning God created the heavens and the earth, but in the actual Hebrew language there is not a preposition of "the" that precedes the word beginning. It says most properly.

"In beginning." Ibid

The seven thunders tell us that this creation of the universe(s) by God has happened seven times. God is in the business of creating universes. How big is our God? See what I mean?

When Jesus said, "heaven(s) and earth will pass away but my word endures forever," He really meant that heaven(s) and earth would truly and literally pass away.

So then with these colossal insights we begin to acquire "angel vision." As we begin to see as the angels, are we not more reasonably assured that we are becoming more like the angels themselves?

The psalms and the gospel of John say, "you are more than mere men."

If that's not the case, then how are we to explain the reconciliation of all things into one at the great reunion? Even while we are being enlarged by seeing, is it not beyond the pale that we are becoming? Your circuits are being stretched. The vanishing points of mind are being pushed beyond present tense limitations.

Yet there is one more problem with the 1st chapter Genesis text. And it has to do with the Word for God.

It is the word Elohim!

Which One Is God?

In the United States of America, there is a great ongoing debate concerning the Ten Commandments. Should they be allowed in public places or not? What is most astonishing about the conflict is that it concerns a document of Laws that was handed down thirty-four hundred years ago.

We hardly give a thought as to how the Law was originally introduced into this world. The debate is whether showing the Law in a court of law, or in a public place, constitutes the government supporting a religious belief. The argument proceeds as to whether or not the public presentation of the Ten Commandments violates the United States Constitution.

The Ten Commandments came from somewhere and now in the twenty-first century it is still hanging around. For most people, who can argue with the content.

These are ten laws that express the righteousness of God! But the Biblical record as to how the Law came into the world is rarely contemplated.

Even to those who revere the Ten Commandments, if asked how the Ten Commandments came into this world, would probably say "it was given by God." Had they been to Sunday school training they might even say it was given by Moses.

But as remarkable as the longevity of the Commandments, the delivery of the Law into the world was even more remarkable than its longevity.

The average Christian holds to the idea that it was God that gave the Ten Commandments to Moses. They would point to their Bible and say look it says here in the book of Exodus that God gave the Ten Commandments to Moses at Mt. Sinai. It's right there in my Bible in the book of Exodus.

Here is the text they would recite and refer to:

"When He had finished speaking with him upon Mount Sinai, He gave Moses the two tablets of the testimony, tablets of stone, written by the finger of God." Ex 31:18

So where is this going?

In these translations there is a big problem because there are other references that indicate otherwise. Look at the book of Acts.

"Which of the prophets did your fathers fail to persecute? They even killed those who foretold the coming of the Righteous One. And now you are His betrayers and murderers— you who have received the Law ordained by ANGELS...... yet have not kept it." Acts 7:53

"Wherefore then serves the Law? It was added because of transgressions, till the seed should come to whom the promise was made; and it was ordained by ANGELS in the hand of a mediator" Gal 3:19

"The word spoken by ANGELS was steadfast, and every transgression and disobedience received a just recompense of reward." Heb 2:2

The angelic entourage that accompanied the delivery of the Law to earth was massive, yet over time the memory of the event seems to have greatly diminished. It has over the millennium faded and almost disappeared. In many ways it could be said it was set aside from view due to the righteousness of the Law itself. But the magnitude of power, glory and prestige of the entourage is critical in understanding who God is and how He operates.

When Moses came to Mt. Sinai the power from the radiant glory on the mount made Mt. Sinai violently shake. There was a frightening earthquake. Not only did the earth quake, but had humans or animals even so much as touched the holy mountain there would have been instant death.

A more complete picture of the event is painted with these references.

It was foretold in a prophecy that Enoch of the 7th generation from Adam would come with ten thousand saints.

"Enoch, the seventh from Adam, also prophesied about them: 'Behold, the Lord is coming with myriads of His holy ones.'" Jude 1:14

And then....

"The chariots of God are myriads, thousands upon thousands; The

291

Lord is among them as at Sinai, in holiness." Psa 68:17

So, it is noticeably clear that those who delivered the Law to Moses were angels. The great Mountain shook because of the presence of angels.

The mighty entourage that accompanied the delivery of the Law was an awesome statement by God of the holiness of His Kingdom. But God Himself personally did not make the delivery. It was delivered by His "proxies." They represented Him!

It was God as represented, and represented by His messengers, the angels.

We know from an earlier explanation that when Moses was at the burning bush that the name of God given by the angel to Moses was Jehovah. But to be carefully noted it was an angel that represented Jehovah. This is an especially important fact that has been glossed over and lost.

Earlier we talked about the fact that Jehovah means Yah and Yah or I AM that I Am, or I Am and I Am.

It is true that even in the oldest book in the Bible, and perhaps the oldest book in the world, is the book of Job. Job was written hundreds of years before Genesis and the word used for God in Job is Elohim.

So it was not until Moses was at the burning bush that he learned the name of God as Jehovah. So then why did not Moses use the name of Jehovah when he penned the book of Genesis one?

Now that we can consider the name of Jehovah as I Am and I Am, and if this is the name of the He who inhabits the Heavens and as well as the Heaven above the Heavens, why was it that the name Jehovah was not the name in Genesis one for God? Why was another name used for God, because in Genesis one the name of the creator was given as Elohim?

Hebrew for Genesis One

"In beginning Elohim had created the heavens and its matter." Ibid

Why was Elohim, the name used in describing creation, and interpreted as God, if in fact the name of God was Jehovah? This is an important consideration and Biblical fact. It is a supremely critical question which must be answered.

The New Testament theologians will tell you that the Elohim is the plural form for God and therefore that name is used to denote the Trinity. The plural form for God, they argue, makes room for the Father, the Son, and the Holy Spirit. So, Elohim in their view, is more theologically applicable and conclusive use for the name of God

But the Triune God of the Trinity, (the Nicaea doctrine of the 4th century AD) was a Nicaea theological construct. By using Elohim, as a plural form for God in the first chapter of Genesis, they were able to retrofit a 4th century AD doctrine to the first chapter of Genesis. They made it sound as though the Trinity was synonymous with Elohim, (please do not think I have a problem with the Father, the Son and the Holy Spirit) but the Elohim of Genesis chapter one where Elohim is designated, should not be construed as a reference to the Trinity.

Elohim?

But there is a massive problem with the word God when in the original Hebrew it is the word Elohim. The word God which is interpreted from the word Elohim appears in virtually all the modern translations.

Here again is a better interpretation of the first ten words of Gen 1.

"From aforetime manifold God **(or Elohim)** *had created the heavens and its matter."*

But here are the first ten words in most every translation.

"In the beginning God created the heavens and the Earth." Gen 1

Is this really a big deal? Isn't this just straining at a gnat? Hang with me and see. It really is a big big deal!

Let's take a closer look at the word, or name Elohim, and how it is used throughout the Old Testament. The number of times Elohim is used throughout all the books is so numerous that we will only collect a sample and variety to demonstrate its elusive ambiguity.

The first time it is used it is to show how Elohim created the heavens and the earth. The next time it is to declare that Elohim will make man "in our image." Please note the plural "our image." And this is the common classic use of Elohim when it is used to make the statement "that man is made in the image of God (Elohim).

Then skipping ahead, we run into some headwinds with the use of the name Elohim. It is in the Ten Commandments. "thou shalt have no other Elohim before me." Only in one chapter (Genesis two) is the word Elohim connected with the word Jehovah. It is in Genesis where the name for the most high God is referred to as Elohim Jehovah.

Now we find there are Elohim other than the Chief Jehovah Elohim. If there were no other Elohim to be worshiped before Me, then this indicates that there are other Elohim! Since this Law itself indicates other Elohim perhaps we should not capitalize Elohim any longer. At least when it is not relating to Jehovah Elohim!

Skipping ahead to the story of Saul at the house of the witch of Endor. The witch was asked by Saul to call up Samuel from the dead. This is kind of a tough story to relate to, but the point of it is that when Saul asked her what she was seeing, as Samuel came up out of the earth, she called what she was seeing an elohim.

Then we come to the great and classic confrontation of David and Goliath. In the story Goliath cursed David by his elohim.

In the book of Daniel we find that in reference to a little horn that the little horn (little horn was Antiochus, and possibly a fore-shadowing reference to the anti-Christ) the individual mentioned herein does not worship "an elohim of his fathers, "but a foreign elohim.

So, there are various references to the word elohim, and it can hardly be equivalent with the name Jehovah Elohim. And these are only a few of the over twenty-five hundred references to elohim.

It seems that elohim is a reference not to be confused with Jehovah, but certainly encompassing a much broader use. In fact, it seems more likely a reference to angelic beings including the fallen ones.

"God takes His stand in His congregation and judges among the 'gods' (i.e., elohim)" Psa 82:1

The gods He is judging in His assembly are the elohim. And now this one.

"For the Lord is a great God, and a great king above all gods/elohim."
Psa 95:3

294

And to make sure we are differentiating between the most high God and elohim look at the configuration of how His Name used to demonstrate the difference.

"For the Lord your God is the'God of gods'. Also the word gods here is elohim" **Deut** *10:17*

But the name spoken here for God, as God of gods is "Yavael." "Ya", as for Jehovah, "va" for of, and "el" for elohim, hence Yavael "God of gods."

But there is another more far-reaching use of the word elohim that was used by Jesus.

It is in the gospel of John. Let's pick up the story as the Jews confront Jesus.

"We are not stoning You for any good work," said the Jews, *"but for blasphemy, because You, who are a man, declare Yourself to be God."*

Jesus replied,

"Is it not written in your Law: 'I said, you are gods? (the word here used for gods is elohim)" Jn 10:33

If he called them gods (elohim) to whom the word of God came, and the Scripture cannot be broken, then what about the One whom the Father sanctified and sent into the world?

"How then can you accuse Me of blasphemy for stating that I am the Son of God?" Jn 10: 34-35

Jesus is quoting scripture from Psalms and here He is citing this very passage to the Jews. Here is the passage from psalms.

"They do not know nor do they understand; They walk about in darkness; All the foundations of the earth are shaken. He <u>said,</u> '<u>You are elohim /gods, And all</u> <u>of you are sons</u> <u>of the Most High.</u> Nevertheless, you will die like mere men, And fall like any one of the princes.'" Psa 82:6

What is going on here? This passage is very difficult for theologians, pastors, and scholars to fit into their earthbound theological minds. What this passage is stating is well beyond our present tense understanding of who we really are! It is why it remains out of reach, but the key to the matter is the word elohim. Jesus essentially is calling His opponents, actually His adversaries, the Jews, elohim. Here He is citing their own scripture (Psalm 82:6-7) which He brings to their attention.

This incredible text is so mind numbing that we must take our time putting it together. But in essence, if you read the whole text, Jesus is saying to them you are more than mere men, "you are elohim." But the psalm goes on to say, "you will die as mere men." He was rebuking them for not comprehending and knowing who they really are.

He brings this psalm into the argument and points to His own deity ship as a clue as to what elohim meant.

It means beyond temporal identity to their spiritual identity. The term elohim is about that which is above the temporal condition of man, and into the spiritual realm of angels, i.e. celestial beings.

You are above mere mankind, but you cannot grasp the matter. That is why you will die as mere men. This is the most mind-blowing use of the term elohim. In using all these passages we can see that the term is intriguing to say the least. In fact, a massive understatement! You are elohim!

The apostle Paul seemed to know exactly what Jesus was talking about when he rebuked the Corinthians. He used the same terminology of the psalm. Take a look.

"for you are still worldly. For since there is jealousy and dissension among you, are you not worldly? Are you not walking in the way of man? For when one of you says, 'I follow Paul,' and another, 'I follow Apollos,' are you not mere men?" 1 Cor 3:4

Paul knew clearly, the great mystery that Jesus was pointing out.

Chapter 62

Who Are You?

Ben ha Elohim! This term is commonly understood to mean the sons of God. But now after having studied the more inclusive meaning of elohim we have to accept that it could mean something far different and comprehensive.

In Genesis six the 'sons of God' are mentioned and recorded as such in the translation, but the term sons of God in Hebrew is ben ha Elohim.

When it is said, *"let us make man in our image"* in Genesis one, elohim is the word used for God not Jehovah. Elohim is a reference to divine beings, divine beings such as angels. So then could the favorite term "we are created in the image of God' rather mean we are created in the likeness of angels?

When Jesus said, quoting Psalms 82:6, *"you are elohim"* could He have been expressing a far deeper divine reality and origination for fallen men? Could it possibly be that we are not just sinners, (which we are) but something more? Something that has escaped our apprehension. Remember we see in a glass darkly. We are blind at birth and go astray from birth.

Remember how Galileo was hated by the orthodoxy of the established Church. Remember the blind man Jesus healed who initially saw men as trees, but who needed a second touch for total healing.

Was it just sinners who Christ came to rescue? *"Ye are elohim!"* I didn't say it, Jesus said it. Take note!

Chapter 63

The Land of Forgetfulness

There are many references to strange matters in scripture we just cannot seem to picture in our fallen and distorted human minds.

When the Jews were carried off to Babylon many people were born there during the seventy years in captivity. While they were there in those years of imprisonment the land of Babylon was called the 'land of forgetfulness'.

This period of time in the history of the Jews also becomes a metaphor of our present existence on earth. Is it not possible that in a broader sense, we who are born here on earth are living in a captivity and therefore in a 'land of forgetfulness'?

The land of Nod in ancient times meant wilderness. Planet Earth is a kind of spiritual land of Nod! And in comparison, just as the Jews in Babylon had forgotten their homeland in Zion neither do we have any spiritual memory of our celestial homeland. If the story has any present significant meaning, could it not reflect on our own present earthly situation? Is not earth a context for a spiritual prison of emptiness?

The comparison is intriguing to say the least. It suggests that just as the Jews began with their homeland Israel, then later exiled to Babylon, and then returned home to Zion, it is also a picture of our redemption back to God our Father. Could not the old historic story reflect and cast light on our own present condition of existence? They, the Hebrews, began at home, then were expelled and then returned home again.

If not, how are we to apply their history?

"To be 'absent' from the Lord is to be present in the body." 2 Cor 5

How can one be absent if not first present? Then it says it again only the other way.

"To be present with the Lord is to be absent from the body." 2 Cor 5:8

The monumental consideration is earth shaking. Could we have begun with the Father in the heavens only to have lost our former home? Then having to be exiled to earth, the land of forgetfulness, which required the redeemer Jesus to rescue and to lead us back home? In that light the Jewish exile to Babylon can be seen as a microcosm of a much greater picture of reality!

Here are some other scriptures which point to this reality, which help to see the big picture.

"I knew you before the foundation of the world." Eph 1:4

"Before you were conceived, I knew you." Jer 1:5

"To whom He did foreknow He also did predestine to be conformed to His image." Rom 8:29

"I created your works before the foundation of the world. Your name was written in the book of life before the foundation of the world." Eph 2:10

"Our heavenly bodies are and were eternal in the heavens." 2 Cor 5:1

Eternity does not start after we die. It was there before we were even born into this world. If our bodies are eternal, then they existed before we existed as human beings!

Chapter 64

What is the Redemption of the Body

Please keep in mind the redemption of our bodies does not refer to our human bodies, but to our eternal bodies which existed before we crash landed into the flesh to be exiled here on this earth! Otherwise, why must our celestial bodies need to be redeemed?

If to be absent from the Lord is to be present in the physical human body, then we must have been with Him before we became absent.

Here is another clue. Look at the famous prodigal son story. The prodigal son began with the father and then returned to him. He didn't start out in the pig pen. He woke up in the "pig pen"! We must wake up in the land of forgetfulness. The land of forgetfulness is the pig pen! We must wake up and learn to remember!

The story does not make sense if the prodigal had not left his father in the first place. We must wake up! But in order to wake up we must also learn to stay awake. In order to achieve this mastery, we must strengthen the inner man. Just as the body of the flesh needs food and drink, so far more importantly, the inner man.

This is what Christ taught concerning His body and His blood. The true food and true drink.

To die like "mere men" as the Psalms 82:7 says, is to fail to recognize that we are fallen divine eternal creatures. "Have I not said ye are elohim!" This is huge!

"Oh Lord why are you so mindful of men?" Psa 8:4

Why did the Father stoop down in the person of Jesus and come to this fallen planet to save a bunch of miserable sinners? The answer is bigger than we thought!

What Happened to Us

The Adam and Eve story does not make sense as in the traditional doctrine of the Church. Look at this. This proverb will no longer be spoken in Israel.

"The fathers eat sour grapes and the children's teeth are set on edge." Ez 18:2

In other words, because of the father's sins, in this case Adam, the children will be judged. Adam sinned and therefore because I am a descendant from Adam, I receive the same penalty. This is the traditional view of Adam. He committed the original sin. I know so did Eve. But look at this scripture.

"Therefore, just as "sin entered" the world through one man and death through sin, so also death was passed on to all men, because all sinned." 1 Cor 5:12

As we have said, sin did not originate with Adam! Sin *entered* this world via Adam/Eve. That is different! So, if Adam and Eve were not the originators of sin, but sin merely entered into this world through them, where did sin originate? And why am I held responsible? Because it also says...

"but death passed to all men even to those <u>who did not commit</u> the sin of Adam." Rom 5:12

How is it that because Adam sinned, I am held accountable? Especially when it says, "we who did not commit the sin of Adam"? We did not commit the sin of Adam!

The ministers say, "Oh but you would have!" What a ridiculous response! These are the same people that argue that you have free choice. Evidently my free choice is not free thanks to Adam. Evidently his choice shut us all up under the choice of Adam's sin. But here we are with all these questions and loose ends.

Yet, we are conceived in sin. We are born into the condition. There is no way out. How did this terrible condition ensue? That is what we must discover because the Adam and Eve story, and the way it has been handed down, does not really explain all that happened to us.

301

First of all we know that sin entered the world via Adam. Therefore, it must have come from the outside. Adam was only the door it entered through. The origination of sin happened first among the angels. They choose to abandon God and follow Lucifer who held at that time the Morning Star office.

The angels left their first love who was the Father. We also know from Revelation twelve that from the angelic defection there commenced a war in the heavens. The angels sinned and the record of that war has been set forth in the book of Revelation. One third of an angelic circuit was cast out.

We find out more information about them from the book of Job.

Job and the Morning Stars

Look again at the remarkable reference to <u>Morning Stars</u> in the book of Job thirty-eight.

"Where were you?" Job 38:4

In the story Job had been complaining to God about his current life situation. Job was expressing and justifying his attitude and why he felt life was unfair. He was having a hellacious time, but then he came before God to complain. Here is God's response and answer to Job.

"Whereupon are the foundations thereof fastened? or who laid the cornerstone thereof; When the morning stars sang together, and all the sons of God shouted for joy? Or who shut up the sea with doors, when it brake forth, as if it had issued out of the womb?" Job 38

God was questioning Job concerning the creation but take note of the Morning Stars. <u>They, the sons of God, (ben ha Elohim) were there</u> and were part of the activity of creation. But curiously in Job thirty-eight God placed him there as well. Look at this.

It is astonishing that the Morning Star office chaired by Jesus and then Lucifer was engaged in creation! And yet the morning star office was also promised to be given to the overcomers of Jezebel as was previously explained.

But, it is clear that this office extended to the sons of God or ben ha Elohim herein mentioned as the morning stars. This is the obvious extension of the office of the Morning Star to ben ha Elohim. The office of those involved with creation were called the morning stars because they were an extension of that office. The entities or those under the authority of the Morning Star were proxies. These were angels involved with creation!

Where were you Job? And then in the 5th verse it says. God speaking,

"Tell me if you have understanding for you know." Ibid

Are we supposed to see this as though God is sarcastically mocking Job or is God stating a fact that Job actually did know, but <u>had forgotten</u> in the land of forgetfulness?

The answer to that question is found in the twenty-first verse and this is what it says,

"You know for you were born then and the number of your days is great." Job 38

No doubt there are many ways to interpret this scripture but for certain it was Satan that brought Job's misery and that is because of this fallen world.

This is astonishing information. "You were born then!" When exactly would that have been if it were not in association with the morning stars and sons of God were singing?

The whole of the book of Job is a man complaining about his terrible plight. In the end he is corrected by God and then rewarded, but what he is missing is the understanding of why the world was so jacked up with trouble which Job blames on God. Certainly, this is what people do today, but the fact of the matter is that the world where we live is in such disarray, because of and due to the "angel wars."

This World was Turned Over to Vanity

It was after the war in heaven that the world had to be turned over to vanity. In the long haul of earth time, which to God is very momentary, we as earthlings must learn what is going on with the world and ourselves, and the point God is trying to make to men and women.

What is the grand lesson?

This is the great mystery that we are called to discover and advance in our daily consciousness over the course of our lifetime.

Over the course of human time most people see dimly in the eyes of their understanding. In this respect we are very much like Job. But God is not unjust because we do not see justice here on the earth. The fact is we have been placed in a temporary unjust world to wake up to the fact that we have strayed from home. We have lost our vision having become estranged from God with no idea who we are. But Jesus said, "you are elohim"!

God has minimized and reduced His presence from off the earth and in the long haul of human time is asking the question, how do you like Me not being with you? How do you like a world without my presence? This is what the angels lost in following the wrong leader. Here is another reference to the morning stars in 2nd Peter.

"We also have the message of the prophets, which has been confirmed beyond doubt. And you will do well to pay attention to this message, as to a lamp shining in a dark place, until the day dawns and the morning star rises in your hearts." 2 Pet 1:19

The true revelation of God in this world is about the restoration of the presence of God, the incredible revelation of who we are! It is about preparing for the reclamation of the "morning star" office. The morning star office is promised to the overcomers, and it begins here and now on earth as we allow our spiritual vision to be restored.

The magnitude of Jesus' mission to earth is so magnanimous it is almost beyond comprehension. He came to forgive sin and recover a lost race of angels.

We are those angels who fell from the heavens having been enchanted by a master beguiler. Then we were expunged, as it were, from our former domain having been sold into the horrific inescapable condition of slavery to sin and placed in a cursed world and a <u>body of death</u>!

It was because of the sin among the angels that a sentence was placed upon us to a temporary earth-bound life, dispossessed from our heavenly eternal bodies.

Job had lost his morning star vision and so have we. And the whole book of Job is an elaborate treatment and dialogue of that very fact. Job was a morning star son of God who upon being born into this world had lost his ability to see clearly! He also had his memory wiped clean. He could not remember spiritually. Job could not see far off. The blessing of God came once he awakened and then he was rewarded.

"Will Your loving kindness be declared in the grave, Your faithfulness in Abaddon? Will Your wonders be made known in the darkness? And Your righteousness in the 'land of forgetfulness'?" Psa 88:11

It wasn't until the Lord reminded Job that he was there when the morning stars and sons of God sang for joy. Then he was able to repent because he could then see his folly. He could see far off because his inner vision was restored.

We must all come to see <u>we are</u> the "morning stars" sons of God who have been severed. When we return to the Lord through Jesus, we begin to see the morning star dawning in our hearts. The transmission of the office promised to the overcomers in the church of Thyatira commences now. It is the restoration to what was lost. We must return and prepare to resume our mission into the heavens that has been temporarily interrupted.

And conclusively in Psalms 135:2 there is the clear recognition of who Father God is, and who we are, and why the directive to give thanks. Here it is.

"Give thanks to the '<u>God of gods</u>' for His loving kindness is everlasting" Psa 135:2

The Meaning of The Two Gunships

"And I saw, as it were two gunships. The gunships were two helicopters. The first was flying aimlessly above a grove of trees and had no purpose of direction. Then soon thereafter when it cleared the trees it came to be joined by a second helicopter. They flew in close proximity to each other by not in tandem as one would assume. The second ship seemed to have fire burning in its center, but this ship had the force of direction and was succeeding in a projected vector. Whereas the first ship was aimless the other with the fire in its center was prevailing in flight. And I sought the meaning of the two gunships."

Two Gunships

They look the same in form but are vastly different. The two gunships are a contradiction. While one is prepared for battle and war the other was not.

The meaning of the two gunships is that they represent the duality of all humans. We are both gunships. The first represents the outer man, the carnal man. The second represents the spiritual man.

But the two gunships also pose a question. Which one of the gunships do you want to be? The one that flies aimlessly or the one with fire with force of direction; thoroughly equipped? You get to choose. Who do you want to be?

In actuality, it's not who you want to be it's who you were. For we are 'Legends from the Heavens'. The Morning Stars!

It is time to fly.

".... for here we do not have a lasting city for we are seeking a city which is to come!" Heb 13:14

Made in the USA
Middletown, DE
21 July 2022

69810448R00177